D1020871

Financing Politics

Financing Politics

RECENT WISCONSIN ELECTIONS

DAVID ADAMANY

The University of Wisconsin Press
Madison, Milwaukee, and London, 1969

Published by the University of Wisconsin Press
Box 1379, Madison, Wisconsin 53701

The University of Wisconsin Press, Ltd.
27–29 Whitfield Street, London, W. 1

Printed in the United States of America
by Kingsport Press, Inc., Kingsport, Tennessee
Standard Book Number 299–05430–6
Library of Congress
Catalog Card Number 79–84948

TO MY FATHER AND MOTHER

Preface

This study was inspired by my own participation, in various roles, in four statewide campaigns. Campaign finance was a matter of continual concern to the candidates, their staffs, and their parties, yet the uses and sources of money, the amounts spent, and the relationship of campaign funds to the rest of the political system were not very clear. An examination of the literature on campaign finance provided some understanding, but it did not probe the matter with the breadth and depth that I would have liked. I therefore undertook this study. As the writing neared its end I was convinced more than ever that those who would explain politics and those who would prescribe reforms in the political system must gain a better understanding of political finance than now exists. I hope that this study will in some way aid in the gaining of that understanding.

It should be noted at the outset that this volume brings together a wide variety of techniques and methods. I relied heavily on the reports of receipts and expenditures filed by candidates, committees, and parties.[1] Published studies and government documents were also used. Such sources would not have been adequate alone. My service in state government from September, 1961, to September, 1965, in a variety of positions

—as assistant to Attorney General John W. Reynolds, as pardon counsel to Reynolds during his governorship, as a member of the Wisconsin Public Service Commission, and as administrative assistant to Lieutenant Governor Patrick J. Lucey—and my active participation in the affairs of the Democratic Party of Wisconsin permitted me a perspective which suggested the right questions to ask and the right places to seek the answers. Obviously, my access to my fellow Democrats was better than my access to the Republicans, but I am grateful for the great help that many Republicans gave me in preparing this study. I thank the politicians of both parties who shared their insights and information with me. I hope this book will justify their faith, both by being impartial and by increasing public understanding of a problem which vexes them unendingly.

I am deeply indebted to Professor Leon D. Epstein. His guidance of my graduate studies prepared me for this undertaking, and his comments on the manuscript pointed the way to changes which have significantly strengthened it. I am also grateful to Professor Austin Ranney, who read a draft copy, for his encouragement and his criticisms.

Professor H. Gaylon Greenhill was kind enough to provide me data on political receipts and expenditures in certain upstate Wisconsin counties and to make available a draft of his own study of labor money in the 1964 political campaign in Wisconsin. These contributions as well as the opportunity to exchange views with him on the general problems of political finance were most helpful to me.

Herbert E. Alexander and Professors Wilder Crane and John Bibby read a second draft of the manuscript and made helpful suggestions. I thank them for their attention to both the theoretical arguments and the partisan balance of the manuscript. Comments by Professors Hugh Bone and Fred Greenstein as the book neared completion strengthened it in many ways.

The tedious tasks of compiling, sorting, and processing data on individual contributors were done by Kathleen Van Galder, Sharon Bauspies, and Alice Lynn Knight. I am grateful to all of them, and especially to Lynn Knight whose assistance extended over a period of almost a year and a half. I wish to thank also my tutorial student, Barry P. Rutizer, for his attention to comparative expenditures in national political systems. His assistance was crucial to parts of Chapter 3 and to the Appendix.

The completion of this manuscript was aided mightily by Mrs. Lloyd Renneberg, Mrs. Joseph Messina, Donna Taylor, and Elizabeth Adorno, who typed full drafts of the manuscript at various stages of its development. The manuscript would still be an incomprehensible collection of hieroglyphics without their efforts.

The staff of the University of Wisconsin Press aided me greatly by raising substantive questions about the subject matter as well as by skilled editing. Those who read this volume will especially appreciate that the editors excised from the manuscript some unbearable academic prose.

This study would have been impossible without the continual assistance of Wisconsin Secretary of State Robert Zimmerman and his staff; they provided me ready and easy access to financial statements filed in recent years by candidates and party committees. The officials and staff of the State Historical Society of Wisconsin, and particularly of its Archives, made available to me the financial statements filed by candidates and political committees in the earlier years covered by this study. Their help was instrumental.

Local officials, and particularly the county clerks in nineteen of Wisconsin's counties[2] were very accommodating in giving access to financial statements filed by local candidates and committees and in making helpful comments on political finance in their own areas. In Milwaukee County, where the Election Commission and its staff resisted my requests to study the filed reports, the city attorney and district attorney were most helpful in enforcing the open-records provisions of the state statutes.

I would be remiss if I did not acknowledge my deep personal and scholarly debts to Judge John W. Reynolds, former Governor of Wisconsin, and the Hon. Patrick J. Lucey, former Lieutenant Governor of Wisconsin, for encouraging me to take an active part in the politics of that state and for making me privy to their political thinking and activities, thus permitting me an extraordinary opportunity for insight.

I hope that in its final form this study will justify the generous assistance extended to me by so many people, but ultimately the responsibility for its content is mine.

D. W. A.

Middletown, Connecticut
March, 1969

Table of Contents

List of
Tables

Financing Politics

Introduction:
Money in Politics

Contemporary Interest in Political Finance

In recent years there has been new interest in the study of campaign finance. Some of this has been generated by rather seamy financing practices, not uncommon in the history of the United States, which have aroused public and journalistic attention and criticism. The 1956 campaign contribution to Senator Francis Case, Republican of South Dakota, by a natural gas lobbyist while legislation affecting that industry was before the Congress was one such incident. Case returned the contribution and denounced the industry and its bill on the Senate floor. An ensuing investigation led to prosecution of several persons and to President Eisenhower's veto of the bill, whose substantive provisions he favored, on the ground that its passage had been aided by improper means.[1]

In 1966 congressional Republicans, particularly Senator John Williams of Delaware, were sharply critical of the so-called President's Club, composed of $1000 contributors to the Democratic National Committee. Williams alleged that business interests seeking government preferment were finding membership in the Club helpful in gaining consideration of their problems by members of the Johnson Administration. At the same time there

3

was sharp criticism of the practice of selling advertising space in political dinner programs because this evaded the ban on corporate contributions to political causes and because some businessmen alleged that it had become a method of shaking down those doing business with the government at the local, state, and national levels. The culmination of this criticism was legislation in the spring of 1966 curbing such advertising.[2]

The 1960 West Virginia primary contest between John F. Kennedy and Hubert Humphrey generated considerable heat on the campaign financing issue. Humphrey's backers and some members of the press corps alleged that the Kennedy organization was not only spending vast amounts of money, but that some of it was being used to purchase saleable blocs of Mountain State voters. These latter allegations have been discredited by careful reporters of the 1960 election, but concern with spiraling campaign expenditures and the unequal distribution of money among different candidates has been a second major focus of increased public debate about money in politics.[3]

A recent Gallup Poll reported that 72 per cent of its national sample believed that campaign costs were too high and that strict limits should be imposed on the amounts spent by or in behalf of candidates for office. Such opinion is likely to be re-enforced by reports of soaring costs of political campaigns. Senator Charles Percy's admission that his successful 1966 campaign to take an Illinois Senate seat from incumbent Paul Douglas cost in excess of $1 million scarcely merited any newsprint in a society accustomed to reports of enormous campaign treasuries. The case of a relatively unknown Pennsylvania industrialist, Milton Shapp, is instructive. His successful 1966 gubernatorial primary campaign against the regular Democratic candidate was based on saturation use of mass media and massive mailings of campaign brochures; the cost to Mr. Shapp of this self-financed effort has been estimated as low as $800,000 and as high as $4 million. Governor Nelson A. Rockefeller reportedly spent more than $5 million, half from his own personal resources, to come from behind to win re-election in 1966.[4]

Recent activity in behalf of campaign finance reform has also caused a heightened interest in and sense of urgency about money in politics. After well publicized deliberations, President Kennedy's Commission on Campaign Costs filed a report urging more comprehensive reporting requirements for political candidates and committees, coupled with tax advantages for campaign contributors.[5] These reforms were considered, but not passed, by Congress. President Johnson continued executive advocacy of such reforms,[6] but the spotlight shifted in 1966 from such minor measures to Senator Russell Long's dramatic proposal to subsidize presidential campaigns from the public treasury. His recommendation began as an invitation to each taxpayer to allocate one dollar of his income taxes to the presidential campaign and has evolved into a proposal to finance Presidential and Congressional campaigns by direct subsidies to candidates based on the number of votes cast in their constituencies in previous elections. This radical suggestion met with remarkable success in Congress. The original plan was approved by both houses and then finally suspended after having been approved by narrow margins on four test votes in the Senate and rejected by similarly close margins on two others. At this writing, the direct subsidy plan has been favorably reported by the Senate Finance Committee and awaits congressional consideration.[7]

Widely publicized reforms have been adopted in some states. A Florida full-disclosure law eliminated spending limits but put sharp teeth into the reporting provisions of that state's campaign finance laws.[8] Reports in various magazines and journals have proclaimed the full-disclosure law a success, and the general pattern of the Florida law has been followed in new legislation in other states, including Massachusetts and Connecticut. A different tack has been taken by the Commonwealth of Puerto Rico which in 1957 enacted a program of direct subsidies to support party and campaign activities and, with some revisions in the law, has retained it as a successful approach to the problem of campaign funding.[9]

A final source of new interest in campaign finance has been the increase in scholarly writing on the subject. Louise Overacker's work in the 1930's and 1940's on presidential campaign financing provided a substantial base of data and middle range theory for contemporary studies.[10] A major cause of the current revival of interest in the field was the publication of Alexander Heard's *The Costs of Democracy* in 1960.[11] Heard not only developed an enormous body of new data, but also integrated the pre-existing data in an attempt to develop and test generalizations about campaign finance, and to fit the discussion of money in politics into existing theories of parties, interest groups, and democracy. Although Heard concentrated most heavily on presidential election financing and developed new data primarily about the 1952 and 1956 presidential contests, he encouraged a number of studies of various aspects of state and local campaign finance from which to make some assessment of money in politics at those levels. Regrettably, few of those studies have found their way into print where they are generally available to political scientists, commentators, and public officials.

In 1959, the Citizens' Research Foundation was formed to encourage research in campaign finance. Although the Foundation's early work was heavily oriented toward reform proposals,[12] a number of its studies have probed actual cases of money in politics. Herbert Alexander, the Foundation's director, has published studies of campaign finance in the 1960 and 1964 presidential elections;[13] these reports supplement and update the work of Heard and Overacker. Other monographs explore the financing of United States Senate primaries in California and Tennessee, the cost of state senate campaigns in Multnomah County, Oregon, the role of labor money in Wisconsin politics, and the funding of the Democratic state organization in Indiana. The most comprehensive of the reports canvassed receipts and expenditures by party committees and political candidates, except those for county offices, in Michigan, and reported the relationship of interest groups to the two parties as revealed by the contribution pattern.[14]

This study is related to all four of these new sources of interest in campaign financing. Its major orientation is toward political science—to develop new data and to relate this information to the wider American political scene. To this end, its coverage is broader than that of previous state finance studies:

it includes analysis of complete data for six elections from 1950 to 1964 and of the preliminary data available for the 1966 election. But it focuses also on problems of soaring political costs: how much does politics cost? for what is the money spent? in what perspective should these costs be seen? It also discusses the problems of fund raising and considers some of the sources of money in a state whose politics is more policy-oriented than is that of the nation as a whole.

Finally, public policies toward political finance are considered in the author's Epilogue, which describes briefly the main approaches to the regulation of money in politics, and provides an opportunity to comment on the merits of these different policies. The policy preference stated there developed during the author's long and frequently frustrating examination of the role of money in an American state political system; it was not a stance from which this study began.

Money as a Political Resource

Although it was at one time argued that those who spent the most money generally won elections, this view is now discredited,[15] and instead money is now thought to be one of many political resources. Robert Dahl found a "common sense" list of political resources adequate for an explanation of patterns of influence in New Haven. His list, which he did not intend to be inclusive for all political systems or situations, consisted of an "individual's own time, access to money, credit, and wealth; control over jobs; control over information; esteem or social standing; the possession of charisma, popularity, legitimacy, legality; and the rights pertaining to public office." In addition, he viewed solidarity of class, religious sect, and of social, ethnic, and racial groups as a political resource when that solidarity permitted a person to evoke support from those who identify as group members. Even the right to vote, and one's intelligence, education, and energy level are political resources in Dahl's list.[16] Other discussions tend to focus on narrower ranges of resources. Nelson Polsby and Aaron Wildavsky call money, control over information, and incumbency the major resources

in American presidential elections.[17] James Reichley lists
money, organization, publicity, the personality of candidates,
and issues as "areas of maneuver" which "compose the tools of
the politician's trade."[18]

William Buchanan and Agnes Bird examined political resources in Tennessee senatorial primaries and devised a "candidate centered" view of these resources. Their list includes the
candidate's personal capacities, the issues and appeals chosen
by the candidate or fixed by his previous positions or thrust
upon him by his opponents or circumstances, his institutional
alliances with interest groups and persons of consequence in
politics or in the media, the organization available to the candidate, and his access to funds to pay the costs of communicating
with voters. They did not list party organization as a resource
because they examined primary elections, but they recognized
that in general elections party organization must be included.[19]

Taken together, despite their overlapping, these lists are a
good compendium of the kinds of resources common to American politics. Dahl's qualification of his own list is pertinent to
the broader review of political resources in this study: "it is not
intended as an exhaustive list as much as an illustration of the
richness and variety of political resources."[20] Indeed, it may be a
fool's errand to try to detail in catalogue fashion every conceiva-
ble political resource on the American scene for they are to a
large degree a consequence of time, place, and technology, and
thus are constantly changing. For present purposes, the appearance of money on all these lists of resources attests its importance in politics.

One of the primary reasons for this importance lies in the
ease with which money can be converted and/or transferred. A
resource is convertible to the extent that it can be exchanged for
other resources. It will be recognized that "[a]ll resources are in
fact more or less convertible. . . ."[21] But money is the most
easily converted because it can purchase most of the other
resources of politics, or their functional equivalents. It is much
more difficult, for instance, to convert manpower into an effective mass media campaign or to convert access to mass media
into manpower than it is to convert money into either media

exposure or campaign workers. Money is not, of course, perfectly convertible into all campaign resources; for example, it obviously cannot be converted into incumbency, but it is to some extent interchangeable with incumbency as a campaign resource. The advantage that the incumbent has because of the familiarity of his name or his easy access to news media can to a large degree be offset if his opponent has sufficient funds to purchase media exposure or to stage "pseudo-events" which gain him news coverage.[22]

The concept of convertibility is a good deal more complex than it first appears to be and some of its complexities must be considered. On one level, campaigns may be seen in simple input-output terms: resources are contributed to the campaign and they are used by politicians or converted into other resources which are then used by politicians to attain the campaign's goals. These resources are contributions of various kinds to the campaign by individuals, groups, party organizations, and candidates. However, it must be recognized that these contributions are themselves often a result of resource conversion: an individual converts his time or skill or possessions into money which he then contributes to a candidate or party or cause, or he may forego devoting his time to the earning of money in order to devote it to politics, thus allocating to politics a convertible personal resource. This study is concerned with money as a campaign resource and focuses most heavily on cash contributions by individuals and groups. In a broad sense, these are really exchanges: for his money the contributor receives such tangible or intangible returns as candidate pledges on specific goals, the satisfaction of supporting approved policy goals, heightened personal identification with an attractive candidate, the sense of having performed a civic duty, etc.

The uses made by politicians of these resources, i.e., campaign expenditures, are the result of a very complex process of conversion. The process of resource conversion may occur several times. Thus a person giving his time to a political campaign may be asked to take part in a fund-raising effort, the product of which is then converted into mass media advertising for the candidate: time is converted into money which is converted into media exposure. Theoretically, these multiple conversions can take place without changing the amount of resources in the campaign, except that some allowance must be made for the amount of resources used to do the work of conversion. For example, the volunteer worker who contributed his time might raise only as much money in the fund drive as his time would have been worth if he pursued his normal occupation; in that case, it would make as much sense for him to put in extra hours at his job and to contribute the money to politics.

Usually, however, resources are pyramided or dissipated as well as converted.[23] Politicians seek to parlay a quantity of resources into a greater amount. The politician hopes, for instance, that the volunteer worker will raise more money by participating in the fund-raising effort than his time would have been worth if he gave its ordinary dollar value to the campaign. Another example is the volunteer worker who succeeds at the task of asking others to give their time to the campaign. Thus resources are pyramided: one resource is converted in such a way as to expand the total amount of resources.[24] Resources might shrink in a campaign if, for example, either of these hypothetical volunteers failed to achieve in money or additional manpower the equivalent of what he had invested in the effort. That such instances are not totally speculative is demonstrated by the case of a Wisconsin candidate whose volunteer workers addressed envelopes for a campaign mailing and then could not raise the money for postage.

Closely related to the concept of pyramiding is the "feedback" from resource use.[25] In simple input-output terms, resources are finally expended when they are directed to the goal of the campaign. This does not describe what actually occurs, because even acts which are directed primarily at winning votes have some side effects or feedback. Mass media vote appeals purchased by money raised by our hypothetical volunteer fundraiser may be intended to convince people to vote for a candidate, but they may also have the effect of causing those who see or hear the message to convert some of their resources to politics in behalf of the candidate. Alternatively, they may cause viewers and hearers to vote for and contribute resources to another candidate. Thus feedback in response to campaign outputs may serve either to increase or to diminish resources. In theory, but clearly not in practice, these effects may be measured.

Central to the conversion of campaign resources is the politician. His is as much an art as a science. The decisions he makes on the uses of resources try to take into account the information available to him about the political situation, but his information is never perfect, and political situations are not stable; he cannot foresee the changes which will occur because of the behavior of other politicians or of altered social and economic conditions. Politicians are thus surrounded by uncertainty. In this environment they try to recognize potential resources, and then to convert and pyramid them in such a way as to attain their goals. The manner in which politicians handle resources depends on their skill and on their values.[26] The role of money in politics depends finally on the conduct of politicians.

It is the ease of convertibility, with all its potential, that makes money so desirable a political resource. Its worth is further enhanced by the attribute of transferability, i.e., money is not only convertible into other resources but it can be used at locales distant from where it is raised. It thus permits greater maneuverability in the waging of a campaign than most other resources. Contrast the transferability of money with the relatively fixed nature of such other resources as manpower or friendly media outlets. Manpower may be plentiful in one locale, but it may not be needed there or at least not needed so badly as elsewhere; yet it cannot be easily transferred since volunteer workers must ordinarily be used near their homes. Similarly, the advantages of access to friendly media are limited by the circulation areas of newspapers and the limits of signals of radio and television stations regardless of where they are needed most. Of course, to the extent that these kinds of resources can be converted into money which is then transferable, their advantage is not totally fixed to their geographic location; but where money is the input of the campaign, there need be no process of conversion before the resource becomes transferable. The combination of easy transferability and ready convertibility makes money a high priority resource in politics.

Money in the Political System

Descriptions of money as a political resource usually focus on the conduct of the individuals who allocate resources and the politicians who convert, pyramid, and transfer resources, but political resource theory also links political finance to the larger political system. At the outset, issues of representation in a democratic polity are raised by campaign giving. Those who allocate resources to politics engage in a form of multiple voting; they seek to expand their influence beyond the single ballot to which all citizens are legally entitled. It might be said in defense of such multiple voting that it permits functional representation in a society whose electoral system is based almost entirely on single-member, geographically defined districts. Most interests in society—at least in the modern day—tend to center upon common economic identifications, ideological and programmatic considerations, and, to a lesser degree, ethnic, religious and racial identity. While such interests may be part of a geographic constituency, they are not assured of the representation—and almost certainly not the vigor of representation—that they would like. At best, they are taken into account in rough proportion to their numbers and, in close districts, according to their ability to swing from one party and its candidates to the other party and its aspirants. To gain representation of their particular viewpoint in a more vigorous manner, they can increase their influence by allocating resources to politics. The contribution of money is a particularly efficacious way to seek additional representation because money can so easily be converted into whatever political activities might be effective in particular political situations and because it is so readily transferable to locales where it can be put to the greatest strategic use. Unlike voting strength, therefore, money permits an interest to make an impact beyond its proportion of the electorate and without regard to the geographical distribution of its adherents.

A somewhat different perspective is to view resource allocation as an expression of intensity of feelings. Most democratic theorists argue that majority rule is an essential element in the definition of democracy, but they are hard pressed by the problem of the intense minority whose views are so strongly held that a casual majority may wish to yield on some issues in order to preserve the consensus of the community. One way in which intense minorities can make their views felt is to allocate resources to politics in order to support those parties and candidates whose postures on issues and ideology—at least on those which evoke such intense feelings—they find amenable. So the allocation of resources, including the making of financial contributions, may be one significant technique for the expression of intensity of political beliefs.

Against this view that resource allocation constitutes a method for representation must be pitted the persistent body of opinion, mainly American, that holds that the making of financial contributions creates inequality in the political system by advantaging those interests which are economically powerful. Much American opinion and some legislation assert that the financing of politics ought to be restricted to small gifts because large contributions eliminate the roughly equal status that citizens have in the conduct of public affairs. At the extreme, of course, representation through financial giving becomes bribery. Yet neither the vociferous advocates of this view nor the statutes which reflect it have condemned the use of other resources as dangerous to the equal status of democratic citizens or as a kind of conduct which is perpetually in the shadowland between propriety and bribery. Certainly those who lead and influence large blocs of voters or who control the media of communications or who possess other kinds of convertible resources have the same opportunity to exert unequal influence—if they allocate resources to politics—as those whose resource is money.

By defining politics in economic class terms, Maurice Duverger revises the argument of those who fear that unequal influence in politics might be gained by financial givers. Legal restrictions on the size of gifts become unnecessary with the advent of the mass party which finances politics on the basis of subscriptions or dues of modest amounts by "a crowd of members" and thereby offsets the financial advantages of "Conservative parties who are backed by the 'financial powers.' "[27] He explicitly stated the issue in terms of democratic theory:

> The mass party technique in effect replaces the capitalist financing of electioneering by democratic financing. Instead of appealing to a few big private donors, industrialists, bankers, or important merchants, for funds to meet election expenses—which makes the candidate (and the person elected) dependent on them—the mass party spreads the burden over the largest possible number of members, each of whom contributes a modest sum.[28]

The analysis of political contributions illuminates these questions about the relationship of resource allocation to representation in a democratic society. It is possible to determine how widespread the allocation of money to politics is. Furthermore, the number of givers who make contributions of a size that might support the unease of those who fear the corruption of representation can be ascertained, as can the share that their gifts constitute of the total financial resources of parties and candidates.

Whether the adoption of the mass party system works the effects on political finance predicted by Duverger can be at least initially tested in Wisconsin, where one of America's few dues-paying membership party systems is found.

An analysis of the sources of contributions—especially of large contributions—may show which groups are particularly active in seeking representation through the allocation of resources. And this analysis permits a determination of whether large contributors seek untoward influence by giving to all parties and candidates in an attempt to sway them from their announced ideologies and their representation of their electoral bases or whether campaign contributions tend to re-enforce the policy stances of parties and candidates set by their public pronouncements and their voter coalitions. The latter pattern of resource allocation would seem less dangerous to a democratic polity than the former.

From this analysis it is a short step to a more accurate understanding of the disparity in the financial resources of candidates and parties. While superior pyramiding of resources by politicians may be one factor, a larger variable would be the constituency of parties and candidates; those whose program has appeal to groups in the community who feel strongly about the issues, who have a sense of political efficacy, and who can afford to allocate money to politics will certainly be advantaged in the raising of campaign cash. In the amassing of other resources, of course, their program may be a disadvantage.

Just as the sources and sizes of contributions speak to significant questions about the nature of the political system, the analysis of political expenditures addresses important questions about the system's politics. Disparities in spending are, of course, a reflection of the availability of political resources and thus related to party program and ideology, to incumbency, to the skill of fund raisers, to the nature of party organization, and to the charisma of particular candidates and party leaders. Furthermore, the level of spending may be conditioned by the need for political activity: the situation may differ vastly with the intensity of electoral competition, with the size of the constituency, and with the kinds of campaign technologies which are available and practicable. The differences in expenditures between state level party units and candidates, on the one hand, and their local brethren, on the other, and between various local political groups may reflect their varying resources and thus reveal an important pattern of intraparty influence. Finally, an analysis of expenditures yields insight into the strategies of politicians: expenditures for television or canvassing or mass mailings are the last step in the chain of resource conversion. Although social scientists have not yet achieved a satisfactory understanding of the impact of various campaign techniques, a study of expenditures does allow at least an initial assessment of the effectiveness of politicians' choices—whether they spend money for campaign activities which seem to make the greatest impact or whether, as one treatise writer has asserted, they waste 90 per cent of their funds.

The examination of political expenditures leads to still another role of money in the political system: the consequences for the political system of the activities supported by the politicians' spending of the campaign funds they raise. It is important to recognize at the outset that so-called functional analysis has become one of the worst morasses of contemporary political science, and especially of the study of political parties. The "functions" of parties are sometimes simply those things which party politicians do intentionally and for self-promoting reasons. At other times, however, "functions" are the unintended, system-affecting consequences of the activities of politicians. And finally, "functions" are viewed as certain activities which are essential for the maintenance of every political system; and the analysis of parties and other political units is a search for the sources of these system-maintaining activities.

The perspective of this volume is that of recent writers who take a modest view of the role of parties in the political system. The intended, self-promoting activities of politicians should be described, and then an attempt made to assess their unintended consequences for the political system. This approach does not regard parties as prime movers; indeed, there is a tendency to regard the structure and the activities of political parties as a response to their larger environment.[29] "Parties . . . are the products of their respective societies, and so their functions [activities] are conceived as relevant to the maintenance of their respective systems."[30] The "myth of party primacy" is rejected by these writers.[31] That is, parties are not viewed as either essential to political systems or as the primary force in shaping them. Rather parties are thought to engage in activities whose consequences may re-enforce the political system, even while effecting some changes through the accepted processes of that system.

To state the argument in its simplest form, parties and politicians use their resources to support self-promoting activities. Yet these activities may well have unintended side effects or consequences for the political system. An examination of the pattern of expenditures therefore reveals the link between political money and the political system; the link is forged, of course, by the politician whose judgment and skill and goals determine the activities to which he devotes his political resources, including money.

The literature on political parties abounds with descriptions of party "functions."[32] Too often, these descriptions do not separate activities from consequences and both of them from "functions" essential to political systems. The most prominent activities of parties and candidates are detailed below, and the consequences of those activities for a democratic polity are suggested. An attempt is made to distinguish the self-promoting and intended activities of politicians from the system-affecting and unintended consequences. When the uses of money by politicians are examined in Chapter 5, there will be an assessment of both the effectiveness of the activities selected by politicians and the consequences for the system of those activities. In this way it is possible to go beyond a cataloging of expenditures and make an evaluation of the role of money in the political system.

Parties recruit activists, candidates, and sometimes appointive officials. The purpose, of course, is to win elections and to run the government. However, the ultimate consequences of such activity may be to provide and train the manpower necessary to operate a political system, to socialize them into the values necessary to sustain the system, and to provide alternate sets of leaders among whom voters in a democracy can choose.

Parties mobilize resources, including workers and money, to build organization, to promote candidates, and sometimes to develop issues. Again, these activities have as their purpose the winning of office or, though this is less frequent in the United States, the formulation, explanation, and achievement of policy objectives. In the course of these campaigns, parties are one of many participants in the process of political socialization of the populace, by educating people in such basic aspects of political participation as registration and voting, and exposing them to candidates, parties, and issues.

In addition, parties simplify the political system in such a way as to make it manageable for a democratic electorate. "[P]arty arranges the confusion of the political world. Its symbols offer [its followers] a point of reference in judging officeholders or in finding the 'right' side of an issue or controversy."[33] Not only do party labels provide convenient guideposts for voters seeking to select candidates to make judgments on issues or just to ascertain the rascals whom they want to throw out, but they provide symbols of allegiance for voters which attach them to the political system.

In seeking electoral success, the parties, during campaigns and in their interelection conduct, provide some "interest articulation": they state programs to which they are committed. In theory, this provides the concerned, informed, and rational citizenry—an exceedingly small number as recent vote studies have revealed—an opportunity to select policy at the ballot box. In the United States such interest articulation is often diluted by the exigencies of electoral combat. In an attempt to build electoral majorities, parties prefer to engage in policy compromises and bargains in order to widen their appeal to all interests and vote blocs. Even this activity, however, may serve the system by lowering the intensity of conflict and diminishing the sharpness of cleavages by assuring all interests representation in the governing process regardless of which party wins the election. Of course the parties represent such interests in different degrees, but by engaging in coalition building they avoid making political choices so unpalatable to interests in the society as to force them to withdraw support from the government if their preferred party loses an election.

One final consequence of party activity may be governmental effectiveness. A party which wins control of the legislative and executive branches, it is argued, bridges the institutional separations which divide sharers of power in the American governmental system. Parties would do this, of course, to build a record for the next election, to serve their electoral base and to extend it. In fact, the fragmentation of political influence in the United States makes the enactment of policy one of the activities which parties perform with less success than their friends would argue, although it is possible that such policy making is performed somewhat better in certain state political systems than at the national level. Nonetheless, the argument is that in striving for their own goals, parties are a source of co-ordinated and effective policy making.

The intense contemporary interest in political finance is perhaps a response to recent political incidents, but the importance of the subject is not so transient. If politics is understood as the employment of some share of the society's resources to contest for the power to govern and then to use that power, the study of political finance is essential because money is one of the major resources sought and used by politicians. At the same time, political finance cannot be viewed as a wholly separate variable in politics: the raising and spending of money, while managed by politicians, is conditioned by the political system. And simultaneously the choices about political finance made by politicians may help shape the system by supporting the performance of some activities which sustain or change it. The conduct of politicians, the ways in which finance is conditioned by the system, and the systemic effects of the uses of money are all examined in the following chapters. The stage is set for this analysis by a description of the Wisconsin political context in which political finance will be examined and of the methods used to gather and analyze political finance data in that system.

Political Setting and the Method of Study

The Political Setting

Wisconsin political history is divided quite clearly into four distinct periods.[1] The first period extended from 1855 to 1894, and was characterized by Republican dominance, that party's candidates winning the governorship in all but three of nineteen elections. Electoral competition was not so one-sided as its results: the Republicans received more than 55 per cent of the vote in only two elections. During this period the Republican party was generally a conservative vehicle, bossed by men of great wealth.

The second period, from 1894 to 1934, was the politics of one-party bifactionalism. After unsuccessful drives for the Republican nomination in 1896 and 1898, Robert M. La Follette won the Republican nomination for governor and was elected to that office in 1900. His Progressive Republican faction took control of the Republican party organization. Soon there was regularized competition between Progressive and Stalwart factions in virtually every county and primaries for offices at all levels were contested by the two factions.

In 1925, the Republican Voluntary Committee was formed as a vehicle for the Stalwart faction's primary efforts. Although not conceived as a mass membership party, it laid the basis for the development of such parties in Wisconsin by seeking the affiliation of individuals outside the statutory party structure to help finance and organize the campaigns of Stalwart candidates. In addition, the clear-cut conservatism of the Republican Voluntary Committee may have contributed to the programmatic orientation of the two major parties in the period after World War II.

Republican electoral strength rose sharply during this period.[2] Republican candidates won every gubernatorial election save one. In all but two elections they received more than 55 per cent of the vote, and in seven contests the Republican vote was more than 60 per cent. The magnitude of Republican domination of the state's politics is suggested by Republican margins of 75 per cent or more in sixteen of twenty state senate sessions, and seventeen of twenty meetings of the state assembly.

The Democratic party's electoral base narrowed to a coalition of Irish, Polish, and some German Catholics. Its organization had the aspects of an immigrant fraternal society rather than a machine for contesting elections. Furthermore, its policy orientation was distinctly conservative. The Democratic gubernatorial candidate won the 1932 election on Franklin Roosevelt's coattails, but in the subsequent years the party was unable to capitalize on this windfall.

The third period began in 1934 when the one-party system disintegrated, and for a decade Wisconsin witnessed multi-party competition. In 1932, the Stalwarts had defeated Governor Philip La Follette in the Republican primary. He and his brother, United States Senator Robert M. La Follette, Jr., then led their followers out of the Republican party to contest for office under the Progressive label. This left the regular Republican organization in the hands of the Republican Voluntary Committee and its conservative following. Philip La Follette won the gubernatorial elections of 1934 and 1936, with both the Democrats and Republicans making strong electoral showings. The Progressives also captured a plurality in the legislature and there teamed up with the Socialist party delegation to enhance their strength. The Socialists, campaigning under the Social Democratic banner, had consistently received between 3.5 and 10 per cent of the Wisconsin vote during the 1920's and 1930's. Their greatest strength was in Milwaukee where they captured the mayor's office with some frequency and always elected several members to the state legislature.

In 1938 occurred the first major step toward the alignment of Wisconsin politics which exists today. R. K. Henry, a conservative Democrat, sought the gubernatorial nominations of both the Democratic and Republican parties. He won the Democratic nomination, but preferred to withdraw and throw his support to Julius P. Heil, who had won the Republican nomination. Thus the state's conservatives were united in a Democratic-Republican coalition. Philip La Follette sought a third term on his own Progressive party ticket and was supported, as he had been in 1936, by the Socialist party. This united the liberal elements in Wisconsin politics around his candidacy. Heil won in a close contest. A seventy-four-year-old assemblyman, Harry W. Bolens, hastily named as the Democratic candidate by that party's State Central Committee after R. K. Henry's withdrawal, received only 8 per cent of the votes. The Democratic party was now a total vacuum, a label without an organizational or an electoral base.

In 1942, Orland Loomis, a Progressive, was elected governor but died before taking office. Walter S. Goodland, the lieutenant governor elected with him, was a Republican and he assumed the office. The Progressives were now without well known ticket leaders except for Senator La Follette. By 1944, liberal and labor elements in the state had begun to move into the Democratic party. Daniel Hoan, a colorful former Socialist mayor of Milwaukee, won the Democratic gubernatorial nomination. Franklin Roosevelt's fourth-term campaign aided the local Democracy. And in the midst of war the internationalist liberalism of the new Democrats was much more appealing than the isolationist liberalism of the Progressives. The Democratic gubernatorial vote, which had been 19 per cent in 1940 and 12 per cent in 1942, rose to 41 per cent in 1944. It was the Progressive party, without a well known candidate and fixed national identification, which now collapsed. Its candidate received only 6 per cent of the three-party vote.

Perhaps 1944 should be marked as the beginning of the present political era, for it certainly witnessed the re-emergence of the Democratic party and the beginning of the realignment of the Wisconsin electorate. We mark 1946 as that year, however, because it was clearly the end of La Follette Progressivism. The Progressive party disbanded at the Portage Convention, where its adherents voted to re-enter the Republican ranks. Robert M. La Follette, Jr., sought to retain his Senate seat by contesting for the Republican nomination. His primary election defeat by Joseph R. McCarthy prepared the way for two-party competition along issue-oriented lines by the Wisconsin wings of the two national parties.

The present period in Wisconsin politics has been marked by the development of close two-party competition between parties composed of program-oriented activists and divided along contemporary liberal-conservative lines. It is within this context that our study of campaign finance takes place. From 1946 to 1957 the Democrats failed to win a major statewide office[3] or control of either house of the state legislature. Their electoral strength grew, however, and in 1954 and 1956 their gubernatorial candidate, William Proxmire, came close to victory with 49 and 48 per cent of the vote respectively. The Democrats increased their congressional delegation from 1 to 3; and their state legislative delegation increased from 11 to 33 in the 100-member assembly and from 5 to 10 in the 33-member senate.

Finally, in 1957 the trend toward two-party competition culminated in the election of William Proxmire to the United States Senate to fill the vacancy left by the death of Joseph R. McCarthy. In subsequent elections Democrat Gaylord Nelson was elected governor in 1958 and 1960, and United States senator in 1962. Proxmire was re-elected to the Senate in 1958 and 1964, and John W. Reynolds was elected governor on the Democratic ticket in 1962. This impressive showing by the Democrats was offset by equally impressive signs of Republican strength. Through the entire period the Republicans dominated the state senate, and in all but two sessions they had working majorities in the assembly. Republicans held most of the constitutional posts below the governorship, although the Democrats elected attorneys general in four of the five elections from 1958 to 1966, lieutenant governors in two of those elections, and a state treasurer in one of them. The Republicans held an edge in the state's House of Representatives delegation, except in 1964 when the state sent five members of each party to that body. The Republicans recaptured the governorship in 1964 and retained it in 1966. This is a picture of close electoral competition with alternating and divided control of public office.

The party organizations which contested these elections were based on the mass-membership principle. The Democratic Organizing Committee (now called the Democratic Party of Wisconsin) was established in 1949 as a vehicle by which liberal Democrats could by-pass the formal party structure. It immediately began to enroll members and imposed a modest dues levy of $2 on individuals and $3 on married couples. Organization centers around counties, except in Milwaukee where there are ward committees. Party units operate on a club basis, with every dues-paying member eligible to attend the monthly meetings and to take part in disposing of the party's business. The state convention elects the state chairman, vice-chairmen, treasurer, national committee members, and the state Administrative Committee, which has legislative powers between conventions. The convention also adopts a party platform on state issues and resolutions on national issues; it has steadfastly refused to alter its rule against the pre-primary endorsement of candidates. Convention apportionment is based on the number of members and the number of votes for the party candidate for governor in each county. The total number of delegate posts has ordinarily been in excess of 1200, making the convention an enormous party rally and a sometimes unpredictable decision-making body. Although party membership was less than 1500 at the party's advent, it rose steadily to 15,000 on the eve of the 1958 gubernatorial election and to a high of 26,000 in 1964. After the Democrats lost the governorship in 1964, membership declined and on the eve of the 1966 election it stood at just below 16,000.

The Republican Voluntary Committee (now the Republican Party of Wisconsin) provided the base for the expansion of the Republican organization. Affiliation is not by dues paid to the state party headquarters, but rather by enrollment in local party units. These organizations may collect dues or not, but in a growing number of instances they have put their membership on a dues-paying basis. In 1964, Republican party membership was estimated at 40,000 to 50,000. State party headquarters takes some steps, such as the circulation of a party newsletter, to maintain cohesiveness among those affiliated with the Republican party. Practices vary from county to county, but usually there is an annual caucus to elect party officers who conduct the party's business during their term of office. In election years the caucuses are empowered to endorse candidates for local and legislative office, although in many cases they choose not to become involved in primary contests. The Republican state convention adopts the party platform and endorses candidates for statewide office; the endorsement carries financial support and generally the assistance of state and local party officers. The state party chairman is elected by the state executive committee rather than by the party convention.

The nature of the Wisconsin party organizations justifies a classification of them as mass-membership parties, a style of political organization untypical of American state politics. The Wisconsin parties have also been described as being more programmatic and more clearly divided on issues than their counterparts in most American states. John Fenton has contrasted the "issue-oriented" politics of Wisconsin, Michigan, and Minnesota with the "job-oriented" politics of Indiana, Illinois, and Ohio.[4] Frank Sorauf has pointed to the "tightly knit and interrelated economic, social and governmental ideology" of the Wisconsin Republican party, premised on "the great value to the individual and to society of unrestricted private enterprise."[5] The Democrats also have a "dominant doctrinal theme" which encompasses local as well as state leaders; this is the liberal position of the national Democratic party and is extended to the state level in the belief that "government has an important role in regulating and controlling the economy, in providing the basic economic and social necessities for all people, and in guaranteeing certain basic rights for all citizens."[6] Leon D. Epstein has reported that sharp differences exist along the usual conservative-liberal lines between the two parties in the areas of labor, social welfare legislation, state finances, regulation of the economy, and foreign policy.[7]

Such characterizations do not describe every member or every leader of the two parties. The Republicans have had a moderate wing, perhaps justly characterized by the Eisenhower term, "modern Republicans." Governor Walter Kohler was so identified, and it is clear that the late Senator Alexander Wiley was both an internationalist and somewhat less conservative on domestic issues than many Wisconsin Republicans. Nonetheless, all commentators on Wisconsin politics focus on the relatively sharp cleavages on issues between the two parties. The Republican state convention demonstrated its conservative preference in 1956 by endorsing Congressman Glenn Davis, a vigorous and outspoken conservative, against Senator Wiley; and most party members preferred Davis to Kohler in the 1957 primary to choose a nominee to contest for the vacancy left by the death of Joseph R. McCarthy. The 1958 Republican state convention approved a right-to-work plank and a sales tax plank for the party platform against the pleas of candidates who felt they could not win on such issues. Party chairman and 1962 gubernatorial candidate Philip Kuehn had been a leader of the McCarthy forces in the state Republican party and he waged much of his gubernatorial campaign on the theme that government "handouts" were destroying the self-reliance of the American people; his advertising argued that welfare programs made people like the "ducks in the lagoon who wait for someone to feed them" rather than like the "soaring, independent eagles" which are symbolic of America. State Republican chairman Talbot Peterson was quoted by John Fenton as saying, "I am not a politican. I am a conservative. We are tired of politicians who coddle the unions and the Communists in order to get votes."[8]

In 1964, party leaders apparently favored Barry Goldwater for the presidential nomination. They discouraged Nelson Rockefeller from entering the state's presidential primary by fielding a favorite son candidate, Representative John Byrnes, whose delegate slate turned out to be unanimous in its support of Goldwater. Then Congressman Melvin Laird chaired the national convention's platform committee which wrote the Goldwater platform, and after the convention the Republican state candidates endorsed the Goldwater candidacy with some enthusiasm rather than take the neutral or hostile stances adopted by moderate and liberal Republicans in other states.[9]

The Democrats, too, have some range of opinion within their ranks. Many Democratic activists in the Polish-American wards of Milwaukee have rejected the party's strong position in favor of civil rights, and especially of open housing legislation, although the leading Polish-American politician in the state, Representative Clement Zablocki, consistently voted for the civil rights bills sponsored by Presidents Kennedy and Johnson. Democrats from the sparsely settled northwestern Wisconsin counties have voted against the party's one-man, one-vote reapportionment position both in party conventions and in the state legislature. Nonetheless, most Democratic leaders have taken clear-cut liberal positions. State party conventions have endorsed the recognition of Communist China and strong civil rights measures as well as a wide range of social welfare programs at the state and national levels. Gaylord Nelson was outspoken in his opposition to the House UnAmerican Activities Committee, and Democratic Attorney General John Reynolds was criticized during his gubernatorial campaign for joining a corporal's guard of state attorneys general who refused to join a brief urging the Supreme Court to reverse its position that public school prayers are unconstitutional.

Democratic factionalism, unlike that of the Republicans, has few ideological or issue-oriented overtones. Instead it has been a shifting factionalism which first pitted the "Madison ring," an aggregation of upstate political leaders centered around a core of party leaders in Madison, against the so-called "Milwaukee ring" which encompassed most of that city's legislative delegation and its party hierarchy. After 1960, the Kennedy and Humphrey-Stevenson partisans formed distinct groups which cut across the old Madison-Milwaukee line of division; and in 1961 the Kennedy and Humphrey-Stevenson wings were overlaid with sharp rivalry between Governor John Reynolds and State Chairman Patrick J. Lucey, on the one hand, and Senator Gaylord Nelson, on the other. Although both Reynolds and Lucey had been prominent Kennedy supporters and Nelson had been a Humphrey partisan, the groups which formed around them were not completely congruent with the factions which

Table 1

Distribution of Liberal and Conservative Vote Scores
of Democratic and Republican Representatives and
Senators, 87th–89th Congresses

	ADA[a]		AFL–CIO[a]		ACA[b]	
Score	Dem.	Rep.	Dem.	Rep.	Dem.	Rep.
80–100	15	0	18	0	0	13
60–79	2	1	0	2	0	2
40–59	1	1	0	1	1	1
20–39	0	1	0	1	3	2
0–19	0	15	0	14	14	0

[a] Americans for Democratic Action and AFL–CIO: High scores are liberal, low scores conservative.
[b] Americans for Constitutional Action: High scores are conservative, low scores liberal.

had grown up in 1960. Whatever overtones this factionalism may have had, they were not programmatic.

It is difficult to provide comprehensive data showing programmatic division between the two political parties. However, the voting records of the state's congressmen and senators provide some insight into the distinction between the parties on issues. The rankings of three interest groups easily identified as liberal or conservative are accessible through the *Congressional Quarterly* service for the 87th through 89th Congresses. High scores on the Americans for Democratic Action and AFL–CIO roll calls are a fair measure of liberalism and low scores of conservatism. Conversely, high scores on the Americans for Constitutional Action roll call are a good test of conservatism and low scores of liberalism.[10]

During these three Congresses, from 1961 through 1967, the Wisconsin delegation consisted of 10 representatives and 2 senators. There were thus a total of 36 roll call scores by each organization during the period, or 1 for each of the 12 members for each of the 3 sessions. There were a total of 18 Republican scores, 17 in the House and 1 in the Senate, and 18 Democratic scores, 13 in the House and 5 in the Senate. Table 1 reports the distribution of liberal and conservative scores of members of the two parties. A sharp polarization emerges, and it is even more distinct when it is recalled that the middle-range Republican scores were in every case those of Senator Wiley and Representative Alvin O'Konski, both regarded as mavericks by the Republican organization. The middle-range Democratic scores generally represent votes by Senator Proxmire, widely criticized within the Democratic party for his conservative voting record between 1958 and 1962, and by one-term Congressman John Race.

These data, the written commentaries on Wisconsin politics, and observation suggest that officeholders, candidates, and party officials tend to be program-oriented and that there are quite distinct issue divisions between the parties. Some survey data are available from the University of Wisconsin Survey Research Laboratory which cast additional light on the question. Their 1964 post-election survey asked respondents their perceptions of the parties and their own preferences in terms of the general rubrics "liberal" and "conservative." In addition, the survey investigated political activism with questions concerning campaign contributions, party membership, and campaign work. It is possible to use these data to examine the ideological orientations of political activists and their perceptions of the ideological positions of the two parties. A severe limitation of this analysis is the highly attenuated definition of activist which is used: a respondent who performed any of the kinds of political activities mentioned above was counted an activist.

Table 2 presents the activists' perceptions of party ideologies and the ideological preferences of the activists who identified with the two major parties. It should be noted that the numbers are fairly small: 149 or 21.2 per cent of the total sample of 702 engaged in political activity and were also party identifiers.

These data show that 56.4 per cent of the activists perceived the parties in ideological terms, and this group was almost unanimously agreed that the Republican party was ideologically more conservative than the Democratic party. As contrasted to these activists, only 32.3 per cent of non-activist party identifiers perceived parties in ideological terms, and 39.5 per cent of

Table 2

Perceptions of Parties and Ideological Preferences of
Wisconsin Political Activists, 1964

Party	Is The Republican Party More Conservative?				Do You Regard Yourself As Conservative or Liberal?			
	Yes %	No %	Other[a] %	Tot. N	Cons. %	Lib. %	Other[a] %	Tot. N
Rep.	60.3	0	39.7	68	60.3	14.7	25	68
Dem.	43.2	9.9	46.9	81	22.2	49.4	28.4	81
All	51.0	5.4	43.6	149	39.6	33.6	26.8	149

[a] "Don't Know," and a few "Not Ascertained."

that small number identified the Democrats as more conservative.

The percentage of activists who identified their own ideological orientations was substantially larger than the percentage who perceived the parties as ideological—73.2 per cent compared to 56.4 per cent. But the congruence between personal ideology and party ideology was less impressive than the correct identification of party ideologies. Among ideologically oriented Republican activists, conservatives predominated by a margin of four to one; while among Democrats, liberals were in majority of substantially more than two to one. The congruence between personal ideology and party ideology was much higher among these activists than among non-activist partisans—the activists having these congruent attitudes in 54.4 per cent of the cases and the non-activists in 37.7 per cent.

Taken together, this evidence shows incomplete ideological identification of the parties by activists, but almost totally correct perceptions of party ideologies among those activists who made such identifications. Furthermore, activists made such identifications and made them correctly in a far larger percentage of cases than non-activists. In addition, there was a substantial difference in the ideological self-identifications of the activists of the two parties, with the Democrats identifying themselves as liberal and the Republicans seeing themselves as conservative. The ideological division between active partisans was sharper than among non-activist party identifiers.

Mere identification of parties or of self as "liberal" or "conservative" might not mean, however, that activists espouse policies which are ordinarily associated with those terms. Or such identifications might represent only the most rudimentary understanding of the sets of issues clustered around the two ideological labels. Testing the meaning of "liberal" and "conservative" for either the general electorate or the activists goes well beyond our scope or means. However, the leading work on belief systems suggests that at least among activists ideological self-identification is ordinarily associated correctly with the policy stances which constitute the liberal and conservative positions. Most frequently these ideologies were identified along a "spend-save" continuum, which of course accurately reflects the willingness of liberals to spend money for domestic social welfare programs and to raise taxes to provide these services and the reluctance of conservatives to embark on these courses. Among the most active, ideology took on additional meanings in the areas of foreign affairs and race relations, and on these issues as well as on the "spend-save" axis there was correct identification of issue positions with ideological labels. Ideological identification meant for some activists consistently friendly or hostile attitudes toward certain groups; here groups rather than issues were central to the belief system. But since many groups in the society, such as business or labor or Negroes, are quite consistently associated with the cluster of policies which constitute the liberal or the conservative ideology, identification with groups rather than with issues may give ideological self-identification important and correct content.[11]

One can conclude that, while neither perceptions of party ideology by activists nor the ideological cleavage between Democratic and Republican activists is complete, the degree of ideological perception and cleavage is quite remarkable in light of the highly attenuated definition of activist used in Table 2 and the ordinary view that American party politics is not very programmatic. Furthermore, other studies suggest that the combination of activism and ideological self-identification is associated with commitments to issues and/or groups which do in fact represent the major divisions between the two ideological positions in America. This evidence and the characterizations of the parties and their leaders by Fenton, Sorauf, and Epstein coincide to portray Wisconsin parties as quite sharply separated along programmatic lines, at least by comparison with the American party system as a whole.

We must add one caveat. The election of 1964 brought Warren P. Knowles, usually thought of as a conservative, to the governor's chair and his close collaborator Ody J. Fish to the post of state Republican Chairman. There is some evidence that after their victory at the polls these men adopted a more moderate stance than that ordinarily attributed to the Wisconsin Republican party. Only preliminary data are available on the direction of Wisconsin party politics in the aftermath of 1964; but as time and research provide a perspective on those years it may be found that the direction of the Republican party has changed. Our extensive campaign funding data are for 1964 and the preceeding years, and for those elections our description of the Republican ideological orientation is adequate. Only preliminary data on fund raising in 1966 are presently available, and we are not able therefore to indicate whether the Republican financial constituency has changed dramatically since the Republican victory of 1964.

Method and Scope of the Study

One reason why campaign finance has been so little studied is the tangled nature of the available data and the difficulty of developing relatively straightforward techniques for dealing with them. These same problems arose in planning the present study; and both the uncertainties about the available data and the specific methods used to deal with the material are summarized here as an aid to understanding the basis for the conclusions.

At the outset, there is the need for the availability of basic information about the sources and amounts of receipts and the objects and amounts of expenditures. Thirty-six states require the filing of reports detailing campaign fund receipts and 43 states require such reports for campaign expenditures. These regulations vary widely on the questions of whether reports are required in both the primary and general election, for political committees as well as political candidates, and before elections as well as after them. Wisconsin's requirements are quite well suited to the purposes of the political scientist, requiring reports of receipts and disbursements of candidates and committees for both primary and general elections, and both before and after each such election.[12]

Even where the statutes make such information available, it is not useful unless accessible to the researcher. The problem of accessibility has two aspects: the location of the reports and the duration of their availability. Thus in 1955, Hugh Douglas Price reported that the then existent Massachusetts law provided for destruction of all filings fifteen months after the general election.[13] The same practice has been followed in Connecticut. In Wisconsin, the reports must be kept for six years, but this requirement is frequently ignored by the county clerks.[14] Fortunately, the Secretary of State gives the financial reports filed in his office to the State Historical Society at the end of the six-year period, and this has made it possible for this study to reach back to 1950.[15]

The location of campaign financial statements also poses a problem for the researcher. White and Owens reported that in Michigan political finance statements were filed with the county clerk in the county of residence of the person making the report. Their analysis of campaign money in Michigan was feasible only because the state attorney general made a complete collection of the reports filed in the various counties.[16] According to a 1957 report by the Kentucky Legislative Research Commission, there

were six other states in which some or all of the campaign
finance reports were filed solely with local officials.[17] The Wisconsin statutes require that the candidate and candidate committee financial statements be filed with the officer authorized by
law to issue the certificates of nomination and election, and this
is usually a county or local clerk.[18] Other political committees
file with the secretary of state if they intend to make expenditures in more than one county or to aid candidates or measures
voted upon in or affecting more than one county.[19]

In effect, this means that in Wisconsin campaign financial
statements for county office candidates and their committees are
filed at the county courthouse, as are the reports of legislative
and congressional candidates and the appropriate supporting
committees if the district is within the borders of a single
county. Other reports are filed with the secretary of state. There
is a general misinterpretation of the statute which has led most
local political committees, both party groups and *ad hoc* organizations supporting statewide candidates, to file in the county
courthouses. Thus county party organizations do not file their
reports in a single office where they would be easily accessible
for research.

To obtain the data for the present study, it was necessary to
travel into 20 of the 72 county seats in order to develop
reasonable estimates of the receipts and expenditures for county
courthouse offices and for legislative seats located within single
counties. For the 1964 election, therefore, our data include
information on the campaigns for 160 of the state's 576 courthouse posts, 79 of 100 state assembly contests, 16 of 17 state
senate contests, and all of the congressional and state office
elections. Because of the six-year rule for keeping these records
and the laxity of some county clerks, the available data were
less numerous and therefore less adequate in the earlier years
covered by the study. The 1966 data, by contrast, are less
complete than the 1964 information because of the time lag
between the election and the development of political finance
data, which is caused by the enormous complications in the
gathering, refinement, analysis, and interpretation of the thousands of filings. Preliminary data for 1966 are available, how-

ever, and are quite useful in estimating candidate and system-wide political expenditures.

For county courthouse, assembly, and state senate contests, there are fairly large numbers of reports available for some of the years studied, but this still leaves the problem of estimating receipts and expenditures for the remaining districts. Two methods for estimating have been used. Those legislative and county reports from urban areas, i.e., counties containing at least one city of more than 25,000 people, were separated from those from rural areas. The calculations for Milwaukee County were handled as a third and entirely separate category. Where the available data covered at least 20 per cent of the total number of offices or districts in the category, the median of the available reports was used to estimate the spending for each of the missing units. This technique easily applied for all estimates made for the 1962, 1964, and 1966 elections.

When reports were available for fewer than 20 per cent of the units, as occurred frequently for the years 1950, 1954, 1956, and 1958, the available data were compared to the data available from the same districts or counties for 1962, a year for which there were a large number of reports available in all categories. The ratio of spending for the two years was computed, and used to estimate spending for the earlier year. For example, assume that spending in all 100 assembly districts in 1962 was $40,000 and that the data available for 1954 encompassed only 12 districts. If the spending in those 12 districts in 1954 averaged 75 per cent of the spending in those same districts in 1962, then total spending for all assembly contests in 1954 would be estimated to have been 75 per cent of all 1962 spending, or $30,000. There are serious shortcomings to this approach, but since most of the financial reports for earlier years have been destroyed, it is necessary to use estimates based on the most reasonable techniques available. The one value of such simple techniques is that they can be used with relative ease for replicative studies elsewhere.

In addition to the problems of availability and accessibility of the basic reports, and the techniques for estimating costs from a limited number of data, there is also the difficulty of the volume of the data which must be examined. American politics is basically state and local politics. The Jacksonian tradition is still felt in many states where minor administrative officers as well as legislative and executive officials are elected at both the state and local levels, often only after contesting a primary election. In addition, party committees are organized around lesser subdivisions of government.

The problem is compounded by the frequency of reporting. Each candidate and candidate committee must file both before

Table 3

Number of Units and Filings, By Political Party, Used to Estimate Total Wisconsin Political Costs in 1964

No. of Filings	Rep. Units	Dem. Units	Total Units	Total Filings
2	134	167	301	602
4	419	335	754	3,016
5	29	30	59	295
Total	582	532	1,114	3,913

and after each primary and general election. The party units must file at these times and on July 1 of each year. There exist, therefore, two reports for each candidate and committee participating in the primary, four reports for those active in the general election, and five reports for party committees. Table 3 indicates the number of reports which had to be examined to gain sufficient data to make reliable statewide estimates for 1964.[20]

The analysis of individual campaign contributions is a special problem, because their sources must be categorized. Most studies of political finance undertake this analysis because it yields some significant insights into the internal distribution of influence within parties and campaign organizations, the relationship of parties and candidates to various groups in the community, and the extent to which there are differences in multiple voting by individuals in a democratic political system.

For the present study, the names of all contributors to the statewide party committees and to the statewide committees supporting United States Senate and gubernatorial candidates for six elections were put on cards and then sorted to eliminate multiple givers, which yielded a file of contributors used to analyze the financial constituencies of the two parties. Even after the multiple givers had been identified, the number of contributors for 1964 alone was in excess of 10,300, exclusive of those who gave less than $5, and therefore are not individually identified under Wisconsin law, the transfer payments from other political committees, the contributions from labor unions, and the receipts from program book advertising.[21]

A final problem of methodology is basic to all the others, namely the question of the accuracy of the data available in public records. Perhaps the best general rule is that there is no general rule. Practices vary from jurisdiction to jurisdiction and may well depend on the quality of enforcement of the campaign finance regulations and the political culture of the jurisdiction. Across the United States, enforcement is generally lax or non-existent, primarily because enforcement officials are themselves involved in the elective process. Some states have experienced wholesale misreporting or non-reporting.[22]

On the other hand, Hugh Douglas Price in his study of campaign finance in Massachusetts and John P. White and John R. Owens in their study of political money in Michigan relied primarily upon the filed reports on the ground that they appear in those states to be quite accurate.[23] Alexander Heard based his estimates of state political costs on reports from political scientists around the country who used official reports and then made revisions in the figures based upon personal interviews and their assessments of the validity of the reports. He then added 15 per cent to the estimates submitted to cover "the vague realm politicians call under-the-table money."[24]

In Wisconsin there is clearly some non-reporting, though it appears to be at a minimum. Several county clerks indicated that they "send out the sheriff" to compel laggards to file the required statements. Misreporting may be a more serious problem. Some committees clearly report less than they spend because they fear adverse public reactions to large-scale political expenditures. Frequently the information is all in the report, but filed in a misleading fashion. One campaign committee, for instance, filed all of its contributors, but on the summary sheet it declared the "net proceeds" from its fund-raising dinners. In excess of $20,000 in receipts and expenditures was thereby excluded from the summary total provided by the committee, even though listed in the body of the report.

A good many of the inaccuracies result from haste or inadvertence or ignorance. Local party organizations have no permanent staff and their officers are typically new each year. The filing forms are a bureaucratic mystery to them, and they file incompletely because they misunderstand the law. This phenomenon is probably more prevalent among Democrats than among Republicans, whose leadership tends to to be drawn more heavily from professional and business occupations where office staff is available to perform the filing duties. The hectic pace of the closing weeks of a political campaign contributes to inaccuracy. Money is received and must be immediately disbursed to cover media costs or other pressing obligations. Records are kept as best as can be, but it is frequently too expensive or inconvenient to assign a staff member full time to the task of processing funds. After all, from the politician's point of view, the filing of campaign reports does not contribute to winning the election, and he is generally reluctant to allocate resources to such an unproductive task. Where the candidate must do his own filing, he moves with as much haste as possible because he obviously has more significant chores to perform a week before election.

The accuracy of filed statements in Wisconsin is sufficient to provide a base of information. Interviews with some political leaders indicate that the reports are usually accurate within a range of 10 to 20 per cent. (This does not include contributions in kind which are very seldom reported despite the legal mandate that they be listed and their value estimated.[25]) One county clerk and former sheriff, for instance, reported that out-of-pocket spending for rounds of drinks at various popular taverns, and for tickets for picnics, lotteries, etc., sponsored by civic, religious, and fraternal groups was a major source of unreported expenditures in courthouse campaigns. On the other hand, another clerk said frankly, "I don't have that kind of personality for campaigning in the bars, and I just have to hope that people are satisfied with the service they get in my office." Apparently they are, since he has been unopposed for three consecutive elections. At least one candidate among all those whose reports were examined from 1950 to 1966 was honest about out-of-pocket expenditures. He reported "refreshments—different taverns: $12.50, $26.30." He won the election, though apparently unaware of a statutory provision making it a felony to "make any gift . . . to procure . . . the vote of any voter at any election."[26]

In addition to misreporting, unreported contributions in kind, and out-of-pocket expenses which are not reported, the problem of accuracy is compounded by the flow of transfer payments between candidates and committees. It frequently happens that money is collected by one committee and then listed as a disbursement when transferred to a second group. That group in turn lists it as a receipt and again as a disbursement when it is spent. This may happen several times to the same sum, thus causing an incredible inflation in the reported figures. The seriousness of the problem can be illustrated by the accounts of the Republican Party of Wisconsin for 1964. Total expenditures were listed as $939,394, but when transfers were eliminated the actual figure was $492,140. This is an extreme case, but a telling one. For the present study, all transfer payments were eliminated by crediting the expenditure of the money to the committee which finally spent it for a campaign purpose and eliminating it as an expenditure on the account of the committee(s) which transferred it to another political organization.

A note should be added about that category of funds described by Heard as "under-the-table money." Extensive interviewing of political leaders suggests that there is almost no spending for such purposes in Wisconsin. There are no local leaders capable of delivering blocs of votes for a fee and no ethnic group leaders whose followers can be purchased for a price. There is some gossip about the purchase of editorial support by the placing of campaign ads, particularly in the ethnic and racial press, but such expenditures usually show up on the filed reports.

Thus it is probably fair to conclude that the filed reports in Wisconsin, when carefully examined for quirks of reporting, yield information about political finance within a range of error of about 10 to 20 per cent, if contributions in kind and some out-of-pocket expenditures by local-level campaigners are excluded. The analysis presented in this study must therefore be viewed within these limitations and in light of the improvisations used to cover gaps in the material.

The present study is a time-series study, as contrasted to a single-year case study; its special value is that it yields the opportunity to compare levels of spending and sources of contributions during the period of Wisconsin's transition from one-party hegemony to intensive two-party competition. It analyzes campaign finance in Wisconsin for seven elections—1950, 1954, 1956, 1958, 1962, 1964, and 1966. The starting date was selected because it is the first year in which the Democratic Party of Wisconsin, in its present form as a mass membership party, operated in a statewide election. Two elections during the period were omitted from the study. The 1952 data appeared to be badly distorted by the flow of out-of-state money to combat and support Senator Joseph R. McCarthy. The 1960 reports reflected a similar peculiarity because of the early effort of the Kennedy campaign organization in Wisconsin and the resources not normally available to Wisconsin Democrats which consequently flowed into the state. In both 1952 and 1960, there are some indications that in-state contributions also increased because of the special appeals of the central figures in those two elections.

Although the balloting for 1968 was completed prior to publication, no attempt has been made to include that election in this analysis. Indeed, as previously pointed out, the time required to analyze the data is such that only preliminary data and analysis are available for the 1966 election. This pattern is the same found in the studies of Heard, Alexander, Overacker, and Price, who required several years after the reports were filed to process and interpret the data.

The concern here is with spending by candidates, political committees, and parties in campaigns to nominate and elect public officials chosen on a partisan ballot. No attempt is made to study campaign finance for Wisconsin's non-partisan judiciary and municipal and town government posts, or for the selection in April of each presidential year of national convention delegates, or for issues submitted to the public on referendum ballots. The study of party committees includes their receipts and expenditures for a period of seventeen months prior to each election. This period is somewhat longer than that usually studied. However, in recent years in Wisconsin the non-incumbents seeking statewide office have usually announced their candidacies about thirteen months prior to election day. Furthermore, the legal requirements call for an annual filing on the second Tuesday in July of each year, as well as filings before and after the primary and general elections. Since a good share of campaign receipts and some significant expenditures occur prior to July, it is necessary to use the annual filing and the campaign filings together to obtain an accurate picture of campaign finance in Wisconsin.

Political finance can only be examined in the context of the larger political system. This study occurs in a system which has recently undergone the transition from one-party politics to intense two-party competition. Furthermore, its party structures are of the programmatic mass party style and therefore atypical in the United States. Nonetheless, it is well suited in many ways to the study of political finance. To begin with, the larger political context within which this investigation takes place has been plumbed with unusual care by a number of political scientists. Furthermore, the availability of political finance data is quite good. The legal requirements for filing finance reports are comprehensive and the reports have been preserved to a greater extent than in all but a handful of other states. The politicians themselves have been accessible and very willing to explore the political finance area with the author, thus offsetting many of the weaknesses of the filed data. Notwithstanding these advantages, it was necessary to improvise some techniques for filling in the gaps created by the destruction of records, the inadequacy of the filed materials, and the fading recollections of past campaigns by men whose concerns are this year's electoral outcomes. The nature of the materials available for this study and the techniques used to refine them have been discussed at length to make easier their evaluation by others. In the rest of this study the emphasis is on the ways in which political finance is a response to the political system, in turn affects that system, and can be evaluated only in the context of that system. The relationships investigated are relatively large ones. They are waves not ripples; hence the quality of some of the data should not mislead, for they are accurate enough to distinguish between a rising and an ebbing tide.

The Cost of State Politics

Estimating the Cost of Wisconsin Politics

In Chapter 2 there was a full discussion of the methods used to project total political spending from the filed reports. Those methods yield the figures "Total Expenditures: Projected from Filed Reports" in Table 4 for cash outlays by candidates, candidate committees, and party committees for seven elections. Transfer payments have been eliminated.

These projections of reported political spending are not, however, a satisfactory statement of total political costs. One major weakness is their failure to include direct political spending by other groups and associations. Thus the direct expenditures for political purposes by labor unions are not included. The extensive data developed by H. Gaylon Greenhill in his study, *Labor Money in Wisconsin Politics, 1964,* suggest that about $100,000 was spent by labor which did not show up as contributions on candidate and committee filings.[1] The bulk of these expenditures went for the extensive telephone banks used by labor to get out the vote on election day in the labor centers across the state. An additional item of direct expense by labor was a Voters Guide Supplement inserted in the *Milwaukee*

Journal. The total cost of these two activities was approximately $70,000.[2]

Labor was the major non-party association engaged in direct political spending, but several others are worthy of mention. In 1964, the Globe Union Republican Committee, consisting of a group of employees of Globe Union, Inc., who contribute monthly to the Committee, reported raising in excess of $11,000, but the amount of spending is uncertain. The Political Education and Action League, composed of young business executives and lawyers in Milwaukee County, regularly campaigns in behalf of Republican candidates and reported expenditures of $1,478 in 1964. The Political Independence Committee, a Falk Corporation association similar to the Globe Union Republican Committee, spent $11,576, most of which, however, appeared on party and candidate reports in the form of contributions.

A final source of direct spending excluded from the estimates is minor party committees and candidates. This spending is inconsequential in the Wisconsin political system. In 1964, the Socialist Workers Campaign Committee reported spending $535; the Wisconsin Campaign Committee of the Socialist Labor party, $1,569; and the Conservative Party of Wisconsin, $257. Even in 1950, the modern heyday of the minor parties, their total spending was under $6,500. In that year the Socialist party, a one-time power in Wisconsin politics, filed a full statehouse slate and a large number of congressional candidates; their aggregate spending was $2,688. The tattered remnants of Henry Wallace's People's Progressive party managed to spend $2,952 on a full slate of statehouse candidates before going out of business for good. The Socialist Laborites spent $643 and the Socialist Workers, $130.

To take into account these various sources of direct spending, an additional $125,000 to $150,000 could be added to the 1958, 1962, 1964, and 1966 estimates. In earlier years, the total was not more than $75,000, and probably less. It was not until the 1957 special election to fill the vacancy left by the death of Senator Joseph R. McCarthy that labor instituted its expensive phone bank operation. And only in 1958 did the merger of the AFL and CIO put vigorous CIO political activists at the head of labor's total political efforts in Wisconsin.

We have mentioned the second major limitation on these projected costs—the probability of inaccuracies in the filed reports amounting to 10 to 20 per cent of the total. One aspect of the 1964 total which tends artificially to inflate the reported cost of state politics also is worth mention. It appears that the Democratic presidential managers directed $64,950 of political committee and union money to the Democratic Party of Wisconsin with instructions that state Democratic leaders pay the money to an advertising agency handling the presidential campaign. This surmise is unconfirmed by state Democratic leaders, but the reports show receipts from various international union headquarters in addition to those directed to the United States Senate and House of Representatives candidates; some of the unions have no apparent interest in local Wisconsin politics. Finally, there are payments of $64,950 to the New York advertising agency of Doyle, Dane, Bernbach, Inc., for "t.v. for state candidates." A close investigation shows that no state Democratic candidate used this agency, and further that the Democratic state organization conducted no independent media campaign in behalf of its state candidates. These facts support Herbert Alexander's argument that Democrats secreted funds in certain states where their spending would not be reported in Washington;[3] this practice tends to exaggerate the reported cost of state politics in 1964 as well as to diminish the reported cost of national campaigning.

A third significant defect in our projected estimates of reported political costs is the failure to include expenditures in kind, for which Alexander Heard suggests that at least 5 per cent should be added to cash outlays.[4] The Republicans have benefited from the use of corporation-owned aircraft for political transportation. The marshalling of substantial stenographic staffs in corporation and law offices to handle campaign clerical chores is also common in Republican campaigning. Republican campaigners frequently call on friendly businessmen to recruit "volunteer" workers, which ordinarily means that junior executives and others in the corporate hierarchy are encouraged to do political work on corporation time. In the 1964 campaign there were reports from members of the Communications Workers of America that telephone company managers in upstate counties had instructed operators to make calls canvassing to identify potential Republican voters. Democrats can occasionally call on lawyers for assistance in kind or for the contribution of services, but the main source of such assistance is labor unions. Office

Table 4

Total Political Expenditures:[a] Wisconsin, 1950–1966

Year[b]	Total Expenditures: Projected from Filed Reports	Total Expenditures: Corrected Estimates	
1950	$ 831,800	$ 990,000 to	$1,073,000
1954	1,027,300	1,205,000	1,308,000
1956	1,284,900	1,488,000	1,617,000
1958	1,297,400	1,577,400	1,707,000
1962	2,436,000	2,830,400	3,073,000
1964	3,292,900	3,772,000	4,101,000
1966	2,757,900	3,245,200	3,526,600

[a] Transfer payments have been eliminated.
[b] 1952 and 1960 omitted (see p. 40).

staffs are committed to political tasks during campaigns; union stewards work hard at politics; postage, telephone services, and other materials are transferred to political purposes from ordinary operations. The 5 per cent estimate of the value of assistance in kind or in services does not, of course, include any estimate of the value of the volunteer man-hours of thousands of political activists. In a state with a mass membership party system, such as Wisconsin, that additional "cost" of politics must be staggering indeed.[5]

In the context of these additional considerations, the "Total Expenditures: Corrected Estimates" in Table 4 suggest the range within which total costs would lie for the seven elections under discussion. These estimates include a 10 to 20 per cent margin for incomplete and inaccurate reporting as well as amounts representing direct expenditures by non-party associations and minor parties. They do not, however, include the value of goods or services in kind or the value of volunteer help. In addition, it should be made clear that these estimates and other cost figures used throughout this study do not include the cost of operating the mechanics of the electoral system, such as the cost of ballots and the salaries of voting clerks, which expenses are borne by the government.

Costs in Perspective—The Candidate's Viewpoint

In *Predicament of Democratic Man* Edmond Cahn argues that a "democratic temper" impels men to look at public problems from a "consumer perspective." He notes that this is a shift of 180 degrees from the vantage point adopted by classic philosophers of government who developed their theories by observing the ways of empires, kingdoms, and other large units which are generally denoted political systems today.[6] Cahn then observes:

Whenever a concrete question arises for decision within a given society, most of the inhabitants recognize the same factors as relevant to resolving it and, if they disagree on the answer, it is only because they see factors in different ratios of size, consequence, and importance. Almost everything in the process of deliberation depends on where they take their stand while they assess them, on what we correctly call their "point of view."[7]

Cahn's analysis of the nature of decision-making clearly applies to normative questions about the cost of politics. The cost may look quite different to the political scientist who views it in terms of system-wide costs and to the candidate who sees it from the point of view of raising the cash to wage an electoral contest. There are no studies available which survey the reactions of candidates and would-be candidates to the costs of campaigns, but the costs of campaigns for a range of offices can give an impression of the magnitude of the financing hurdle which must be overcome in seriously waged political contests.

The costs of campaigns vary widely, of course, in response to such factors as the size and nature of the constituency, the importance of the office contested, the intensity of electoral competition, the vigor and strength of the opposition, the skill and will of the candidate and his supporters in gathering and pyramiding their resources, the availability of resources, and a host of other factors. Our assessment of political costs from the perspective of the candidate includes only the estimated cash expenditures on behalf of individual office seekers. Yet it must be kept in mind that candidates also bear the burden of gathering in-kind resources and volunteer labor. And they must co-ordinate their efforts with those of party organizations and other candidates so that they may take advantage of opportunities for joint campaigning. In Wisconsin, for instance, both parties regularly circulate pamphlets and brochures on behalf of the entire party ticket and they engage in other kinds of joint campaign efforts. Determining the value of these efforts to particular candidate campaigns would befuddle even trained accountants.

While relatively few of the nation's politicians share in the direct responsibility for financing the costs of presidential campaigns, a statement of the magnitude of the expenditures in campaigns for that office is useful for gaining a perspective on the funding problems which face those at the summit of American politics. Republican national level committees spent $8.9 million on behalf of their presidential nominee in 1956, $10.1 million in 1960, and $17.2 million in 1964. Democratic and labor union outlays were $6.3 million in the first of those elections, $10.6 million in 1960, and $15.6 million in 1964.[8] These totals reveal a doubling of costs in eight years, yet this rate of increase may not be so great as that in campaigns for some state and local offices. On the other hand, the $0.41 per vote spent on the presidential campaigns in 1964 represents a higher per vote expenditure by candidates than in all but a handful of the state and local contests for which data are available.

Nonetheless, the costs of statewide campaigns in the nation's large industrial states are also clearly at levels well beyond the reach of many of those well qualified to seek office, and these costs have in recent years spiraled as sharply upward as presidential campaign costs. Thus Alexander Heard's estimates that in 1952 and 1956 campaign costs for major statewide offices ranged from $150,000 to $250,000 in Connecticut, $400,000 to $600,000 in Illinois, and $800,000 to $1 million in New York, now seem modest.[9] Senator Abraham Ribicoff reported well in advance of his 1968 senatorial campaign that he would spend $350,000 wooing the voters in his Connecticut constituency; his actual outlays exceeded $550,000. In Illinois, Charles Percy spent $1 million to oust Senator Paul Douglas, who in 1952 had set the figure for a United States Senate campaign in "a fairly large industrial state" at between $150,000 and $200,000,[10] and had thus campaigned through an era when campaign costs had quintupled. Similarly, the 1966 New York gubernatorial campaign of Nelson Rockefeller cost $5 million, five times more than Heard's top estimate for candidate expenses in that state. A secular study of spending in Tennessee United States Senate primaries reports that Senator Estes Kefauver's campaign expenditures more than quadrupled from his first campaign in 1948, which cost $75,000, to his third-term campaign in 1960, which required $325,000.[11]

Evidence of the high costs of individual campaigns is also available from other states for which there are no time-series comparisons to measure the rate of increase. In the early 1960's the cost of running for governor of California was set at $853,000 and of Michigan at $500,000.[12] In 1956, Coleman Ransone, Jr., suggested that a figure of $100,000 would cover the average spending necessary in behalf of a gubernatorial candidate in a medium-sized American state, although he warned that such factors as the quality of the opposition, the need to battle a primary as well as a general election, the existence of real issues, and other such factors would affect the estimate.[13] Frank Sorauf estimated a decade later that typical United States Senate races in fairly competitive states cost between $200,000 and $500,000,[14] and it seems obvious that gubernatorial costs are in the same range because they occur in the same constituencies.

Even for offices of much less visibility, campaign costs seem high. Sorauf reports that expenditures on behalf of candidates for the House of Representatives in fairly competitive urban districts may run as high as $100,000, and that congressional campaign costs in all contested districts range from a minimum of $10,000 to a maximum of $100,000.[15] A study of ten congressional campaigns in the San Francisco Bay area in 1962 indicated that candidates with stiff opposition felt that between $50,000 to $60,000 was necessary to wage an effective campaign and likely winners in less competitive districts estimated their needs at $20,000 to $30,000.[16] The actual expenditures were somewhat lower than this, however: the average spending by six candidates in three competitive districts was $34,000, by seven winning candidates in non-competitive districts $16,000, and by the seven men defeated in those districts $12,500.[17] In Connecticut, 1966 congressional costs ranged from $14,600 to $48,600 for the Democrats and from $25,000 to $83,900 for the Republicans; the average Democratic expenditure in the six districts was $30,200 and the average Republican spending $42,600.[18]

Even at the state legislative level costs are often quite high. The largest expenditures have occurred in California where spending in excess of $42,000 in behalf of a single assembly candidate and $64,000 in behalf of a state senate aspirant was reported.[19] Donald Balmer has reported much more modest costs in state senate campaigns in Multnomah County, Oregon; the largest expenditure was by an incumbent Democrat who spent $2,973 to gain renomination and $1,948 to come through the general election.[20] But even those costs were not nominal when considered in the context of the candidate's other resources and the nature of his district: his was a relatively safe at-large district, and he had both Democratic county committee endorsement and newspaper editorial support.

The costs of individual campaigns in Wisconsin follow the same trend as in other states. Although the earlier expenditures for statewide offices were lower than in other jurisdictions, the recent spending levels compare with Sorauf's generalization that statewide campaigns cost between $200,000 and $500,000 dollars. In 1950, the reported expenditures for the Democratic gubernatorial and senatorial candidates were a modest $26,300 and $35,900 respectively. By 1964, these reported costs were $215,800 and $196,000, increases of 717.4 and 446 per cent. The estimated cost of each of these two campaigns in the latter year was in excess of $250,000, and Democratic party officials admitted that $300,000 had been expended in the gubernatorial race.[21] The 1966 gubernatorial expenditures were reportedly $192,400, and were actually in excess of $225,000. Comparable data are not available for the Republican expenditures for statewide offices because most spending is handled by the Republican party headquarters and is not differentiated according to the campaign to which it was allocated.

Wisconsin congressional and state legislative costs appear to be slightly less than those reported in other jurisdictions. In 1950 spending by Democratic candidates for the House of Representatives ranged from $900 to $10,900, with the average candidate spending $3,900. The comparable figures for the Republican candidates were $2,400 to $17,700, with the average standing at $6,100. By 1964, the Democratic range was $3,200 to $39,300, the average being $16,400; the Republican reports indicated a range of $3,700 to $64,500, and an average of $25,600. For both parties, average spending in the ten congressional districts more than quadrupled in the fourteen-year period from 1950 to 1964.

Secular data for state legislative districts are not at hand, but the level of costs for 1962 and 1964 is available. In the former year, Democratic state senate candidates spent as little as $230 and as much as $3,050, while that party's assembly candidates ranged from no expenditures at all to $2,117. Two years later the range of costs in state senate contests was $164 to $6,380 and in state assembly contests $6 to $2,726. Republican contestants for the state senate spent as little as $43 and as much as $5,417 in 1962 and their ticket mates for the assembly varied in their financial efforts from no expenditures to $2,509. In 1964 the range of spending by Republican upper-house candidates was from $377 to $6,877, and by lower-house aspirants from no outlays to $2,901. These figures, while apparently quite modest, are in fact quite high when one takes into account that there are relatively few sources of funds for candidates for state legislative office and that a large share of these expenditures must be financed from the candidate's pocket.

All of these estimates of campaign costs for offices ranging from the presidency to seats in the state legislature compel one conclusion: it is now difficult at best, and in most cases impossible, for an individual to campaign for office on his own resources. For most Americans, the financing of a candidacy for office is beyond their ability, even with the help of personal friends and associates. But even conceding this inability of candidates to finance their own campaigns, the question remains whether even a consumer approach to campaign costs requires this. If a candidate can raise the necessary funds in small sums without obligating himself on matters of public policy or the stewardship of his office, those who object to the high cost of politics for the candidate should be satisfied. However, it has been frequently pointed out that, while ample small contributions are theoretically available, the difficulty of financing politics through small sums from contributors without an interest in post-election favors is enormous: one money manager argued that "it costs a dollar to raise a dollar" through drives for small contributions,[22] although there is some evidence that systematic efforts to raise campaign cash in small sums can meet at least a nominal part of the campaign budget.[23]

In essence, the problem of the high cost of politics for the candidate is inherent not in the spending of money, but in the raising of it. The general difficulty of raising money at all is compounded by the potential dangers in raising money from persons or groups who wish to obligate the aspiring official to specific kinds of conduct. In this light, the cost of politics is probably "too high" for the average candidate. (This problem is examined later in the context of the sources of political finance.)

Costs in Perspective—Analysis of the System

In addition to the political costs for individual candidates, there is the overall cost to the entire political system of the competition for nominations and elections. System-wide political costs are difficult to state. One can simply relate the estimates of total dollars spent. Thus the total cost for the American political system in 1964 was estimated at $200 million; Wisconsin costs were between $3,772,000 and $4,101,000 in 1964 and between $3,245,200 and $3,526,600 in 1966. This kind of statement of costs is not very useful for comparative purposes, since it does not take into account the variations among the political systems being compared. Alexander Heard argues that "per capita expenditures are a more convenient indicator of relative costs than expenditures per eligible voter or per vote cast. They are probably more appropriate, too, given the varieties of settings and institutions from nation to nation."[24] He also suggests that the vote per capita per office on the ballot refines the data for comparative purposes, since the number of offices contested is probably a factor in determining costs.[25]

On the other hand, Herbert E. Alexander in his studies of the 1960 and 1964 elections relies upon the cost per presidential vote as a device for comparing the spending by national level committees from 1912 to 1964.[26] By pegging his cost index for national level committees to the number of presidential votes, Alexander seems to take into account the cost per vote per office. However, since national level committees spend at least a portion of their funds for other than the presidential candidates, his index does not square precisely with Heard's formula.

Arnold Heidenheimer suggests still a different approach. He devised an Index of Expenditure which he used to compare political spending in the nine political systems for which data were available as a result of the 1963 *Journal of Politics* symposium and the extensive studies of American costs. His Index of Expenditure was calculated by dividing the cost per vote by the average hourly wage of a male industrial worker. This was an attempt to relate political costs to a measure of wealth in each political system. Heidenheimer, like Heard, suggests that a further refinement might take into account the number of offices to be filled in any given election.[27]

Confronted with this variety of comparative techniques, the student of campaign finance must ask the question: "What is being compared?" Using per capita costs as a measuring stick is misleading to the extent that it pegs costs to the number of inhabitants, many of whom cannot vote because of various suffrage restrictions such as age, literacy, sex, and so forth. On the other hand, it may come closer to being accurate in wealthy modern societies where the major cost of politics appears to be mass media advertising for which politicians pay to reach those ineligible to vote as well as the enfranchised. The contrasting advantage of an index based on per voter costs is that it measures the cost of motivating a person to make a voting decision and then carrying out that decision by casting a ballot.

Heidenheimer's addition of a measure of economic wealth in his index is probably essential, especially for cross-national comparisons. Furthermore, a measure of wealth related to individual income seems wise since it suggests the actual burden to ordinary individuals of operating the system's politics. However, his use of the average hourly wage of *male* production workers seems especially unfortunate, since such data are not available for the United States or its state political systems. To be really useful, the Index of Expenditure should be revised as follows:

$$\text{Index of Expenditure} = \frac{\text{Total Expenditures}}{\text{Number of Votes Cast}} \div \text{Average Hourly Wage of Industrial Workers}$$

The suggestion of Heard and Heidenheimer that the number of offices contested be included in analyses of political systems is persuasive. In practice, however, this is especially difficult; there is a vast variation in amounts spent for various offices because of their relative importance. For comparative purposes the importance of offices, rather than their number, is significant in realistically assessing costs.

Contrast, for example, the estimated $300,000 spent by the 1964 Democratic candidate for governor in Wisconsin with the $45,000 spent by his running mate for lieutenant governor and the $2,000 spent by their ticket mate campaigning for secretary of state. With no measure of the significance of the offices being contested, there is no basis for including the number of offices in schemes for the comparison of political system costs. A second

difficulty with using the number of offices in comparative spending analyses is that joint campaigning for party tickets, common
in some places, makes it unlikely that costs will rise at a regular
rate for each additional office contested. Political finance as well
as industrial economics may experience the phenomenon of
"economies of scale."

Table 5

Estimated Political Costs in Wisconsin for Seven Elections
According to Various Indexes of Measure[a]

Election Year[b]	Cost Per Capita	Cost Per Vote Cast	Index of Expenditure
1950	$0.31	$0.94	0.64
1954	0.36	1.12	0.61
1956	0.43 (0.53)[c]	0.93 (1.21)[c]	0.60
1958	0.44	1.42	0.67
1962	0.76	2.43	0.97
1964	0.99 (1.17)[c]	2.42 (2.91)[c]	1.09
1966	0.85	3.01	1.05

[a] Based on "Total Expenditures: Corrected Estimates" in
Table 4.
[b] 1952 and 1960 omitted (see p. 40).
[c] Includes per unit costs of presidential campaigns.

Table 5 presents the estimated cost of politics in Wisconsin
on a per capita basis, on a per vote basis, and according to the
modified Index of Expenditure. The outstanding characteristic
of the data in Table 5 is the sharp increase in Wisconsin
political costs, especially after 1958. The significance of these
cost increases is realized more fully when Wisconsin costs
through this time period are compared with total costs for the
American political system as estimated by Heard and Alexander. These comparisons are detailed in Table 6. It is quickly
apparent that the cost of politics in Wisconsin has risen much
more rapidly than the cost of politics in the nation. The national
cost per capita rose 28 per cent, but the Wisconsin cost per
capita increased 174 per cent during roughly the same period.
The cost per vote reflects the same trend, with national costs up

20 per cent and Wisconsin costs up 220 per cent. The Wisconsin Index of Expenditure's rise of 64 per cent was less sharp, but was nonetheless a startling contrast to the United States Index of Expenditure, which declined 28 per cent.

Despite the increase in costs, system-wide costs do not convey an impression of being "too high." A cost of $2.83 per vote

Table 6

Estimated Political Costs in Wisconsin[a] and the United States Since 1950 According to Various Indexes of Measure

Election Year	Cost Per Capita		Cost Per Vote		Index of Expenditure	
	U.S.	Wisc.[b]	U.S.	Wisc.[b]	U.S.	Wisc.[b]
1950	$ —	$0.31	$ —	$0.94	—	0.64
1952	0.89	—	2.27	—	1.36	—
1954	—	0.36	—	1.12	—	0.61
1956	0.92	0.53[c]	2.50	1.21[c]	1.26	0.60[c]
1958	—	0.44	—	1.42	—	0.67
1960	0.97	—	2.54	—	1.12	—
1962	—	0.76	—	2.43	—	0.97
1964	1.04	1.17[c]	2.83	2.91[c]	1.12	1.09[c]
1966	—	0.85	—	3.01	—	1.05

[a] Based on "Total Expenditures: Corrected Estimates" in Table 4.
[b] 1952 and 1960 not analyzed (see p. 40).
[c] Includes per unit cost of presidential campaigns.

in the nation and $3.01 in Wisconsin is not a high price to pay for the operation of a democratic political system, which by its nature involves the expenditure of resources to sustain an adversary process between competing political groups or parties. The cost looks even less significant when stated as a ratio of the average hourly wage of industrial workers, namely 1.12 for the United States and 1.05 for Wisconsin. A cost per vote of one hour's wages to conduct biennial elections is unlikely to seem high when contrasted to expenditures for other purposes made in the society.

Furthermore, Wisconsin political costs do not seem high in a comparative context. The 1964 cost per vote of $2.91 was only slightly higher than the $2.83 cost per vote for the nation. And the $3.01 cost per vote in 1966 was lower than the comparable figure of $3.37 in Connecticut, the only other state political system for which a 1966 system-wide estimate is available.[28] In a broader setting, neither Wisconsin nor nationwide political costs are high when compared to those for the countries studied in the *Journal of Politics* symposium. Table 7 shows that the

Table 7

Index of Expenditure for Spending in Various
Political Jurisdictions

Jurisdiction	Election Year	Index of Expenditure
Australia	1958	0.27
Wisconsin	1958	0.67
Britain	1959	0.83
Wisconsin	1962	0.97
United States	1960	1.12
Germany	1961	1.40
Japan	1960	1.40
Italy	1958–1960	4.50
Philippines	1961	18.90
Israel	1960	21.20

Sources: see Appendix.

Indexes of Expenditure for Wisconsin and the nation rank at the lower end of a scale which includes the indexes for seven foreign nations. Only Australia and Great Britain have cost indexes as low, while the remaining five foreign jurisdictions have substantially higher cost indexes.

The one count on which Wisconsin political costs might be deemed high is the rapid rate of their increase. Not only did the percentage increase in costs outrun those of the nation as a whole and of Connecticut, the two political systems for which secular estimates are available, it increased at a much faster rate than measures of wealth and income. Thus total political spending in the nation increased 43 per cent, or 4 per cent per year, from 1952 to 1964. Connecticut political expenditures rose 88 per cent, from $1,852,500 in 1952 to $3,476,900 in 1966, or about 6 per cent per year. Wisconsin costs, by contrast, rose 229 per cent from 1950 to 1966 for an average annual increase of 14 per cent.

Similarly, from 1950 to 1966 the Gross National Product rose from $284.8 billion to $739.6 billion, a total increase of 159.7 per cent or an average annual increase of about 10 per cent. The national and Connecticut political expenditure increases of 4 and 6 per cent per year respectively were well below this, while Wisconsin's annual increase in political spending of 14 per cent per year was well above it. A comparison of increases in political costs with increases in total personal income tells the same story. The increase in the nation's total personal income averaged 7 per cent per year from 1952 to 1964 while political costs increased about 4 per cent. The increase in Connecticut's total personal income from 1952 to 1966 was about 9 per cent per year as contrasted with its increase of 6 per cent per year in political spending. Wisconsin also increased its total personal income by an average of 9 per cent per year but its political costs rose 14 per cent from 1950 to 1966. On the other hand, all of these jurisdictions had greater average annual increases in political costs than the average increase per year in the Consumer Price Index, which rose from 83.8 in 1950 to 113.1 in 1966 (1957–59 = 100) or an average of only 2.2 per cent per year. From a systemic perspective, political costs in the nation have not risen as fast as increases in wealth and income. On the other hand, they have increased at a faster rate than the prices of non-political goods and services purchased by consumers.

That Wisconsin political costs rose at a faster rate than wealth and income as well as the Consumer Price Index merits additional comment at this point because of its relevance for later discussion. Heidenheimer suggests that political costs may be dependent on various factors, including: the degree of partisan politicization in the system; the degree of competition between parties; the nature of the constituencies and the electorate, including the number of offices contested, the size and geographic dispersion of the electorate, and its cultural homogeneity; and the degree to which public funds and services are provided for political purposes and/or tight public controls are applied to political spending.[29]

Although marginal differences may exist, it seems unlikely that there has been any significant change in the degree to which institutions were politicized in Wisconsin or the United States from 1950 to 1964, and this variable does not seem relevant to explaining the patterns of political spending. Unlike the practice in some jurisdictions, in the United States and its subsystems the political parties do not have their own labor union affiliates, cultural organizations, schools, and so forth. A high degree of cultural homogeneity characterizes the United States, at least to the extent that expensive appeals to separate language and cultural groups are not a significant part of the political system. Both the length of the ballot and the degree of voter dispersion vary within the United States, but most states, including Wisconsin, still elect large numbers of local and state officials; and Wisconsin has followed the national trend toward the concentration of its people in urban areas. As in most parts of the United States, there are in Wisconsin no significant public subsidies for political activity and, while legal regulations are on the books, there is no effective control of political spending.

The one factor mentioned by Heidenheimer which on its face suggests a direction for further investigation is the degree of party competition, especially from the viewpoint of "what they [parties and candidates] believe to be the potential for persuading large, or marginally decisive, numbers of voters to change their political choice."[30] Wisconsin underwent a change in the balance of party strength during this period. The long-dominant Republican party was successfully challenged in a series of statewide elections by resurgent Democrats. It is notable that the sharpest increases in costs occurred after the Democrats demonstrated in 1958 that they were able to win elections in Wisconsin. There have been a growing number of offices which are of a politically marginal character, and statewide contests in recent years have been decided by only a few percentage points on one side of the ballot or the other. Furthermore, there is substantial evidence that both parties became organizationally stronger during the period. In the next chapter, therefore, some systematic attempt will be made to test the relationship between the degree of electoral competitiveness and the magnitude of political spending.

The thrust of this chapter has been to establish some statement of the costs of politics. Such statements take varying forms, depending on one's perspective. From the candidate's perspective—and indeed from the perspective most widely adopted by commentators and the public—political costs are those incurred in the waging of specific campaigns. From a systemic perspective, however, political costs are the aggregate costs of sustaining all the party activities and waging all the election contests in the entire political system. The two perspectives lead to different evaluations of political costs. The expenditures required to wage specific campaigns undoubtedly seem staggering to the politicians who must raise the money and to the public. But from a systemic perspective the costs seem slight, whether stated in absolute dollar terms, in relation to the system's wealth, or as a comparison with costs in other political systems. Both these evaluations may, however, be too narrow. Neither takes account of the reasons for the levels of costs. To understand the costs of politics—and therefore to evaluate those costs more rationally—the variables which contribute to the level of spending must be explored. Furthermore, a systemic perspective requires that the purposes and effects of spending be assessed. These questions are discussed in the following chapters; in the context of this larger understanding of political costs public policy approaches to political finance are considered in the Epilogue.

The Pattern of Spending

The Pattern of Spending: An Overview

The discussion in Chapter 3 of the total cost of politics does not illuminate the question of what factors are related to the level of spending, nor does it indicate where in the political system money is spent and why. Yet it is clear that the amounts spent vary from system to system and that spending within systems is uneven. It will soon enough be clear that the limits on data and on analytical techniques make these difficult questions to plumb. Nonetheless it is possible to use the available data to move toward an examination of those factors which are related to the amount and distribution of political spending.

The next two sections of this chapter will attempt to isolate a range of factors which seem to be significant for the level of costs. The subsequent sections will show how these same factors affect the distribution of political spending within the Wisconsin political system. At the outset, however, it is useful to report the location of spending in Wisconsin for the seven elections under study here. Tables 8 through 14 show the amounts spent by each party and its candidates at each government level. Transfer payments are deducted from the spending unit which made the transfer and reported as an expenditure by the unit which disbursed the money for goods and services. These tables do not show direct spending by labor, other non-party associations, or minor parties. It will be recalled that their estimated total spending was $75,000 in the years 1950 through 1956 and between $125,000 and $150,000 since then.

Table 8

Distribution of Reported Political Spending in Wisconsin in the 1950 Election

Spending Unit	Dem.	% of Dem. Total	Rep.	% of Rep. Total	Total	% of Total
Statewide candidates and committees	$105,900	39.8	$ 98,400	17.4	$204,300	24.6
State party committees	42,700	16.0	242,600	42.9	285,300	34.3
Congressional candidates and committees[a]	42,900	16.1	91,100	16.1	134,000	16.1
State senators[b]	8,700	3.3	23,700	4.2	32,400	3.9
State assemblymen[b]	16,400	6.2	36,400	6.4	52,800	6.3
Courthouse candidates[b]	18,900	7.1	40,400	7.1	59,300	7.1
Local party units	30,800	11.6	32,900	5.8	63,700	7.7
Totals	$266,300	100.1%[c]	$565,500	99.9%[c]	$831,800	100.0%

[a] Includes congressional district committees of political parties.
[b] Includes committees in behalf of these candidates.
[c] The result of rounding of figures.

Tables 8 through 14 not only report the increase in political spending, they pinpoint where the increases took place. In addition, they provide data on other significant patterns such as the disparity in spending between the two parties, the division of spending between party organizations and candidates, and the distribution of spending between state and local level political units. Each of these patterns will be separately considered after the variables which seem most determinative of both the level of spending and the distribution of expenditures have been set forth.

Table 9

Distribution of Reported Political Spending in Wisconsin in the 1954 Election

Spending Unit	Dem.	% of Dem. Total	Rep.	% of Rep. Total	Total	% of Total
Statewide candidates and committees	$109,100	28.2	$ 18,500	2.9	$ 127,600	12.4
State party committees	60,300	15.6	266,100	41.6	326,400	31.8
Congressional candidates and committees[a]	66,100	17.0	85,300	13.3	151,400	14.7
State senators[b]	15,000	3.9	42,400	6.6	57,400	5.6
State assemblymen[b]	26,300	6.8	61,100	9.5	87,400	8.5
Courthouse candidates[b]	30,200	7.8	53,900	8.4	84,100	8.2
Local party units	80,500	20.8	112,500	17.6	193,000	18.8
Totals	$387,500	100.1%[c]	$639,800	99.9%[c]	$1,027,300	100.0%

[a] Includes congressional district committees of political parties.
[b] Includes committees in behalf of these candidates.
[c] The result of rounding of figures.

Table 10

Distribution of Reported Political Spending in Wisconsin in the 1956 Election

Spending Unit	Dem.	% of Dem. Total	Rep.	% of Rep. Total	Total	% of Total
Statewide candidates and committees	$ 86,500	21.6	$143,000	16.2	$ 229,500	17.9
Statewide committees— presidential candidates	15,800	4.0	50,900	5.7	66,700	5.2
State party committees	87,500	21.9	332,900	37.6	420,400	32.7
Congressional candidates and committees[a]	71,400	17.9	110,800	12.5	182,200	14.2
State senators[b]	12,800	3.2	19,900	2.2	32,700	2.5
State assemblymen[b]	22,500	5.6	48,500	5.5	71,000	5.5
Courthouse candidates[b]	25,900	6.5	53,900	6.1	79,800	6.2
Local party units	77,200	19.3	125,400	14.2	202,600	15.8
Totals	$399,600	100.0%	$885,300	100.0%	$1,284,900	100.0%

[a] Includes congressional district committees of political parties.
[b] Includes committees in behalf of these candidates.

Table 11

Distribution of Reported Political Spending in Wisconsin in the 1958 Election

Spending Unit	Dem.	% of Dem. Total	Rep.	% of Rep. Total	Total	% of Total
Statewide candidates and committees	$186,100	35.8	$127,100	16.4	$ 313,200	24.1
State party committees	78,300	15.1	238,600	30.7	316,900	24.4
Congressional candidates and committees[a]	86,700	16.7	112,600	14.5	199,300	15.4
State senators[b]	9,100	1.7	31,800	4.1	40,900	3.2
State assemblymen[b]	38,100	7.3	57,300	7.4	95,400	7.4
Courthouse candidates[b]	44,000	8.5	64,100	8.2	108,100	8.3
Local party units	77,800	15.0	145,800	18.8	223,600	17.2
Totals	$520,100	100.1%[c]	$777,300	100.1%[c]	$1,297,400	100.0%

[a] Includes congressional district committees of political parties.
[b] Includes committees in behalf of these candidates.
[c] The result of rounding of figures.

Table 12

Distribution of Reported Political Spending in Wisconsin in the 1962 Election

Spending Unit	Dem.	% of Dem. Total	Rep.	% of Rep. Total	Total	% of Total
Statewide candidates and committees	$315,200	34.2	$ 221,100	14.6	$ 536,300	22.0
State party candidates	262,000	28.4	534,700	35.3	796,700	32.7
Congressional candidates and committees[a]	127,100	13.8	209,000	13.8	336,100	13.8
State senators[b]	27,000	2.9	41,900	2.8	68,900	2.8
State assemblymen[b]	53,600	5.8	67,400	4.5	121,000	5.0
Courthouse candidates[b]	69,800	7.6	114,400	7.6	184,200	7.6
Local party units	68,200	7.4	324,600	21.5	392,800	16.1
Totals	$922,900	100.1%[c]	$1,513,100	100.1%[c]	$2,436,000	100.0%

[a] Includes congressional district committees of political parties.
[b] Includes committees in behalf of these candidates.
[c] The result of rounding of figures.

Table 13

Distribution of Reported Political Spending in Wisconsin in the 1964 Election

Spending Unit	Dem.	% of Dem. Total	Rep.	% of Rep. Total	Total	% of Total
Statewide candidates and committees	$ 510,800	39.4	$ 588,700	29.5	$1,099,500	33.4
Statewide committees—presidential candidates	41,000	3.2	34,600	1.7	75,600	2.3
State party committees	294,900	22.8	492,100	24.6	787,000	23.9
Congressional candidates and committees[a]	137,600	10.6	328,600	16.5	466,200	14.2
State senators[b]	29,600	2.3	65,500	3.3	95,100	2.9
State assemblymen[b]	87,200	6.7	86,100	4.3	173,300	5.3
Courthouse candidates[b]	71,700	5.5	143,600	7.2	215,300	6.5
Local party units	122,700	9.5	258,200	12.9	380,900	11.6
Totals	*$1,295,500*	100.0%	*$1,997,400*	100.0%	*$3,292,900*	100.1%[c]

[a] Includes congressional district committees of political parties.

[b] Includes committees in behalf of these candidates.

[c] The result of rounding of figures.

Table 14

Distribution of Reported Political Spending in Wisconsin in the 1966 Election

Spending Unit	Dem.	% of Dem. Total	Rep.	% of Rep. Total	Total	% of Total
Statewide candidates	$ 324,000	29.0	$ 146,700	8.7	$ 470,700	16.7
State party committees	239,500	21.4	524,100	30.9	763,600	27.1
Congressional candidates and committees[a]	179,200	16.0	296,400	17.5	475,600	16.9
State senators[b]	57,900	5.2	85,600	5.1	143,500	5.1
State assemblymen[b]	119,600	10.7	175,000	10.3	294,600	10.5
Courthouse candidates[b]	98,300	8.8	198,500	11.7	296,800	10.5
Local party units	100,400	9.0	268,600	15.8	369,000	13.1
Totals	*$1,118,900*	100.1%[c]	*$1,694,900*	100.0%	*$2,813,800*	99.9%[c]

[a] Includes congressional district committees of political parties.

[b] Includes committees in behalf of these candidates.

[c] The result of rounding of figures.

Variables in the Pattern of Spending: An Overview

One element in the level of spending is the importance of the office or offices contested. The importance of an office is a protean concept, changing its shape in the eyes of its various beholders. The extent of authority and of influence in administrative matters, in appointments, in legislation are important considerations. The visibility and prestige of the office add to its importance. Its position on the ballot may be important for those who are concerned with the fate of the offices below it on the same and the opposition tickets. For virtually everyone, however, offices such as governor and United States senator loom as important while offices such as state treasurer and secretary of state are viewed with little interest. At the same time, an aggregation of offices may take on a collective importance which no single one of them holds. Thus the state assembly and state senate or majorities of their members may have almost the same importance as the governorship because they share with it a wide range of powers.

Perhaps the most convenient way to test the impact of the importance of office on political spending is to examine the amounts spent in campaigns for offices whose constituencies are identical. In 1962, reported spending on behalf of the Democratic candidate for governor was $122,700 and for United States senator $180,300. These figures contrast with expenditures of $4,445, $883, and $3,803 for those on their ticket seeking the offices of lieutenant governor, secretary of state, and attorney general respectively. In all, expenditures for the two "important" offices accounted for 96.1 per cent of total spending for statewide offices.

Even in 1964, when the Democrats fielded unusually vigorous candidates for lieutenant governor and attorney general, gubernatorial spending accounted for 46.1 per cent and senatorial spending for 38.4 per cent of the statewide total, so that only 15.5 per cent of spending for statewide offices was generated by the campaigns for the other four posts. Similarly, in 1966, when there was no United States Senate contest, the "important" office accounted for most campaign expenditures: the governorship was the object of 81 per cent of total state office expenditures. Recently developed Connecticut political finance data show that in 1966 reported Democratic expenditures for six statewide offices (no United States Senate seat was filled that year) were $286,708, but that $241,974 or 84.3 per cent was expended by committees supporting Governor John Dempsey.[1]

It seems clear that the level of expenditures is related to the importance of the office contested, and that the more such offices that are contested the greater total spending will be. Furthermore, the distribution of spending is affected to the extent that in some years an important office, such as a United States Senate seat, is contested and in some years it is not. In the former years the proportion of total spending occurring at the state level will undoubtedly be larger. We will return to this point subsequently when we examine the distribution of spending in a series of Wisconsin elections.

A second factor in the level and distribution of expenditures has already been touched on indirectly: the number of offices contested.[2] If one could hold constant other variables, political spending should increase at about the same rate as the increase in the number of offices contested. Other variables are seldom constant, and we do not often add offices to the ballot so there is no very precise way to test this proposition. It is instructive however to compare campaign expenditures in years in which both the governorship and a United States Senate seat are being filled with spending in years in which only the former office is on the ballot.

In 1964 the Democrats spent $215,800 in the gubernatorial contest and $196,000 in the United States Senate race. An additional $41,000 was spent by committees campaigning for the Johnson-Humphrey ticket. In 1966 only the governorship was contested and spending was $196,000. There is no indication that the elimination of spending for a senate seat and the presidency freed additional money to be spent elsewhere. Indeed, the contrary appears to be true when it is noted that total reported spending by the Democrats declined from 1964 to

1966 by somewhat more than the sums involved in the senate and presidential races in the former year.

John Owens' study of Connecticut yields an unusually clear example of the relationship of the number of offices to the level of spending. In 1950, Democrats spent $244,000 to contest two United States Senate seats and the governorship. Two years later candidates with unusual personal financial resources spent $233,000 to contest two United States Senate seats. And in 1954, when only the governorship was contested, the Democrats spent $69,000 to win that office.[3] While the amount spent for each additional office was not proportional because of "the exceptional ability of the 1952 Democratic candidates to raise funds,"[4] it nonetheless seems clear that costs were much higher when several important statewide offices were contested than when only a single such office was at stake.

The size of constituency is a third factor which contributes to the level and distribution costs.[5] At the outset it is necessary to differentiate between the size of constituency as measured by the number of electors or the population and its geographical size. Only the first of these measurements can be readily dealt with here, but an attempt will be made at least to suggest the relationship between geographical size of constituency and political spending. The number of electors has one obvious effect on spending: it determines the number of contacts that must be made in the canvass, whatever its form. Costs will increase as the number of contacts increases, though not necessarily proportionally. The clearest example is that of direct mailing: an electorate of 40,000 will be more costly to reach than one of 10,000 because four times as many pieces must be prepared and mailed. Thus if all other factors remained constant, the growth of the electorate would require increased political expenditures. In some cases, increases in the population rather than in the electorate cause cost increases. This is true, for instance, of mass media, because advertising rates are set according to the number of readers, listeners, or viewers regardless of their status on election day. In any case, the expansion of the suffrage and the growth of the population both contribute to increased political costs. And for the same reasons, larger constituencies are more expensive to campaign in than smaller ones.

This element in political costs is not, however, merely a matter of increased numbers of electors or inhabitants. There is also good reason to believe that the cost per vote increases as the electorate or the population of a district increases. Or, to put it differently, the cost per vote is higher in larger districts than in smaller ones, even in the same political system. In small constituencies, personal campaigning by the candidate and his friends can make a significant political impact. Furthermore, personal visibility and reputation are likely to be established in a small constituency and need not be projected through campaign activities. The media which can practicably be used in small constituencies are less numerous and less expensive; thus television is not practicable in most state legislative districts because it buys exposure to more people who are ineligible to cast ballots in the district than to those who are. In larger constituencies, neither personal campaigning nor personal reputation have so great an impact. Consequently there is a need to employ the mass media of communication, especially such expensive media as television and the metropolitan daily press. In addition, expenditures must be made for travel, for the hiring of staff to plan and advance candidate trips, for headquarters and organizational staffs, and for professional media advisors. The cost of reaching each voter is thereby multiplied.

A convenient way to examine the impact of constituency size on per vote expenditures is to compare such expenditures in legislative elections with those in gubernatorial contests; this assumes that control of the state assembly is almost as important as the governorship. Since gubernatorial contests were electorally competitive, comparison is limited to competitive assembly seats. Focusing only on competitive districts has the additional advantage of allowing examination of the costs of wooing those voters who determined dominance in the assembly, which was closely divided between the parties, and whose majority alternated between the parties several times in recent years. The proposition is not retested with data from state senate contests because Republican dominance of that body was quite well established throughout recent Wisconsin political history, and because the substantially larger number of competitive assembly seats permits us to make more reliable comparisons between per vote spending in smaller districts and in the governor's statewide constituency.

In 1962, the mean per vote spending by Democratic candidates in 10 competitive assembly districts where the nomination was not contested was $0.04, and the median $0.03. In that year, per vote expenditures by the Democratic candidate for the United States Senate were $0.14 and for the governorship $0.10. In 1964, the comparable figures for 16 assembly districts were $0.06 and $0.04. Gubernatorial expenditures were $0.13 per vote and senatorial spending was $0.12 per vote. A study of expenditures in Connecticut showed mean per vote expenditures by Democratic candidates in 23 state senate districts of $0.06 and in 46 state House districts of $0.12. Much higher expenditures were found in the state's 6 congressional districts, where the average per vote expenditure was $0.18, and in the gubernatorial contest, where $0.24 per vote was spent.[6] These data provide tentative confirmation that costs increase not only absolutely but also on a per vote basis as the size of the constituency increases.

It is not clear whether a similar phenomenon occurs when the geographical size of constituencies is enlarged. Candidate travel costs will increase, and there might be a need to spend money on more intensive organizational activities since it is easier to canvass the same number of voters when they live in close proximity, as any discussion with a rural precinct chairman and his urban counterpart will quickly reveal. Furthermore, when voters are spread out geographically, the visibility and reputation of the candidate may be less well known in the various parts of the district. Also, there may be media which could be practicably used in the district but which are relatively expensive. It is surely the case, for instance, that no assembly candidate in Milwaukee County finds it efficient to purchase advertising in the metropolitan press; but many legislative candidates in upstate districts feel compelled to budget funds for advertising in the daily and weekly newspapers in the smaller cities and towns which are wholly encompassed within the borders of their districts. Regrettably, there are not enough data from Milwaukee County districts and from significantly larger outstate districts to permit a comparison of costs in geographically compact and extensive legislative districts. This discussion suggests, however, that a variety of factors would contribute to a larger per vote cost in the latter, even when the populations and electorates of the districts were of equal size.

The nature and strength of party organization is a fourth factor which is related to the level of political costs and their distribution. Where there is strong and effective precinct organization, it may not be necessary to spend as much money on other forms of campaigning. Personal contact has been shown to be an especially effective form of campaigning. But in Wisconsin—as in other areas with middle class mass membership parties—the parties are not particularly effective electoral units.[7] Program-oriented partisans tend to be more interested in debating issues than in precinct work. Furthermore, the greatest Democratic organizational strength is located in middle class areas which are electorally Republican, and Democratic party members are consequently expending their energies in the least productive precincts. Meanwhile, the working class districts are seldom canvassed because the party is weakest there. The Republicans have a different, though equally vexing, problem. Their organizational strength is in neighborhoods populated by the well off and well educated; canvassing probably does not yield a substantial increment of additional votes here because these voters are already committed to the Republicans and have a very high turnout rate. On the other hand, organizational weakness in the small towns which are heavily Republican, but where turnout is not so high, prevents the Republicans from capitalizing on a major source of potential votes. In these situations, the need to spend money for substitute methods of campaigning, such as media advertising, increases political costs. The relationship between party organization and spending will be dealt with again in considering the rationality of the expenditure choices made by Wisconsin politicians. At this point, however, it can be suggested that the level of costs is affected by the nature and strength of party organization.

A fifth element which affects the level and distribution of costs is the campaign technology which is available in a district. Available means existent, practicable, legal, and publicly acceptable. Television simply didn't exist in many parts of Wisconsin in the early 1950's and therefore had no impact on the level of costs. Even after it began reaching virtually all areas of the state, it was, as previously noted, not practicable in many small districts. Of course, campaign techniques are not really available if banned by law (at least where the ban is enforced with reasonable effectiveness) or if viewed by the public as improper.

As new political techniques develop, their use causes additional expenditures. Seldom do new techniques displace old ones so completely that no increase in the cost of running campaigns accompanies innovations in political technology.[8] In Chapter 5 the increases in spending caused by television will be more closely analyzed, but it is enough to note here that both the per unit cost and the number of units used have increased sharply in Wisconsin. Public opinion polls are another recent advance in campaign technology whose extensive use increases costs. Computers are now employed in some states to personalize appeals to voters and, while that practice has not yet been used in Wisconsin, its success elsewhere makes its adoption and the concomitant increase in costs almost inevitable. Thus, the range of campaign techniques available is a factor which affects the level of costs.

The availability of resources is a broad sixth factor in the amount and distribution of expenditures. All of the factors previously discussed create the need for spending, but there must also be the money available to meet the need. Among the most important convertible political resources in Wisconsin are party ideology, candidate and party program, incumbency, candidate charisma, and the degree of electoral competitiveness. In addition, the intervention in the state's politics of outside forces has from time to time had a substantial effect. Finally, the fund-raising apparatus developed by a party or a candidate has significance because it determines the skill with which resources are pyramided.

Each of these elements determines the availability of funds, and the effect of each will be seen in subsequent sections. At this point, however, it is well to note briefly their relevance. Party ideology determines in large measure the party's financial as well as its electoral constituency. Thus, because they are the more conservative party in the system, Wisconsin Republicans have developed a strong constituency among the upper socio-economic ranks in the state,[9] and especially among those associated with manufacturing concerns and financial institutions. This constituency is not only able to give money, it is more likely to have the sense of political efficacy which encourages contributing.[10] Furthermore, from these ranks can be drawn men and women whose experience, self-assurance, and contacts make them effective fund raisers.[11] The Democrats, on the other hand, have no such natural financial constituency aside from their labor allies. Their fund-raising efforts tend therefore to be more chaotic and they appeal to a substantially smaller base.

Program should perhaps be separated from ideology as a resource. Some groups may be interested in quite specific programs which are unrelated to a larger ideology. Highway contractors, brewers, truckers, and similar groups are in this category. Candidates or parties who espouse these specific programs can usually convert that advocacy into cash during the campaign season.

Incumbency is also a resource. It may yield patronage, status, visibility, connections, the opportunity to do minor favors, and a wide range of other advantages to those who hold office; and each of these can, in turn, be helpful in raising funds.

The personal charisma of political candidates and occasionally of a party leader may be a convertible resource, but this is much more difficult to demonstrate. Buchanan and Bird found that the "personality" of gubernatorial candidates in Tennessee primaries was the most significant incentive identified by those who contributed to their campaigns; issues were identified as the second most important incentive.[12] In senatorial primaries in that state the rank order of the two incentives was reversed. That personal appeal should rank either first or second is an indication of the importance of candidate charisma as a resource.

Although the relationship between electoral competition and political spending will be considered more fully in the next section, it should be viewed here as a resource. To the extent that closely competitive electoral politics provides a motivation for individuals to respond to politicians' appeals for money either by making contributions or by increasing the amounts they give, it is an important resource which can be converted into campaign funds.

Finally, the effectiveness and skill of the fund-raising arms of political organizations should be considered. As previously indicated, it is easier for a conservative party or candidate to develop a corps of effective fund raisers. The constituency of a candidate or party also determines the effectiveness of fund raisers. A homogeneous constituency permits centralized fund raising and systematic appeals to a well-defined group of potential givers. This is emphatically the Republican case in Wisconsin and elsewhere. The Democrats, on the other hand, must appeal to such a fragmented and shifting constituency that their fund-raising apparatus tends to be disorganized. Incumbency too affects the quality of the fund-raising organization, since office-holders tend to develop a corps of associates and staff members who can use the advantages of incumbency in raising funds. Aside from these conditioning factors, however, is the skill and the will of those who have responsibility for fund raising. It will be seen in a subsequent section that in both parties in Wisconsin the leadership of particular men who brought particular skills and energies to the task vastly increased the amounts raised within the framework of conditioning situational factors.

Variables in the Pattern of Spending: Electoral Competition

One factor related to the pattern of spending which needs more extended treatment is the intensity of electoral competition. Such a relationship has been widely posited in the political finance literature. Coleman Ransone, Jr., pinpointed the "quality of the opposition," including the seriousness of the challenge, as one of the variables determining the level of spending in gubernatorial contests.[13] V. O. Key, Jr., argued that "the perceived stakes of an election and the intensity of the feelings it arouses may bear on the level of expenditure."[14] The closeness of party competition, particularly in a state such as Wisconsin where parties are highly programmatic, causes interested persons and groups to perceive that relatively high stakes rest on the outcomes. Alexander Heard stated the proposition more directly when he pointed to "the intensity and extent of competition within and between the parties" as a factor affecting campaign costs.[15] And Arnold Heidenheimer attributed cross-national differences in political expenditures to, among other factors, "the potential for persuading large, or marginally decisive numbers of voters to change their political choice."[16] Yet in all these commentaries there is no systematic testing of the hypothesis that intensity of electoral competition and the level of political expenditures are related. Only in Leuthold's recent study of ten congressional campaigns is there even preliminary evidence of such a relationship. He shows not only that candidates in four competitive districts perceived their financial needs as higher, but also that spending in these districts was in fact much higher than in six non-competitive areas.[17]

The real importance of closely competitive electoral situations is their effect on the perceptions of politicians and contributors. In the last section was suggested one impact of such perceptions: those who have previously contributed may be moved to increase the size of their gifts and those who have not may give to the party or candidates they favor. Similarly, candidates and party leaders, perceiving themselves in precarious electoral situations, have a greater incentive and will to gather their resources and to pyramid them as fully as possible. In the next several pages an attempt will be made systematically to demonstrate a relationship between the intensity of electoral competition and the level of political spending, but it is necessary to keep in mind that the politicians' perceptions and conduct are the intervening link between these phenomena.

The ideal way to test the relationship between competition

and spending would be to have available spending data of a
comparable kind for specific offices or for total political systems
for a large number of the American states. It would be necessary to isolate other factors, such as those previously considered, which affect costs. In its present primitive state of development, the study of political finance does not even offer cost data
on a significant number of jurisdictions, much less the additional
material that is required.

The present study is limited to a single state and there is no
comparable study for other states for the years under examination. Within the confines of the data the best way to approach
the relationship between competition and spending is to study
campaign expenditures in legislative contests. We have available
full reports of spending in 1964 by Democrats in 79 state
assembly districts and by Republicans in 68 such districts. In
addition, there are similar data for 72 Democratic campaigns
and 69 Republican campaigns in 1962. Wisconsin legislative
districts were not seriously malapportioned during this period so
that the populations of the districts were roughly equal. Furthermore, the study takes place in a setting where the parties were
similar in organization and leadership from one district to another, and campaign techniques showed signs of substantial
uniformity, probably because of an exchange of campaign ideas
between legislative candidates at party campaign schools and
through more informal channels of communication. Generally
Wisconsin assembly districts have been so small that there is
little use of mass media, except small radio stations and newspapers. Metropolitan dailies and television were not heavily relied
on, according to the best information that could be obtained by
interviewing legislators about their own and other legislative
campaigns. Thus the differences in cost figures should not
usually have been caused in Wisconsin by differences in the type
of media used.

A further consideration in the use of these data is the impact
of primary campaign spending upon the comparisons. Candidates and committees are required to file financial statements
for both the primary and general elections. However, these
statements may misrepresent the actual allocation of expenses

between those two election efforts in any particular campaign. For instance, a candidate without a primary but with a close general election contest may purchase cartop signs, pamphlets, bumper stickers, and other campaign materials in August for a November election. Nonetheless, these expenditures show up on his September report, filed for the primary election. On the face of the record it would appear that he spent money "in the primary" although it was actually for the general election campaign. To avoid this methodological pitfall, districts have been categorized and the analysis compares total district spending in the various categories rather than relying on the division of spending as it appears in the primary and general election financial statements.

A competitive general election has been defined as one in which the winning candidate received less than 55 per cent of the two-party vote. A competitive primary election has been defined as one in which the winner did not receive 20 per cent more of the vote cast than his nearest rival. Since candidates cannot rely on a past history of party identification in the district to aid them in a primary, it seemed likely that outcomes would be more uncertain in their minds and they would perceive potentially competitive situations where margins were somewhat wider than the 10 per cent figure used to distinguish general elections.

Using these simple definitions, assembly contests in each party were categorized as (1) no primary—non-competitive general election, (2) non-competitive primary—non-competitive general election, (3) competitive primary—non-competitive general election, (4) no primary—competitive general election, (5) non-competitive primary—competitive general election, and (6) competitive primary—competitive general election. In some categories there were inadequate numbers of cases to use for analysis. However, there were sufficient numbers of districts in categories (1), (3), and (4) to compare campaign spending in districts with neither primary nor general election competition to districts which had, first, only primary competition and, second, only general election competition.

Figure 1 illustrates the clear tendency for spending to be

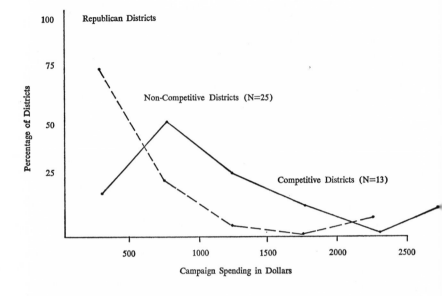

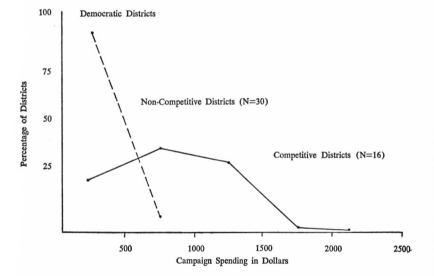

Figure 1. Assembly District Spending and Electoral Competition in Wisconsin, 1964

greater on behalf of candidates of both parties where the general election was competitive, as previously defined. To assure that primary spending did not influence these comparisons, the districts used for analysis in Figure 1 were those with no primary contests in 1964. The same kind of analysis of spending on behalf of legislative candidates of both parties in 1962 yields similar results. There did not appear to be any consistent differences in spending in urban as contrasted to rural districts, even when the degree of electoral competition was held constant, although admittedly the number of cases on which these comparisons were based became rather small when the data were

Table 15

Campaign Spending on Behalf of Assembly Candidates in Districts With No Competitive Contests, With Competitive Primaries and With Competitive General Elections, 1964

Range of Spending In Dollars	*Non-competitive Districts*[a]		*Competitive Primaries*[b]		*Competitive General Elections*[c]	
	No.	*%*	*No.*	*%*	*No.*	*%*
	DEMOCRATS					
000–500	28	93.4	1	8.3	3	18.7
501–1,000	2	6.6	0	0.0	6	37.5
1,001–1,500	0	0.0	5	41.7	5	31.3
1,501–2,000	0	0.0	2	16.6	1	6.3
2,001–2,500	0	0.0	0	0.0	1	6.3
2,501 and over	0	0.0	4	33.3	0	0.0
Totals	*30*	*100.0*	*12*	*99.9*[d]	*16*	*100.1*[d]
	REPUBLICANS					
000–500	18	72.0	1	11.1	2	15.4
501–1,000	4	16.0	2	22.2	6	46.2
1,001–1,500	1	4.0	2	22.2	3	23.1
1,501–2,000	0	0.0	1	11.1	1	7.7
2,001–2,500	2	8.0	0	0.0	0	0.0
2,501 and over	0	0.0	3	33.3	1	7.7
Totals	*25*	*100.0*	*9*	*99.9*[d]	*13*	*100.1*[d]

[a] No primary contest and a non-competitive general election, as previously defined.
[b] A competitive primary election and a non-competitive general election, as those terms were previously defined.
[c] No primary contest and a competitive general election, as previously defined.
[d] The result of rounding of figures.

divided according to both the degree of competition and the urban or rural nature of the districts.

A further analysis of the relationship between spending and competition shows that costs tended to be higher where there were competitive primaries as well as where competitive general elections occurred. Table 15 shows that the amounts spent on behalf of Democratic and Republican assembly candidates in 1964 were greater both in districts with competitive primaries and in districts with competitive general elections than in districts with competitive contests in neither election. Again, there appeared to be no significant relationship between spending and the urban or rural character of the districts.

One interesting aspect of these data is that spending in districts with competitive primaries appears to be somewhat higher than spending in districts with competitive general elections, although the cases are too few to make any firm generalization. One explanation of such a tendency might be that general election campaigns are usually limited to two candidates, each drawing on his own sources of funds, while primaries often are contested by a larger number of candidates, each bringing to the race separate resources. Within the context of a competitive situation, a larger number of candidates may sometimes send costs higher than they would be if there were only two candidates, as in general elections.

The data presented in this section seem to indicate that spending rises rapidly in electorally competitive circumstances. Further evidence of this relationship might be detected by ascertaining what division of spending occurred between the two parties in different sets of competitive circumstances. Where the two parties are closely competitive within a district, it would seem that each party would muster its resources as fully as possible to win the election. This would cause the two parties to be relatively evenly matched in spending, with the Republicans having some advantage. Similarly, the amount of spending by the two parties would be roughly the same, again with some Republican advantage, in non-competitive districts where each party would make merely a token effort, expending just enough to go through the motions of a campaign. In these non-competitive districts, of course, spending would be less than in competitive districts, though the ratio of spending between the parties would be roughly the same. Previously presented data indicate that this hypothesis is accurate at least insofar as the Republicans tend to spend more on assembly campaigns and more money is spent in competitive districts than in non-competitive races.

The same kind of theorizing suggests that the ratio of spending between the parties would be substantially unequal where one party, particularly the predominant party, had a primary contest and the other did not. This reasoning rests upon the assumption that the competition of a primary contest would generate spending within the ranks of the party whose nomination was contested. Thus in a one-party district with a primary contest for the majority party nomination, the majority party's percentage of the total spending would be greater than in any district without a primary.

A refinement of this speculation would suggest that a non-competitive primary in the majority party would cause the majority party's percentage of the total spending to be greater than its share in competitive or non-competitive general election situations where there is no primary, but somewhat less than it would be in a competitive primary circumstance. This hypothesis is grounded simply in the assumption that the intensity of primary competition influences the amount spent in the primary and thus the majority party's share of total spending.

The theory developed here is, then, based on a presumed relationship between the level of spending and the intensity of competition. First, costs are higher in competitive two-party districts than in non-competitive districts, assuming an absence of primary contests. This proposition has been successfully tested in Table 15 and in Figure 1. Second, primary competition, like general election competition, generates additional spending. It can be seen in Table 15 that costs in districts with competitive primaries are higher than in districts without primaries, where the intensity of general election competition is constant. Third, the intensity of primary competition will affect the ratio of spending between the parties, assuming that the degree of general election competition is constant, in some rough relationship to that intensity. Table 16 attempts to confirm this statement.

Table 16 was prepared by calculating the share of spending by the winning party for 85 assembly districts in the years 1962 and 1964. The first major category of districts included those with no primaries, and either non-competitive general elections or competitive general elections. The second major category

Table 16

Share of Total Spending by Dominant Party According to Competitiveness of General Election and Primary Contests: Wisconsin Assembly Districts, 1962 and 1964

% of Total Spending By Dominant Party	No Primary				Non-competitive General Election			
	Non-competitive General Election		Competitive General Election		Non-competitive Primary Election		Competitive Primary Election	
	N.	%	N.	%	N.	%	N.	%
00.0–20	1	3.4	1	7.1	0	0.0	0	0.0
20.1–40	4	13.8	5	35.7	0	0.0	1	4.3
40.1–60	11	37.9	4	28.6	5	26.3	2	8.7
60.1–80	10	34.5	3	21.4	4	21.0	4	17.4
80.1–100	3	10.3	1	7.1	10	52.6	16	69.6
Totals	29	99.9[a]	14	99.9[a]	19	99.9[a]	23	100.0

[a] The result of rounding of figures.

was those districts with non-competitive general elections and with non-competitive primary contests or competitive primaries.

The sharp difference between the share of total spending by the dominant party in districts without primaries and the share in those with nomination contests is notable. More than half the districts with primaries in the predominant party had over 80 per cent of total spending accounted for by committees and candidates of the majority party. Where there was no primary, the balance of spending between parties tended to be somewhat more equal, with the majority party generally responsible for anywhere from 20 to 60 per cent of the spending. Furthermore, intensely competitive primaries apparently increased the dominant party's share of the total spending more than less closely decided nomination contests.

It is risky to overstate the conclusions to be drawn from the available data. Nonetheless, some tentative patterns can be suggested. First, in circumstances which hold constant such variables as the size of the constituency, the national and state issues, the nature and ideological content of party organizations, and the nature of campaign techniques, there are strong indications of a relationship between the closeness of electoral competition and the level of campaign spending. Second, competitive primaries may be as productive of spending increases as competitive general elections. Less closely contested primaries are more costly than non-competitive general elections, but not so costly as either competitive primaries or competitive general elections. Third, the sharp increase in total political spending in Wisconsin may be at least partly attributed to the rise of a sharply competitive two-party system which replaced a one-party system, generally marked by only feeble primary competition for at least a decade.

Before concluding this discussion of the relationship between electoral competition and political spending, it is necessary to consider a normative question, to speculate on trends in spending, and to render one caveat. We must first note the preference of the public and of many political scientists for closely competitive electoral situations. Sixty-eight per cent of the respondents to a University of Wisconsin Survey Research Laboratory poll agreed, for instance, that "democracy works better where competition between parties is strong." V. O. Key, Jr., in his classic work on *Southern Politics,* summed up the inferiority of one-party factional systems to two-party competitive systems. He argued that the discontinuity of factions, as opposed to the permanence of parties, confuses the electorate in identifying policies with officeholders and fails to organize voters into more or less like-minded camps on public policy. Discussion of public issues tends to decline in such a system, while a high premium is placed on demagogic personalities and techniques as necessary

to obtain public attention on the campaign trail. Favoritism is
more likely in factional than party politics, he suggested. And
the "have nots" tend to be disadvantaged in the political system
because their needs require strong organization within the government in order to enact and administer affirmative programs
for their benefit. Multifactional one-partyism heightens the separation of powers, thus hindering such affirmative action in
behalf of "have not" elements. Furthermore, the multiplication
of access points, where money and influence are useful in
blocking legislation, aids the "have" elements in the community
in blocking social welfare legislation.[18]

It has been argued that continuing bifactionalism within a
one-party state may be preferable to multifactional one-partyism, though not so desirable as a competitive two-party situation. The bifactional system takes on many of the characteristics
of the two-party system, but it lacks long-term continuity because one or both factions are generally built around a dominant personality who passes off the scene in a relatively short
time and because of the lack of continuing identification of local
level candidates and political organizations with state factional
leaders.[19]

Key's hypothesis that the increased party cohesion, greater
clarity of electoral choices, narrowness of electoral margins, and
diminished influence of interest groups in two-party competitive
states permits "have not" elements more effectively to make
demands upon government for social welfare programs which
are to their benefit[20] has been challenged in recent years by a
number of political scientists. Richard E. Dawson and James A.
Robinson reported that socio-economic variables, such as ur-
banization and per capita income, bear a more significant relationship to high levels of welfare expenditures than does the
degree of party competition.[21] Support for this position comes
from Richard I. Hofferbert, who argues that "welfare orientation" in the public policy of the states is for the most part a
function of social and economic factors rather than the competitiveness of the party system or the degree to which legislative
apportionment approaches the one-man, one-vote model.[22]
These studies have drawn a rejoinder from John Fenton, who

employs similar methods to show a significant relationship between the intensity of competition and such public policy outputs as per capita expenditures for welfare, aid to dependent children, education, and general governmental spending. This relationship holds up, he argues, even when socio-economic variables are held constant.[23]

Despite the intensive analysis of the effects of electoral competition on both the process and outputs of government, few commentators have linked it with accelerating political expenditures. If the evidence adduced here correctly portrays the general situation, then sharp increases in political costs and two-party competition are closely linked. Those who prefer intensive two-party competition must be prepared to include in their normative calculus the enormous and perhaps dangerous burdens of fund raising that competitive politics places on the politicians. If this is an unacceptable concomitant to their preferred style of politics, they must consider the financing alternatives available and be prepared to offer policy options to cope with the sharp increases in costs that arise from competitive politics. One such policy option is proposed in the Epilogue.

Long-term trends in expenditure levels in closely competitive two-party situations should be projected. Costs might continue to rise at about the same rapid rate, or they might continue to rise, but at a reduced rate, after electoral competition becomes the established norm. The Wisconsin data are neither extensive enough nor extended through a sufficiently long period to test these alternatives. This question of expenditure trends can therefore be approached in only the most tentative way by citing the previously presented rates of increase in total spending in Connecticut and Wisconsin. In the early 1950's two-party electoral competition had already become the established norm in Connecticut. During the 14 years from 1952 to 1966, the increase in statewide costs was 88 per cent, or about 6 per cent per year. Wisconsin costs rose 229 per cent from 1950 to 1966 for an average annual increase of 14 per cent. During this period Wisconsin was undergoing a transition from one-party to two-party competitive politics and the greater rate of increase might be attributed to this. Indeed, an examination of the amounts spent in gubernatorial campaigns in 1964 and 1966 suggests that there was no significant increase in costs. And the cost per capita, cost per vote, and index of expenditure presented in Table 6 show a slowing of the rate of increase. On the basis of this scanty and only suggestive data, the better hypothesis seems to be that after a very sharp acceleration in the rate of spending during the transition from one-party to two-party competition, there is a flattening of the rate of increase. Nonetheless, Connecticut's higher per vote costs suggest that costs in dollar terms are likely to be much higher in areas with established two-party competition than in either non-competitive situations or transitional jurisdictions.

Finally, a caveat on our findings must be registered. It is not possible on the basis of the present data to determine the cause-effect relationship between intensity of competition and levels of spending. The data show a clear relationship, but they do not demonstrate which is the dependent and which the causal variable. An intuitive approach suggests that there is a reciprocal relationship, with increases in the intensity of electoral competition, which occur largely as a result of changes in the social and economic conditions in the constituency, causing sharp increases in political expenditures. An increase in the degree of electoral competition provides an incentive for politicians to redouble their fund-raising efforts in order to purchase additional campaign activities to win the decisive extra votes. Furthermore, the sense of urgency about electoral outcomes created by closely contested elections undoubtedly increases both the number and the size of financial contributions. At the same time, the increase in spending may make competition closer and increase the intensity of feelings surrounding elections, thus generating still further fund-raising efforts by politicians and an additional willingness among the electorate to make financial contributions.

The Distribution of Spending: The Disparity Between Parties

Tables 8 through 14 provide data on the distribution of spending between the two parties; Table 17 summarizes the percentage of total spending accounted for by each party in seven elections.

As in most other competitive states, the Republicans have a substantial edge in political spending. A spending ratio of about 60:40 in their favor usually prevails in Wisconsin. This compares with 1952 ratios in favor of the Republicans of 61:39 in Connecticut, 57:43 in Maryland, 51:49 in Massachusetts, and 69:31 in Pennsylvania.[24] Heard found that in 1956 aggregate figures compiled from the reports of 351 statewide and 350

Table 17

The Disparity in Spending Between Political Coalitions
in Wisconsin, 1950–1966

	Reported Spending		Estimated Spending Including Non-Party Units[a]	
Year[b]	Dem. %	Rep. %	Dem. %	Rep. %
1950	32	68	35	64
1954	38	62	40	59
1956	31	69	33	66
1958	40	60	43	56
1962	38	62	40	60
1964	39	61	41	59
1966	40	60	41	58

[a] Includes direct outlays by such non-party organizations as labor unions. Figures do not always sum to 100 because of minor party spending and rounding of figures.
[b] 1952 and 1960 omitted (see p. 40).

local committees indicated overall Republican advantages of 64:36 and 59:41 respectively.[25] The White and Owens study of Michigan showed a ratio of 75:25 for 1956, but this did not take into account the substantial increment to the Democrats resulting from direct labor spending.[26] A 1966 study shows a Republican spending advantage in Connecticut of 56:44.[27] Presidential campaign spending, excepting 1960, shows roughly the same disparity as in state spending. Thus, in 1956, the Republicans outspent the Democrats and their labor allies by 59:41 and in 1964 by 63:37; in 1960 the Democrats had a slight edge of 51:49.[28]

The persistence of the Republican advantage in political expenditures indicates the importance of party ideology and constituency as political resources, which was touched on earlier. There is evidence from the voting studies that those of higher socio-economic status are generally opposed to the expansion of governmental social welfare programs and government regulation of the economy.[29] These same people are relatively more involved in politics, and one manifestation of this involvement is the making of campaign contributions.[30] The Republican party in the nation is the more conservative party, and in Wisconsin's polarized programmatic politics its conservatism is even more apparent. Its resistance to the expansion of the government's role in providing social welfare services and in regulating the economy is in line with the preferences of upper socio-economic groups. And, as might be expected, survey data clearly show that these groups identify with the Republican party in Wisconsin as elsewhere in the North.[31]

In this situation, it is not surprising that the Republicans have a substantial advantage in political spending. Their program attracts a constituency both able and willing to give. And among their constituents are those who are most effective as fund raisers. These facts will be demonstrated again in the analysis in Chapter 6 of the major sources of large gifts to the two parties.

Other evidence shows the relationship between ideology and financial resources. Data developed by Louise Overacker and extended by Alexander Heard indicate that prior to the New Deal the Democratic party relied heavily for financial support in presidential campaigns upon some of the same sources as the Republicans, namely those persons involved in manufacturing, banking, stockbroking, etc. By 1936, with the New Deal enacted and operative, the representation of these elements in the Democratic financial constituency had declined precipitously.[32]

Similarly, in Michigan, where there is the same kind of highly programmatic mass party politics as in Wisconsin, party ideology is related to the availability of funds. In 1956, Democrats there received fewer than one-third as many large contributions as the Republicans. Furthermore, Democratic contributions tended to come from unions, from officeholders, from professional people, and from those engaged in a variety of small business enterprises. Republican contributions came most frequently from those associated with the automobile industry.[33]

Party program seems a major determinant of financial sources even in a state like Connecticut whose politics is not markedly programmatic. In 1966, Republicans there received 32 per cent of their large contributions from those affiliated with manufacturing concerns, insurance companies, and financial institutions, while the Democrats received only 3 per cent of such funds from these sources.[34]

In sum, the evidence points to a high congruence between party program and the availability of financial resources. There may be some groups whose goals are not related to party ideology, and their contributions might be expected to be more evenly distributed between the parties as they seek access to government. This is indeed the case with breweries, distillers, contractors and truckers, both in Wisconsin and nationally.[35] Nonetheless, the overall pattern is one which advantages the more conservative party in the system because its constituency includes a disproportionate share of those both able and willing to give and of those who are effective fund raisers.

The Distribution of Spending: Campaign Spending and Party Organization

One of the continuing issues which divides journalists, politicians, and political scientists is the desirability of a responsible party system in the United States. The proponents of a responsible party model generally argue that political parties ought to be controlled by a membership which democratically elects party officers and drafts a platform; the public officials elected on the party ticket would, in turn, be obligated to support and effectuate the platform so adopted. To maintain the party's discipline over candidates and public officials, the party organization should be able to control the nominating process and campaign finance, according to the usual arguments.

It needs little demonstration that political parties in the United States do not come close to such a model. That does not

mean, however, that party organizations do not have a significant place in the overall constituency of a public official. To the
extent that the party is an important part of his political base,
the candidate or public official is likely to be attentive to the
party's viewpoints and needs.

Table 18

Percentage of Total Reported Spending by Local and State Party Committees, Directly or to Candidates and Their Committees, 1950–1966

Year[a]	State Party Committees			Local Party Committees			Total
	Direct	Transfers	Total	Direct	Transfers	Total	
DEMOCRATS							
1950	16	5	21	12	1	13	34
1954	16	2	18	21	4	25	43
1956	22	1	23	19	2	21	44
1958	15	0	15	15	2	17	32
1962	28	4	32	7	2	9	41
1964	23	3	26	9	2	11	37
1966	21	2	23	9	3	12	35
REPUBLICANS							
1950	43	5	48	6	1	7	55
1954	42	1	43	18	2	20	63
1956	38	6	44	14	5	19	63
1958	31	0	31	19	6	25	56
1962	35	10	45	21	5	26	71
1964	25	20	45	13	7	20	65
1966	31	7	38	16	2	18	56

[a] 1952 and 1960 omitted (see p. 40).

The data in Tables 8 to 14 yield some sense of the magnitude
of party roles in the financial constituencies of candidates and
elected officials. Such an analysis is, in itself, only a suggestion
of the party's total role. The relationship between parties and
candidates has numerous aspects: parties may provide volunteer
workers or skilled campaign technicians or issue information as
well as money. Ideological commitment and personal charisma
may affect the relationship between party workers and candidates. Thus the present data reveal only one facet of the link

between parties and candidates. Nonetheless, it is a facet worth examining as one brush stroke on a much larger canvas.

Table 18 shows the role that party organizations in Wisconsin played in the total reported political spending for the seven elections under study. The direct spending by state and local party units as well as their transfers to candidates or candidate committees is presented. The Table shows that Democratic party organizations ordinarily accounted for about one-third of total reported Democratic spending; this contrasts with about 60 per cent by Republican party organizations. This level of participation by parties suggests that party organizations have been a significant part of the candidates' constituencies in both parties. Even the lower Democratic figure represents an important part of the total Democratic effort, for a financial effort amounting to one-third of the total resources expended cannot be ignored by party candidates and public officials.

The large role played by the Republican party in financing the campaigns of its candidates is, as previously indicated, a function of that party's ideology and the constituency it attracts. Those in the upper socio-economic groups are not only able and willing to give, their identification is with the Republican party proper rather than with only certain of its candidates. They are therefore prepared to contribute to the party organization through its finance structure. Similarly, the commitment of those prominent business and professional men who are the most effective fund raisers is to the Republican cause generally and they are willing to devote their efforts to the party's fund-raising program rather than to the finance drives of individual candidates.

Alexander Heard has described the centralized structure of Republican fund raising, with its separate but closely co-ordinated finance committees at the national, state, and local levels. These finance committees are generally composed of prominent businessmen and civic leaders who have established access to potential donors.[36] The Wisconsin Republican party has a similar fund-raising apparatus. In most counties there is a finance committee whose members devote their major political efforts to the raising of money. Each county has a quota and the finance committee forwards money to the state finance committee until the quota is met. Within the Republican state headquarters certain staff members are assigned to carrying out the program of the state finance chairmen and his committee. The state headquarters generally provides local committees with lists of past contributors and develops leads on additional prospects. In addition, the county finance committees develop whatever new sources they can.

The Republican canvass for funds is carried out on a highly systematic basis, with each donor asked to pledge certain amounts and follow-up collections made by the finance committee member who make the original contact. The door-to-door solicitation in the executive wings of major Wisconsin corporations is revealed by the filed reports where the names of all the executives of a given corporation appear in tandem with contributions of the same amount. The sums may be somewhat larger if an executive of that corporation is also a member of the county or state finance committee, and in Milwaukee the Republican Finance Committee is apparently attempting to develop a program of having a finance committee agent in every major corporation.

Not only is Republican fund raising more centralized, but the entire financial management of Republican campaigns follows this pattern. Until 1964, the Republican state headquarters handled the campaigns of all statewide candidates. Budgets were submitted by the candidates to a committee which included the state chairman, finance committee representatives, and party organization leaders. The budgets were then reviewed and approved, sometimes with modifications. Republican headquarters dispensed money in behalf of the candidates as needed and in accordance with the budgets. With the money both raised and spent by the Republican party organization, the candidates and their managers were freed to work on other aspects of the campaign. This campaign finance process, of course, made the candidates almost entirely dependent upon the party for financial support, and obviously strengthened the link between the party and its candidates and officeholders.

In 1964, each Republican candidate set up his own separate

committee and the Republican headquarters transferred funds, in accordance with the agreed budgets, to these candidate committees. This left the candidates and their managers with the responsibility for actually disbursing and managing the money. The decision to adopt this format, which did not alter the role of the party organization in raising the money, was apparently a result of severe disputes about budgeting between the party headquarters and the 1962 Republican gubernatorial candidate. In 1966, however, the Republicans returned to the system of handling most candidate expenditures through the party headquarters.

In contrast to the orderly Republican system, the Democrats have operated in an atmosphere of financial chaos. The state party headquarters has provided certain minimal aids, such as nominal direct contributions, "mutual assistance" literature featuring the entire Democratic ticket and key points from the party program, long distance telephone lines, lists and equipment for mailings, and similar contributions in kind. In recent years the actual money contributions have been about $10,000 to gubernatorial and United States Senate candidates, $2,500 to $5,000 to lesser statewide candidates depending on the office, and from $25 to $400 to legislative candidates depending on the nature of the district. In 1966 a legislative campaign committee was established which increased the financial aid given to legislative candidates in critical districts either by transferring funds to them or spending directly in their behalf. In statewide campaigns involving cash outlays between $200,000 and $300,000, the party's direct financial contribution has not been of major significance. Its expenditures to organize and direct local party units which have provided most grass-roots campaign efforts for all candidates have, of course, been a very significant indirect contribution to those who run for public office on the Democratic ticket. Furthermore, there have been some monetary contributions, usually of a nominal amount, from local party committees to candidates for various offices.

Democratic candidates are expected to raise the funds necessary to wage their campaigns by direct solicitations of individuals and groups. Thus a typical Democratic partisan may be solicited by the candidates for governor, United States senator, Congress, the state legislature, and perhaps by an occasional aggressive courthouse aspirant. Furthermore, each of these candidates must set up some fund-raising machinery, so that different groups of fund raisers come to be associated with particular political personalities or sometimes with certain public offices. Both fund raising and financial management in Democratic campaigns is carried on separately from the party organization by the same political committees responsible for the other aspects of the campaign.

The contrast between the centralized, systematic Republican finance system and the chaotic fiscal operation of the Democrats has not been a matter of Democratic choice or incompetence. Rather, it has been related to the distinctly different nature of the Democratic financial constituency.[37] First, the Democrats have relied upon organized labor for a substantial portion of their funds—about 20 per cent in Wisconsin according to the best current study.[38] The captains of the labor movement firmly maintain the independent stance of endorsing candidates rather than affiliating with parties. Furthermore, labor's contributions do not come in a single lump sum: the endorsed candidate must set up some machinery for actually soliciting the money from the various COPE committees at the national, state, and local levels as well as from the regional union offices and the union locals.[39]

A second source of Democratic contributions is the non-programmatic economic interests. The relationships of these groups to the two parties are different, fitting well with the centralized Republican fund-raising system but probably adding to the disorganization of Democratic fund solicitation. The leaders of these groups tend to be Republican in their personal viewpoints and thus willing to contribute to the Republican organization, especially since the party headquarters and finance committee have generally had excellent access to Republican elected officials. Thus a contribution to the Republican party organization both provides the access to decision-making which is desired and serves the general political philosophy of the donor. On the Democratic side, by contrast, there has not been such a clear link between the party headquarters and the elected officials; and during the six-year Democratic gubernatorial incumbency the party chairmen were almost continually associated with different party factions than the governor. To obtain the desired access to the officeholder then, these interests want to be solicited by someone closely linked with the candidate and this necessitates some separate fund-raising machinery for each candidate.

A third factor which has contributed to the chaotic Democratic finance picture has been the irregular contour of the individual contributor base. Whereas the Republicans have been able to approach a sympathetic business community on a systematic basis, the Democrats have had no well-off occupational or social support group that could be comprehensively canvassed. There are, of course, individual businessmen and professional people who prefer the Democratic cause, and there is the program-oriented party membership drawn heavily from the middle class. It has frequently been difficult to identify the potential donors among these groups, and often they have been motivated to contribute by the personal qualities of a particular candidate or by the development of a certain issue by a specific office-seeker. Solicitation from such sources is often successful only when made by a candidate or his organization, since the candidate rather than the party is the focus of attention.[40]

A fourth obstacle to centralized Democratic fund raising has been that party's difficulty in finding effective fund raisers. Financially successful men with the necessary experience and connections are unlikely to be Democrats, and if they are Democrats they are unlikely to be active partisans. Such men may, however, be available to candidates for governor or United States senator because of personal friendships, past business or professional contacts, specific policy or personal interests, or other relationships which are not party-oriented in nature. In recent years there have been signs that members of Democratic state administrations were instrumental in raising funds for the campaigns of the chief executive. These people gain prestige and "clout" from their intimate association with the governor. At any rate, effective fund raisers have been more easily mobilized by candidates than by the party on the Democratic side.

Finally, the Democratic party rule against party endorsement of primary candidates has probably been an obstacle in Wisconsin to effective centralized fund raising. The Wisconsin primary is not held until early September, and party funds do not become available to Democratic candidates until the primary is over. Campaigns, of course, begin much earlier and there is a need to finance them for the many months prior to the primary. Thus a separate fund-raising apparatus has been essential to Democratic candidates to finance the critical initial stages of the campaign, to wage the primary fight if there was one, and to begin building a bank account for use in the closing weeks when money is scarce and time too short to raise it. Since 1961, Democratic candidates for governor and senator have been the beneficiaries of testimonial dinners in the non-election years in order to build up the financial reserve necessary to begin the campaign. These dinners have generally netted between $25,000 and $45,000, or between 10 and 20 per cent of total campaign needs. Generally there has been a further fund-raising effort in the spring of the election year which raised some additional portion of the campaign budget. All of these early efforts have been conducted by the candidates and their supporters because neither party funds nor fund-raising machinery becomes available until after the September primary.

The Republican practice is quite different. The Republican state convention endorses candidates for state offices and United States senator; congressional candidates are endorsed by congressional district caucuses. Upon endorsement, substantial financial resources become available to candidates from the party treasury. Republican candidates may, of course, be forced to wage some kind of fund-raising effort before the party's endorsement convention in late May or early June. Pre-convention campaigns have not been notably expensive, and the filed reports suggest that some major party contributors give to the pre-convention campaigns of the candidates favored by the party's more conservative wing. After endorsement, Republican candidates can ordinarily leave the major problems of campaign finance to the party headquarters with a feeling of confidence that their campaign budgets will be met; some candidates do, however, engage in separate fund-raising campaigns to make up a portion of the budget or to supplement it.

All of these factors contribute to the greater significance of party organization in the overall Republican finance picture as opposed to that of the Democrats. The fact, however, that fund raising is structurally more centralized in the Republican party has not meant that Republican elected officials have been subject to stronger pressures from a programmatically united support coalition than have Democratic officeholders. As will be shown more fully, while Republican party finance may be more centralized, the evidence seems to indicate that the more jumbled Democratic fund-raising efforts draw funds nonetheless from a programmatically homogeneous base.

There are difficulties in attempting to divide political spending into one category designated as party organization spending and another as candidate committee spending. The overlap between these categories makes clear distinctions difficult, and there is some credible evidence that the party organizations have been used as a conduit for channeling money from certain sources to be spent in behalf of candidates without their committees reporting such expenditures. Motives for this strategem have not necessarily been pernicious. Both Democrats and Republicans have apparently appealed to candidate-oriented donors to contribute directly to the party organization in order to build up the organization's fund-raising prestige and ability. Funds so contributed were automatically earmarked for a particular candidate, and the state party headquarters actually had no significant role in raising the money nor any choice in how to dispense it.

In other situations, the motives were less pristine. Often such channeling of funds was intended to avoid the full disclosure that is required by law. Candidates wishing to forestall anticipated public ire about high levels of spending have urged contributors to give to the party, which then spent the money as directed by the candidate or his managers. In other instances, candidates have preferred not to show on their own reports large contributions from certain sources. Bank taxes have been a partisan issue in Wisconsin for some years, and interviews with party leaders suggest that Republican gubernatorial candidates have preferred to have contributions from banking interests funneled into the party; and the Democrats have become somewhat sensitive on the issue of large labor contributions so that union money has often been forwarded to the party organization which expended it according to the candidate's prescriptions.

In 1964, the Democratic Party of Wisconsin showed on its reports approximately $65,000 received from various sources and earmarked by them specifically for the presidential campaign, and another $49,000 designated for Senator William Proxmire's campaign, all but $10,000 of which came from non-party sources. These sums were reported as expenditures of the Democratic Party of Wisconsin, although specifically raised by and spent on behalf of particular candidate campaigns. By contrast, in 1962, only about $14,000 of this kind of accounting seems to have occurred, all of it directed to the senatorial and gubernatorial campaigns, and in 1966 the sum channelled through Democratic headquarters on behalf of the gubernatorial campaign was under $10,000.

The extent of this practice is difficult to gauge, but persons connected with the two parties indicate that, except for the Democratic experience in 1964, it has not been so widespread as to invalidate the general pattern found in Table 18. Nonetheless, the very existence of the practice raises a signal flag which warns of the difficulty of separating party organization spending from candidate spending in any meaningful and accurate way.

The Distribution of Spending: State and Local Level Spending

The previous sections have suggested some of the ways in which the factors discussed at the beginning of this chapter affect the distribution of spending. Their full impact on spending patterns is best seen, however, by an examination of the distribution of spending between state and local candidates and party committees. Heard estimated that 14 per cent of nationwide spending in 1952 occurred at the national level, 48 per cent at the state level, and 38 per cent locally.[41] If only the total expenditures by state and local political units are considered, the former account for 56 per cent of the state-local total and the latter for 44 per cent. It is clear, however, that the proportion of total spending at various governmental levels is not static. Rather it is determined by the interplay of the variables which affect the levels of spending. Table 19 indicates the dynamic nature of the state-local spending relationship.

Table 19

Percentage of Reported Spending by Candidates and Committees at the State and Local Levels, 1950–1966

Year[a]	Democrats		Republicans		Total	
	State	Local	State	Local	State	Local
1950	56	44	60	40	59	41
1954	44	56	43	57	44	56
1956	47	53	59	41	56	44
1958	51	49	47	53	49	51
1962	62	38	50	50	55	45
1964	65	35	56	44	59	41
1966	50	50	40	60	44	56

[a] 1952 and 1960 omitted (see p. 40).

The pattern of Democratic spending at the two levels seems most closely related to the rise of electoral competition, but it is modified by a number of other variables. The predominance of state level spending in 1950, for instance, was largely due to the impinging influence of national politics. In 1949, liberal Democrats formed the Democratic Organizing Committee (DOC), a mass membership, liberal, voluntary political organization, to convert the Wisconsin Democracy from a conservative, patronage-oriented, immigrant fraternal society, into a seriously competing political party clearly committed to New Deal-Fair Deal domestic and international programs.[42] The Truman administration chose to support this Democratic faction over the moribund traditionalist Democratic group. Furthermore, the national administration was anxious to build a strong new liberal political

base to defeat Joseph R. McCarthy in 1952, and the prospects
for this maneuver seemed encouraging in light of Mr. Truman's
Wisconsin victory in 1948. The Democratic National Committee and the national CIO–PAC channelled money into the
coffers of the DOC and the committees supporting the Democratic United States Senate candidate, Thomas Fairchild.
Though not large by most measures, these sums were substantial
compared to the meager resources which the newly founded
DOC could raise from its corporal's guard of dues-paying members. In 1950, therefore, the dominance of the state level spending committees was due not to their own resources, but to the
transfer of funds from the national administration to meet certain of its political objectives.

The small state level percentage of total Democratic spending
in 1954 was certainly related to the non-competitive nature of
the Wisconsin Democracy. Democratic candidate William Proxmire had received only 37 per cent of the gubernatorial vote in
1952, and few took his 1954 candidacy seriously. Consequently,
he was able to raise little money and the unavailability of
resources was a major factor in the low proportion of Democratic funds spent at the state level. At least as important was
the absence of a United States Senate campaign from the ballot;
even the reduction by one of the number of major state level
offices contested had the expected impact of reducing state level
spending. A further factor was the reapportionment of legislative seats which occurred in 1954; this encouraged local Democrats to field more candidates and to support them more vigorously because of the prospect of making gains in the legislature,
especially in the assembly. Finally, the loss of federal patronage
in the aftermath of the Eisenhower victory in 1952 eliminated
one of the significant convertible resources which the Democrats
had possessed in 1950. Frank Sorauf reported as early as 1953
that with the termination of federal patronage and with no other
significant lever for raising money, the state Democratic party
had few financial resources and was largely dependent upon
county party organizations to sell tickets to state headquarters
fund-raising events.[43]

The steady rise in 1956 and 1958 of the state level share of

Democratic spending was associated with the increase in Democratic electoral competitiveness for governor and United States senator. In 1954, Proxmire gained 49 per cent of the gubernatorial vote and in 1956, 48 per cent. In this newly competitive circumstance, both he and the state party organization were able to raise additional funds. Added to these were the expenditures on behalf of the United States Senate candidates in 1956 and 1958. Still, the Democratic party was not incumbent at either the national or state levels, and the state party headquarters had not developed an effective finance wing. Even though expenditures at the state level were a rising proportion of the whole during these elections, they were only about half of total state-local spending.

The dominance of state level spending in 1962 and 1964 represents a convergence of virtually all the variables previously mentioned. The Democrats had captured a United States Senate seat in 1957 and the governorship in 1958; and they held these offices through 1964. After John F. Kennedy's victory in 1960, they had both state and national level incumbency with the concomitant fund-raising advantages. In addition, their series of Wisconsin victories had established that the close electoral competition of the mid-1950's was not merely a sometime thing. And in both 1962 and 1964 there were two major state level offices in contest, the governorship and a United States Senate seat. In 1964, as in 1950, state level spending was increased by the impinging politics of the presidency when the Johnson campaign managers transferred almost $65,000 to the Democratic state headquarters for disbursement on behalf of the Johnson-Humphrey ticket.

Not only were the Democratic candidates stronger, the Democratic party organization was more vigorous. Under the leadership of state chairman Patrick J. Lucey, Democratic membership had grown steadily and in 1964 it stood at 26,000. This membership was extensively canvassed for funds. Furthermore, Lucey's early alliance with John F. Kennedy and his subsequent standing as the President's Wisconsin agent strengthened the party headquarters' fund drives. In 1962 Mr. Kennedy agreed to speak at the Jefferson-Jackson Day Dinner, and ticket prices were raised from $25 to $100. The new price was kept in force in subsequent years. Lucey also instituted a Century Club which allowed party members to purchase their membership, certain party publications, and a Jefferson-Jackson Dinner ticket on the installment plan, thus expanding the number of those who made the effort to give as much as $100 to the party. The use of program book advertising by the Democrats began on a large scale in 1962, and this device permitted the Democratic party headquarters, armed with the argument of tax deductibility and the plea for equality of treatment for the two parties, to solicit funds from corporations. Finally, Lucey, himself a businessman, developed a corps of effective fund raisers to make more successful the Democratic party's canvass.

During this entire period, as we shall see in Chapter 5, the rise of television as a political weapon stimulated state level spending by increasing enormously the need for funds in gubernatorial and United States Senate campaigns. Proxmire's upset United States Senate victory in the special election of 1957 was attributed by Democrats largely to the candidate's indefatigible handshaking efforts and to his effective use of television. From 1957 to 1966, Democratic state level candidates felt compelled to raise enormous sums to finance extensive schedules of television spot announcements. Thus, because the newly available technology was both more expensive on a per unit basis and was used more extensively, the cost of politics at the state level rose sharply.

The decline in the state level share of political spending in 1966 seems anomalous. Not only was the gubernatorial race relatively close—Republican Warren Knowles won with 53.7 per cent of the vote—but there was a fiercely fought three-way primary for the Democratic gubernatorial nomination. Yet these surface considerations cover a configuration of variables which operated to minimize state level spending. While the Republican percentage of the vote was within the range regarded as competitive by political scientists, few observers in Wisconsin believed that the Democrats would win; money was more difficult to raise as a result. Furthermore, as in 1954, state level spending dropped because no United States Senate seat was being filled.

Indeed, a glance at Tables 13 and 14 shows that the decline in total spending from 1964 to 1966 was substantially less than the reported $196,100 that was spent on behalf of William Proxmire in 1964. If a United States Senate campaign of the same expense had been waged in 1966, state level spending would have been 58 per cent of total Democratic spending.

Unusually heavy campaign activity for the state assembly and several congressional seats increased the local share of spending. Labor and the Democratic National Committee made a major effort to save two marginal congressional seats won in 1964. As a result, reported Democratic expenditures in the First and Sixth Congressional Districts rose from $30,927 to $69,361. Although losing the governorship in 1964, Democrats had a slim majority of the seats in the lower house of the legislature. In 1966, a major effort was made by a special legislative campaign committee and by the state Democratic headquarters to save that majority. Total spending for lower house seats rose from $87,200 to $119,690.

From 1964 to 1966 the fund-raising capacity of the Democratic headquarters declined. The Democrats no longer had the benefit of gubernatorial incumbency. The vigorously contested gubernatorial primary made it difficult for party leaders to raise money because partisans of the various candidates were reluctant to contribute to a fund which might ultimately go to a candidate they opposed. In addition, party membership declined and so did the party's fund-raising activities; the new state chairman, J. Louis Hanson, did not have the same network of connections and the same cadre of fund raisers that had made Patrick J. Lucey a successful party financier. Finally, Democratic strategy changed in 1966 so that television was de-emphasized as the major mass medium; newspaper advertising was more heavily relied on. Whether this decision was wise strategically is not important here; its impact on financing was to diminish somewhat the amount of money needed to sustain at least the same level of media activity as in recent campaigns. In short, the same variables that operated in prior years were operating in 1966, but they now moved in a different direction, to diminish the proportion of spending at the state level.

The division of Republican spending between the state and local levels does not show the same rising state share in response to the growth of competition from 1954 to 1964 that was found for the Democrats. But the same variables which determined spending for their opponents also set the pattern of Republican spending. In 1950, the heavy spending at the state level can be partly attributed to the contesting of both the governorship and a United States Senate seat. More important perhaps was the nature of the Republican Party of Wisconsin. From 1925 until the mid-1950's, the Republican Party of Wisconsin was basically a state level political organization. Both its support and its leadership came mainly from the business elements of the state and those who shared their viewpoints. These people were primarily interested in issues such as taxing, spending, and governmental regulation of business. These issues were state and national issues, rather than courthouse matters. Thus the orientation of the Republican party tended toward state and national issues, and its primary function was to nominate conservative Republicans for statewide offices. Furthermore, Republican campaign finance was primarily a state organization function, with money raised and spent at the state level.[44]

The Republican party's local units were very informally organized and were often only mailing lists of "sympathetic" citizens. Frequently the county organizations were so weak that they had to be financed by subventions from the state Republican organization.[45] The annual county Republican caucuses seldom endorsed legislative or courthouse candidates seeking Republican nominations, so that little money was spent in local primaries. And most counties were dominated by the Republicans so completely that little effort was necessary in the general election campaign. It is not surprising that in these circumstances, spending at the state level overshadowed that at the local level.

In 1954, the distribution of Republican spending was reversed. That no United States Senate seat was filled that year undoubtedly diminished state level spending. Probably as important was the perceived lack of a competitive gubernatorial contest: Governor Walter Kohler, Jr., had defeated his Democratic challenger by a landslide in 1952 and no one foresaw that his margin would be reduced to 2 per cent in 1954. Furthermore, reapportionment of the state legislature encouraged numerous primary battles within the Republican ranks and required considerable additional sums to beat back the aggressive challenges of the Democrats who attempted to make gains in the newly constituted districts.

The dominance of state level spending in 1956 was caused largely by a reversal of the factors that had operated in 1954. Not only were both the governorship and a United States Senate seat at stake, but there were disbursements by state level committees formed on behalf of President Eisenhower. Furthermore, there was an enormously bitter and expensive United States Senate primary between conservative Republican Congressman Glenn Davis, who had won the endorsement of his party's convention, and incumbent Senator Alexander Wiley, who was affiliated with the Eisenhower moderates, especially on matters of foreign policy. The Republicans perceived a serious Democratic challenge in the aftermath of 1954, and they spent heavily at the state level to beat back William Proxmire's third gubernatorial challenge.

In 1958, the preponderance of Republican spending was again at the local level, probably because an expensive United States Senate primary and special election in the late summer of 1957 had partially exhausted the resources available to the Republican state level committees. This erosion of state level resources was further compounded by the unpopularity, even within his own party organization, of the sitting Republican governor, Vernon Thomson, and by the disenchantment of the party's conservative wing because of its failure in successive senatorial primaries to nominate Glenn Davis over Eisenhower Republicans Alexander Wiley in 1956 and Walter Kohler, Jr., in the special election in 1957.

The Democrats in 1958 captured the governorship, retained the United States Senate seat held by William Proxmire, captured a majority in the state assembly, and won three of the lesser statewide constitutional offices. In the aftermath of this defeat, the Republicans began in earnest to build up their local organizations. Not only did the state headquarters seek to develop regular membership affiliations in the counties, but the county organizations began raising and spending money locally both to aid statewide candidates and to meet the increasingly vigorous Democratic local campaigns.

Spending by the Republicans increased sharply to combat the resurgent Democrats, but the spending was now spread more evenly between the two levels. Heavy state level expenditures to win back the statehouse were matched by heavy spending to retain challenged courthouse positions and to regain firm control of the legislature. The division of Republican spending between the state and local levels in 1962 and 1964 reflects the ability of the Republicans to raise large sums at both levels to wage both state and local campaigns. After their defeat in 1958, the Republicans reorganized and greatly strengthened their fund-raising arm under the leadership of finance committee chairman Daniel Parker of the Parker Pen Company. The Republican finance structure was further strengthened after the Republican victory of 1964 with state party chairman Ody J. Fish expanding the finance committee staff and broadening membership on the committee itself. The more even division of spending in 1962 than in 1964 does not reflect any weakness in Republican fund-raising capacity in the former year, but rather the much smaller financial effort in 1962 on behalf of Senator Alexander Wiley, who had long been unpopular with his party, than in 1964 on behalf of Wilbur Renk whose unsuccessful senatorial campaign cost as much as the successful gubernatorial race of Warren Knowles.

In 1966, state level spending was far overshadowed by local level expenditures. The reasons seem the same as for the Democrats: the lack of a United States Senate contest, the feeling that Warren Knowles was not faced with a serious challenge, the extraordinary sums devoted to congressional campaigns. It should be noted, however, that 1964 and 1966 were the years of the heaviest Republican reliance on television in their mass media campaigning. Previously they tended to rely more heavily on newspaper and radio advertising and on billboards. The resulting increases in state level costs were not, however, great enough to offset the forces toward higher local level spending which occurred in 1966.

In sum, the factors of the number and importance of offices contested, the intensity of electoral competition, the distribution of such resources as incumbency and ideology, the nature of party constituencies and their fund-raising structures, the availability and use of various campaign techniques, and the impingement of national politics on state political systems are all related to both the level of spending and the distribution of spending in a political system. The total costs reported in Chapter 3 are meaningful only when seen as responses to these factors, and the uneven distribution of spending from election year to election year can be explained only when the changing configuration of these variables is examined for each election. In the next chapter the choices of goods and services made by politicians in the expenditure of their campaign dollars will be considered. To a significant extent, the variables which determine the amount and the distribution of spending are also important in the politicians' choices about the directions or purposes of spending.

The Uses of Money in Politics

Constraints on Expenditures

Chapter 1 dealt at length with the problem of resource conversion. To recapitulate briefly, resources can be allocated to such purposes as the further pyramiding of resources or the purchase of campaign "outputs" designed to attain the final goals of the campaign. Even expenditures for campaign outputs may, of course, feed back into the campaign so as to pyramid or dissipate the stockpile of resources, but that is not their main purpose. The object of this chapter is to investigate and evaluate the purposes to which Wisconsin politicians allocated their monetary resources.

It is well, before presenting and analyzing these data, to point out the difficulty of developing any general theory about the uses of money in politics. It has been shown that money is desirable as a resource because of its easy convertibility: theoretically politicians can convert their financial resources into whatever money will buy in the society. Despite this wide latitude which exists in theory, it appears that in practice there are significant regularities in the uses of resources by politicians.

Louise Overacker has pointed out that campaign practices common in ancient Athens and in republican Rome are still common today.[1] Candidates were sponsored or supported by political clubs which bear a striking resemblance to those familiar to Americans, and the members of these clubs undertook the chores of campaign management much as do modern day politicians. "Preliminary campaigning and canvassing took place, dinners and banquets were given at which the candidates were the guests of honor, and on election day the agents of the candidates went about the business of 'getting out the vote' in a thoroughly business-like fashion. . . ."[2] Ancient campaign practices extended from simple endorsements ("Vesonius Primus requests you to choose Gaius Gavius duumvir; he will be a valuable public servant")[3] to enormous expenditures designed to ingratiate candidates with the voters, who came to expect lavish entertaining and the provision of games or gladiatorial contests on a magnificent scale.[4] The practice of endorsement is with us today, as full-page advertisements taken by college professors in the *New York Times* bear witness. And the entertainment of voters continues only slightly abated, as observers of politicians like former Louisiana Governor Jimmy ("You Are My Sunshine") Davis and the late Idaho Senator Glen Taylor, both of whom campaigned guitar in hand, can attest. The 1960 campaign of John F. Kennedy was lent "glamour" by the appearances of such Hollywood notables as Robert Vaughn and the Frank Sinatra-led "Rat Pack." While politicians in all ages have employed entertainment as a campaign device, in the 1960's the process has been carried to its logical conclusion— the displacement of some politicians in elective office by the entertainers they formerly used as campaign attractions. Such a practice has its logic for both the public and the celebrities: it eliminates the middleman.

Obviously, neither the wide latitude which politicians theoretically have in their use of campaign funds, nor our somewhat overdrawn demonstration of the recurrence of certain centuries-old campaign practices are adequately descriptive of the contemporary conversion of campaign funds into political efforts. A more precise approach requires two lines of analysis. Here it is helpful to discuss in a general way some of the limitations which narrow the range of choices which politicians make in the employment of their resources. Later it will be useful to detail the campaign activities to which politicians actually allocate their resources.

At the outset, politicians may be restrained in their use of campaign resources by the legal framework of the political system. They will ordinarily not spend money for purposes which they perceive to violate legal bans. In some cases, they are limited not by their perceptions of the legal prohibitions, but by their assessment of the probabilities that they will be detected or prosecuted for activities which they perceive to violate legal codes. Such rare vote buying as still occurs in America is engaged in by politicians who know that the practice is illegal, but who do not see a real likelihood of its detection or of the enforcement of the laws against bribing electors.

Beyond these legal limits, politicians may further narrow their own choices by their value systems. Certain types of campaign appeals or certain methods of campaigning may be seen as unethical or improper, even though they are not perceived as illegal.

A different restraint is the perceived public acceptability of campaign techniques. If politicians believe that the electorate will react negatively to certain campaign styles or messages, they will not engage in them even though they perceive them to be neither illegal nor unethical. In the Netherlands, for instance, door-to-door canvassing is viewed as an invasion of privacy, and politicians do not employ this campaign technique. In both the United States and Great Britain, a very large percentage of respondents are not hostile to the idea of being called on by party workers, and in both countries politicians freely mount doorbell-ringing campaigns.

Inadequate information is another factor which limits a politician's use of his resources. The most obvious instance is where a politician is unaware of certain campaign techniques or messages which might be available to him. For example, at the present time, many politicians do not use computers to collate information on electors and then categorize voters into groups to whom specialized appeals can be directed. This may be partly due to cost; but it is in even larger measure a result of the lack of knowledge of such techniques. Or a politician might be unaware of some aspect of the public record of his own candidate or of his opponent which might be exploited and so does not convert resources to this purpose.

The fact that in every campaign there is some limit to the available resources is, of course, a restriction on the kinds of campaigning politicians may engage in. Although theoretically resources might be pyramided indefinitely, there are in practice real limitations such as skill, time, and the resistance of those who possess the resources which a politician seeks to capture. Thus no campaign has a stockpile of resources large enough to buy all of the campaigning which might be desirable. Politicians are therefore forced to select which kinds of campaigning they will purchase; the effectiveness with which they do this is of course a measure of their skill.

A politician's supporters and allies impose additional constraints on his use of his resources. Often this takes the form of demands on the politician to allocate some portion of his resources to them. It is common in many American states for candidates to make subventions to precinct workers or committees to get out the vote. Heard has pointed out that these "subventions . . . blend a concern over needed costs with recognition of local leaders whose aid is essential in their areas."[5] He estimates that these costs may have been as high as $18 million in 1952 and 1956.[6] They accounted for 20 to 45 per cent of local level expenditures in Connecticut, Maryland, and Pennsylvania in 1952.[7] In 1956, local Democratic committees in 23 states and similar Republican committees in 24 states reported allocating 42 and 33 per cent of funds respectively to these election day expenditures.[8] These kinds of demands on the politicians' resources appear in other and less justifiable forms. Richard Rose reports that the Labour party purchases advertising in Labour's official paper, *The Herald,* and the Co-operative movement's *Sunday Citizen* in response to pressures from leaders of those groups.[9]

Supporters and allies may impose a somewhat different restraint, not by demanding a share of the politician's resources, but by applying overt or implicit pressures to prevent their being used in certain ways. This is especially pertinent in Wisconsin, where the programmatic nature of party membership imposes a threat of high costs—in the form of defections or slackened enthusiasm among party workers—on politicians who make electoral appeals at sharp variance from the membership's understanding of the party's program.

A quite different limit on the use of resources by politicians may be the unavailability of certain kinds of competence and skills. In theory it is possible to retain specialists to perform tasks for which political leaders lack the technical training, but what is theoretically possible may be exceedingly difficult to achieve in practice. In Wisconsin, for instance, there is almost no patronage for the minority party and such patronage as is available is not very desirable. As a consequence, the minority party finds it difficult to sustain from election to election a corps of staff members who understand the technical aspects of campaign management and who have the necessary knowledge of issues, the records of the parties and their candidates on them, and the maneuvers which accompanied their development. And few people with these kinds of skills and knowledge will be available for the campaign season only.

To the extent that certain special skills or talents are not readily available and cannot be easily hired, politicians cannot effectively use their resources for strategies which require such expertise. In recent years some Democratic candidates in Wisconsin have found it difficult to obtain adequate assistance and advice in the waging of mass media campaigns. Only one advertising firm in the state has been willing to take Democratic accounts; the others deem them a threat to their retention of accounts of businesses whose executives are known to favor the Republicans, or regard them as too limited in duration, or assess them as too dangerous (because of the loss of prestige which accompanies an election defeat) to be worthwhile. In Democratic primaries the contestants who are unable to obtain professional advertising assistance even though they are quite willing to pay the usual fees for such services are significantly disadvantaged. The problem also arises in the general election when all of the state, congressional, and local candidates who might wish to employ professional media specialists find that there is simply not enough talent to serve all of the Democratic candidates.

An additional limit on the use of resources derives from the candidate's own capabilities: his personality, speaking manner, and physical appearance may limit the uses to which campaign resources can be put. In 1964, Governor John Reynolds, who embarked on his re-election campaign as an underdog, experimented with a series of "walk-on" television spots in which he personally explained the tax policy which was thought to be a major cause of his unpopularity. Both the Governor and party leaders agreed that his television manner was simply not effective, even though his personal presentations of his case at public meetings were quite well received. As a result, the television spot series was discarded after a brief test period. Reynolds' inability to get across on television probably hindered him in dispelling the image that he was a weak executive who had defaulted on his campaign promises; a stronger television appearance might have conveyed a quite different impression of his personal qualities and offset the Republican campaign attacks which hammered at his alleged weakness and perfidy.

Still another restraint on the use of campaign resources is the practicability of certain types of campaign strategies which might be pursued. For state legislative candidates to use television or major metropolitan dailies as media for reaching their constituents is simply not practicable. These may be the media most relied on by voters for political information, but their reach or circulation is so great that the candidate is compelled to buy exposure to many times the number of voters in his constituency.

This latter limit is really a special case of a much broader constraint which can perhaps best be stated in the current Pentagon phrase for calculating strategies in terms of the "cost-effectiveness ratio." Some political activities clearly are so costly that they cannot be reasonably pursued; the example of the legislative candidate attempting to wage a media campaign is a case in point. It will be recognized that in many instances there is room for the politician to employ his skill in making nice calculations of the relative "cost-effectiveness ratio" of resource expenditures to pursue certain political activities. In other instances, however, it will be obvious that some uses of resources are vastly inferior to others and that these uses may be viewed as impracticable. This becomes a significant deterrent to, though not an absolute limit on, allocations of campaign resources by politicians.

Like the list of resources in Chapter 1, this list of constraints on the uses to which politicians can put their campaign resources may vary in different situations and through time. It does represent the constraints which are obvious in the Wisconsin political situation. Because of the tendency for the public to overstate the significance of money in politics, it is especially useful to demonstrate that politicians operate within quite significant boundaries in the conversion and use of resources. Even within this context of limitations, however, politicians have a wide range of choices which they can and must make in using their resources to attain campaign goals. This is a subject which must be studied by reviewing the specific uses to which resources are put in specific campaigns. If the pattern of resource use is a recurring one in different state political systems or at different times, some generalizations can be made about political conduct. Where changes in such an established pattern occur, they merit investigation to determine what changes in the political system or among politicians are causing new patterns of resource use. Finally, the uses to which money is put ought to be evaluated both in terms of their effectiveness in attaining the goals of politicians and their significance for the performance of certain functions or activities, such as those described in Chapter 1, which are thought useful to the maintenance of the political system.

The Uses of Money in Wisconsin Politics

A discussion of the uses of money in Wisconsin politics must begin with the methodological questions of how to obtain data and within what general categories of "uses" the wide range of specific expenditures should be grouped.

The filed campaign reports are less helpful in studying the

uses of money than in any other aspect of this inquiry. The law requires that the amount of an expenditure, the person to whom the amount was paid, and the purpose of the payment be reported.[10] These reports, however, generally show the specific goods or services purchased and not their purpose or function. Thus, an entry may show that $X was paid to the ABC Co. for printing. The purpose or function of the printing remains a mystery to those who examine the reports. Whether the money was expended for the printing of campaign literature aimed at the voters, or organization manuals to strengthen local party units, or fund-raising letters to finance the mass media campaign is the significant question.

Some evidence concerning the actual uses of money can be obtained from the filed reports, especially as to the amounts spent for purchasing mass media to win votes and for hiring political staff members. For the most part, however, information on the uses of money must be gained from personal access to those charged with actually spending the money. Even then, reports may be inconsistent or uncertain, because political managers do not think in general functional terms during the short-run crises of campaigns and because they themselves do not keep close account of the money spent on a day-to-day basis.

The data used in this study are largely derived from the author's experience in several statewide Democratic campaigns, from his access to leading Democratic political figures in the state, and from examinations and interpretations of the filed reports. The role of political activist which yielded such excellent access in the study of Democratic uses of money resulted, of course, in negative access to the Republican politicians; the Democratic spending pattern is therefore studied and presented more completely and with greater confidence than that of the Republicans.

These same methodological considerations limit the scope of this study to the uses of money by statewide major party committees, and by major party candidates and their supporting committees for the offices of governor and United States senator. It was feasible to survey the filed reports of these committees and to obtain interview data concerning their spending; to survey the uses of money by the thousands of candidates and their supporting committees involved in contests for lesser office would not be possible. Occasionally some data are presented concerning system-wide costs, and the basis of this information is clearly noted. The study concentrates on the 1964 campaign because the recollections of those who participated are still fairly accurate. In considering expenditures for mass media, however, some reported data were available as far back as 1954 and this information was used when appropriate. Within these limitations, then, it is possible to present a general picture of the purposes for which political money has been used in Wisconsin and, to a lesser extent, to indicate the relative distribution of money to these various purposes.

A survey of the uses of political money must first establish some general categories into which specific kinds of expenditures can be grouped. These categories should be of a functional nature to best relate spending to other aspects of the political system. The eight categories which have been established in this study may be as significant for what they exclude as what they encompass. There is no evidence, for instance, of any vote buying in Wisconsin. Nor is there any indication that precinct leaders or ethnic bloc leaders are paid to deliver their precincts or their blocs. Wisconsin politics shows up, then, as almost completely free from the uses of money which are generally regarded in America as illegal. The following paragraphs set forth and describe the eight major categories into which political expenditures in Wisconsin have been grouped.

1. *Candidate expenses.* This involves the personal expenses and travel costs for a statewide political candidate and for his driver. The necessity for candidates to maintain the exhausting pace which has become the norm in American politics is sometimes challenged. In Wisconsin, the candidate's personal campaigning serves a range of purposes, from inspiring his partisans across the state to generating free political news in the state's media to winning votes by the personal handshake and appearance. Every campaign includes a substantial allowance for travel expenses.

2. *Candidate headquarters' expenses.* The practice varies widely in establishing political headquarters for the candidates. A few candidates have simply operated out of the office of their political party. Generally, however, major office candidates have established separate headquarters in both Madison and Milwaukee. The costs of maintaining such headquarters include staff salaries, communications (telephone, telegraph) expenses, postage, rent, and so forth. From headquarters, the candidate is scheduled, his publicity staff wages his public relations effort, campaign materials are dispatched to local candidate support committees and party units, volunteer workers across the state are given direction, and the candidate's campaign is co-ordinated with whatever efforts are being made by party committees and by other candidates on the party ticket.

3. *Party organization expenses.* In addition to the temporary headquarters and organizations established by the candidates, the state party committees maintain headquarters for the purpose of sustaining the local political organizations between elections and guiding them during the campaign. The party committees maintain permanent staffs to administer their offices and perform organizational chores across the state. Among the most important of these chores is developing large dues-paying memberships, training the local volunteer activists in the mechanics of politics, and recruiting candidates for local offices where none come forward. Each party committee, in conjunction with its local units, advises officeholders on whatever state or federal patronage matters may arise. In a mass membership party system, such as Wisconsin's, the party offices maintain membership records, arrange for the conventions which adopt platforms and elect party officers, develop and expound issues in the non-campaign season, and so forth. The operation of the party office is a separate function from the operation of the candidate headquarters, although in the closing months of a campaign there is likely to be close collaboration between them.

4. *Fund-raising activities.* The raising of money is itself a major political cost. Dinners with program advertising books were the most common fund-raising device, until recent amendments to

the tax laws made program book advertising non-deductible. The cost of mailings, telephone calls, staff, purchase of dinners, hall rentals, and printing of program books accounts for a substantial portion of total political spending.

5. *Public relations costs.* For the present study, public relations costs are those costs involved in gaining news coverage. The costs are relatively high when the frequency of statements, program papers, announcements, and other press releases is multiplied by the cost of sending such materials to hundreds of news outlets throughout Wisconsin. The cost of staging press conferences and preparing brief television or radio tapes for use on news programs causes the totals to rise still farther. Finally, staff help is generally needed to write the press releases even though the issues material is sometimes researched and written by volunteers.

6. *Campaign materials.* This study defines campaign materials as published matter prepared for distribution and use other than through the mass media: pamphlets, tabloid newspapers, brochures, bumper stickers, cartop signs, position papers, so-called "throw-away sheets" dramatizing a single issue, and related materials fall in this category. The sheer volume of such items used in Wisconsin campaigns is surprising, especially since party organizations and similar outlets in Wisconsin cannot be viewed as very strong. In one recent gubernatorial campaign, approximately 1.4 million pieces of such campaign materials were prepared and, for the most part, actually distributed, in behalf of the Democratic candidate.

7. *Mass media advertising.* This category of political costs includes purchased outlets for campaign viewpoints. Television, radio, and newspaper advertising constitute the predominant share of such expenditures, with small amounts allocated to billboards, advertising in convention or club programs, and other lesser commercial outlets. Sharp increases in the cost of mass media advertising have in recent years been pinpointed as a major cause of rapidly spiraling costs for the total political system.

8. *Opinion polls.* In recent years there has been an expanded use in the United States of the public opinion poll as an aid in planning campaign strategy, and particularly in the determination of which issues and what candidate "image" should be projected to the public through mass media. Surprisingly, this has not yet become a major new political cost in Wisconsin despite the heavy reliance of both parties on mass media. The private polls available to the Democrats in 1960, 1962, and 1964 were commissioned by the Democratic National Committee and national labor organizations as part of national strategic planning. Only in 1964 was a separate poll commissioned by Wisconsin politicians, and that was a ten-city survey taken by the Reynolds campaign group. It appears that in 1964 the Republicans began to use polling on a systematic and periodic basis during the course of the campaign. Apparently polls were taken in limited geographical areas at fixed intervals leading up to election day. The use of opinion polls is expensive (from $5,000 to $7,000 per survey) and its expansion would lead to a significant increase in political costs. This category of spending is included in the present study more for its potential future significance than for its role in the spending pattern of the campaigns under study here.

Table 20 divides the total 1964 expenditures by the Democratic party, the Democratic candidates for governor and senator, and the committees operating in their behalf among the categories elaborated above. The figures represent, at best, careful estimates based on filed reports, interviews, and experiential data. In some cases it is almost impossible accurately to attribute certain known expenditures to a given category, as, for instance, the salary of a staff member who sets up a candidate's schedule, issues press notices on the schedule, and then works with the local party organization to develop a distribution of materials while the candidate is in town.

Two qualifications of these data ought to be registered. First, no state level Democratic committees showed expenditures for election day activities. Since local Democratic committees have normally had very small financial resources, it is improbable that they devoted large sums to this activity. Yet the pattern of

Table 20

Distribution of Political Expenditures by State Level Party,
Gubernatorial, and Senatorial Committees;
Democrats, 1964

Category of Spending	Spending in Dollars	% of Total Spending
Candidate expenses	$ 18,000	2.8
Candidate headquarters' expenses	40,000	6.1
Party organization expenses	120,000	18.4
Fund-raising activities	45,000	6.9
Public relations costs	12,000	1.8
Campaign materials	67,000	10.3
Mass media advertising	343,000[a]	52.6
Opinion polls	6,500	1.0
Totals	*$651,500*	*99.9%*[b]

[a] Excludes $64,950 which was directed into Wisconsin on behalf of
the Johnson-Humphrey campaign and then transferred to a New
York advertising firm. This transfer of funds was apparently
for the purpose of secreting certain national level expenditures and
did not reflect an actual state political expense.
[b] The result of rounding of figures.

spending in other states includes considerable outlays for getting
out the vote, as noted in the previous section. In Wisconsin this
expense is borne almost entirely by labor unions, who spent
approximately $55,000 for their 1964 phone bank operations.
A second qualification relates to staff expenditures. In 1964, the
Democratic candidates for senator and governor were incumbents and their personal staffs handled most of the campaign
operations for which manpower would ordinarily be employed.
Thus Democratic expenditures for staff in 1964 actually understate the personnel costs of a campaign. As we will see, Republican organization costs were substantially higher than those of
the Democrats. This is partly explained by the need for the
Republican party to spend money for staff and get-out-the-vote
expenses which, on the Democratic side, were met in other
ways.

A review of the Republican committees operating at the state level shows total spending of $1,019,070 after transfer payments. Expenditures for mass media were $334,000, a few thousand dollars less than similar expenditures by the Democrats. Yet total spending by the Republicans was almost $375,000 more than the total of Democratic spending. Some Republican money went directly for billboards which were not included in the $334,000 for mass media paid to advertising agencies. Observation of Wisconsin campaigns since 1958 suggests that a further cause of higher Republican expenditures is the large amounts expended for campaign materials. The Republicans have usually far outdistanced the Democrats in expenditures for cartop signs, posters, bumper stickers, and other display-type materials. These are the most expensive of the various types of campaign material. Republicans have also usually had longer, more expensive tabloid newspapers printed on higher quality paper for statewide distribution. Also, the Republicans have tended to rely more heavily on expensively printed pamphlets, while Democrats have usually purchased less expensive campaign cards or single-issue flyers. Thus materials costs have probably been a larger share of the total Republican budget than of the Democratic spending pattern.

Perhaps the greatest difference between Republican and Democratic spending occurred, however, in the category designated as party organization expenses. First, the Republicans traditionally have spent a great deal more money for such items as membership newsletters, party conventions, precinct schools, printed organizational materials, travel to national political functions, and a whole range of other headquarters costs. Second, Republican staff costs are much higher than those reported by the Democrats. The Republicans reported a staff of 12 persons for the non-campaign period and 15 people from July through November, 1964. Staff costs alone were $73,400 for the period. This contrasted to a five-man Democratic staff and an annual operating budget for *all* headquarters purposes, excluding capital expenditures, of $70,000. Third, in 1964 the Republicans had almost twice as many members in Wisconsin as did the Democrats—approximately 40,000 to 50,000 activ-

ists as opposed to about 26,000. Organization expenses involved in staying in contact with and directing the efforts of this
large number of members were undoubtedly greater than the
similar costs for the smaller Democratic cadres.

A reasonable appraisal of Republican spending would seem
to suggest, therefore, that while Republicans spent somewhat
more in all major expenditure areas, Republican state level
spending especially outdistanced Democratic efforts in the areas
of party organization expenses and campaign materials. To the
extent that the well-co-ordinated Republican organization
shifted certain expenses to local level party units, Republicans
may also have had significant spending advantages in other
areas such as mass media. There is some scattered interview
evidence that local Republican clubs, and particularly the Republican Women's Federations, spent money locally for radio
and newspaper advertising in behalf of state candidates. Democrats, by contrast, have not been so well directed from state
headquarters and their local party groups seldom have had more
than nominal amounts to spend for campaign purposes.

The Democratic allocation of 65 per cent of total spending
for public relations, media advertising, and campaign materials
is quite similar to allocations for these purposes elsewhere; in
1952, propaganda, publicity, and media expenditures for Democratic state level committees were 77 per cent in Maryland, 66
per cent in Ohio, and 85 per cent in Connecticut.[11] In each of
these states the Republicans spent a somewhat smaller percentage of their funds for these purposes and a somewhat larger
percentage for salaries, overhead, and field activities;[12] this is
similar to the pattern noted above for Wisconsin Republicans. If
candidate committee spending were to be considered alone, it
seems clear that media expenditures would loom much larger,
since the state party headquarters in Wisconsin handle mainly
organizational matters and engage in very little direct media
campaigning. In the Democratic gubernatorial and senatorial
campaigns prior to 1966 between 75 per cent and 85 per cent of
total expenditures went for media, materials, and publicity. In
1964, 70 per cent of the Republican gubernatorial campaign

budget was devoted to media, an allocation about 10 per cent less than in the Democratic gubernatorial campaign.

Although expenditure data from 1966 are still not fully enough developed to allow the precise statements of resource allocation that are possible for 1964, several general contours are visible. The absence from the ballot of a United States Senate contest affected the percentage of state level expenditures devoted to mass media campaigning. Just as total spending decreased when no United States Senate seat was at stake, so the kinds of spending associated with candidates as opposed to party organizations decreased in that situation. To the extent that party committees emphasize organizational spending and candidate committees media outlays, the elimination of a major statewide office from the ballot reduces the proportion of total spending devoted to mass media. Only 27 per cent of Democratic expenditures and 17.3 per cent of Republican outlays were allocated to mass media in 1966; two years before these proportions had been 53.5 per cent and 32.8 per cent, respectively.

Of equal significance was the changed expenditure allocation in the Democratic gubernatorial campaign. In 1966, media spending accounted for $99,800 or 52.6 per cent of expenditures, while in 1964 the gubernatorial campaign devoted $194,000 or 71 per cent of its budget to media advertising. The 1966 Democratic nominee, Lieutenant Governor Patrick J. Lucey, did not have the staff and facilities advantages associated with gubernatorial incumbency and he was required to use a larger share of his campaign budget for staff salaries and expenses, travel, headquarters operations, and similar basic expenses. It becomes apparent that, for the Democrats at least, incumbency is not only a convertible resource which is significant for fund raising, but that it provides important services in kind which permit more flexibility in the use of the campaign funds raised.

Finally, it is worth reiterating that the picture drawn here of the uses of money only describes outlays by statewide party and candidate committees. Local campaigns are quite likely to have a substantially different pattern. Candidate travel expenses are usually small because the districts and counties are relatively compact. Local party organization expenses are ordinarily nominal because the machinery is operated almost completely by volunteer activists. Few, if any, local candidates open headquarters, so that the category of candidate headquarters expense would be eliminated except in occasional congressional campaigns. There are some fund-raising expenses, especially in the form of printing and food and drink costs for testimonial dinners or cocktail parties, both of which are common at the local level. Public relations costs are probably slight because local candidates have only infrequent opportunities to make speeches or issue statements, press releases are written by the candidate or volunteer helpers, and releases are unlikely to be sent to those media which cover the district or county only as part of a much larger circulation area (e.g., television stations or major metropolitan daily papers).

Local campaign spending in Wisconsin has probably been directed to a much greater extent to campaign materials and certain of the mass media than state level spending. Posters, campaign cards, pamphlets, bumper stickers, matchbooks, and cartops have undoubtedly been the most frequently used tools of local campaigns. In addition, advertising was purchased if media were available whose circulation area was reasonably contiguous with the boundaries of the district. Small daily or weekly newspapers and local radio stations were thus much more likely to receive local campaign advertising accounts than television stations or metropolitan dailies. It would obviously be impractical for a candidate in a single assembly district to purchase advertising in the *Milwaukee Journal,* whose circulation intensively covers thirty assembly districts and significantly reaches into at least a dozen more.

The pattern of spending described here is basically a pattern set by state level party committees and major statewide candidate campaigns. A quite different pattern for the whole political system would emerge if it were possible to include reliable data on local level spending, but such data are not available. While the extent of the difference cannot therefore be detailed, the

direction of the difference can be suggested: the proportion of
money spent for campaign materials and perhaps for advertising
in weekly and small circulation daily papers and on radio would
be greater, and expenditures for staff, publicity, travel, and
headquarters, as well as for advertising in such media as television and the metropolitan press would be substantially less.

The Uses of Money: Mass Media Expenditures

The foregoing discussion has emphasized the importance of
mass media in total campaign expenditures. Heard has pointed
to the sharp increase in media expenditures as a major factor in
the overall increase in American political costs.[13] The data from
Wisconsin suggest that until 1966 media expenditures increased
faster than spending for other purposes and much faster than
per unit costs of media advertising. Apparently the politicians
chose to put increasing emphasis on mass media, and especially
on television, in their quest for votes. But the expenditures for
media apparently did not displace equal sums which had previously been used for other campaign purposes, and total spending spiraled upward.

Analysis of the use of media in Wisconsin politics must begin
with the 1954 election campaign. In 1950, Wisconsin had no
television outlets, but in 1952, WTMJ-TV, affiliated with the
Milwaukee Journal, was operating in Milwaukee. It was used on
a very limited basis that year in Thomas Fairchild's unsuccessful
campaign to unseat Senator Joseph R. McCarthy, an election
not under consideration here. On a partial basis, the analysis
continues through 1966, but that year poses peculiar methodological problems because no United States Senate seat was contested and because per unit cost data for the various media are
not yet available. On a number of points, therefore, the analysis
encompasses only the decade ending with the 1964 election.

The filed campaign financial reports in Wisconsin seldom
distinguish among the kinds of media purchased with campaign
money. Usually the reports only show transfers of funds to
advertising agencies which then purchase the time or space for
candidate advertising. A further methodological difficulty is in

distinguishing between increased costs of media and increased use of this form of political campaigning. An attempt to gain a gross impression of whether rising media expenditures represented the expanded use of media as well as its increased cost per unit has been made by comparing the percentage increases in per unit media costs with the percentage increases in spending for media purposes. The data tell us the direction of the spending pattern, but not its exact magnitude. A letter of inquiry to radio and television stations and daily and weekly newspapers brought a sample of replies about changing media costs from 1954 to 1964. The sample of television stations and daily newspapers was reasonably good.[14] The response from radio stations and weekly papers was not so helpful.[15] The relatively small response from the radio and weekly press outlets makes more qualified and uncertain the media cost figures used here. It is worth pointing out, however, that these two kinds of media are much less widely used and have increased their advertising rates at a much slower rate than daily papers and television. They may, therefore, play a smaller role in political campaign costs than the media for which we have more complete information.

Table 21 shows the increase in total spending and the increase in media spending by statewide party committees, candidates for governor and United States senator, and their supporting committees. The figures do not include amounts spent in primary campaigns by unsuccessful contenders for nominations for governor and United States senator.

Spending for mass media increased at a faster rate than total spending, except for the Republicans in 1966. The higher rate of increase in media spending could, of course, result from the displacement of expenditures for other campaign activities. This does not seem to be the case. The number of dollars spent by the Republicans for activities other than media advertising was higher in each subsequent year than in 1954, and the same pattern was true for the Democrats for all campaigns except 1956 and 1958, when a certain amount of displacement seemed to take place. Republican expenditures for these activities rose from $212,161 in 1954 to $685,221 (323.0 per cent) in 1964

Table 21

Total Spending and Media Spending by State Level Party,
Gubernatorial, and Senatorial Committees, 1954–1966

Year[a]	Total Spending	% of 1954 Total	Total Media Spending	% of 1954 Total
	DEMOCRATS			
1954	$ 142,346	100.0	$ 26,040	100.0
1956	145,683	102.3	56,350	216.3
1958	237,113	166.5	147,097	564.8
1962	564,988	396.9	167,032	641.4
1964	641,789	450.8	343,677	1319.8
1966	462,490	324.9	125,058	480.2
	REPUBLICANS			
1954	$ 266,435	100.0	$ 54,274	100.0
1956	411,357	154.3	88,130	162.3
1958	353,641	132.7	123,942	228.3
1962	675,042	253.3	247,486	455.9
1964	1,019,070	382.4	333,849	615.1
1966	896,847	336.6	155,667	286.8

[a] 1952 and 1960 omitted (see p. 40).

and $741,180 (349.3 per cent) in 1966. Similar Democratic spending increased from $116,306 in 1954 to $298,112 (256.3 per cent) in 1964 and $337,432 (290.1 per cent) in 1966. While it is true that media expenditures increased at a faster rate than total spending and non-media spending increased at a lesser rate, it is nonetheless clear that the increase in media spending did not result from the displacement of non-media campaigning since the number of dollars spent for those activities rose appreciably from 1954 to the mid-1960's.

It might also be argued that the sharp increases in media spending merely reflected increases in cost levels of advertising rather than increases in the amounts of media advertising used. Table 22 shows that from 1954 to 1964 the average increase in costs for each of the four major kinds of media outlets in Wisconsin—television, radio, daily press, weekly press—was substantially less than the increase in media spending. Thus increased per unit costs are only a partial explanation for

Table 22

Increases in Per Unit Cost of Major Media Contrasted
with Increases in Total Media Spending by Party,
Gubernatorial, and Senatorial Committees: Democrats
and Republicans, 1954–1964.

1964 Media Costs Per Unit as a Percentage of 1954 Media Costs Per Unit	
Television (5 of 14)[a]	298.0%
Radio (8 of 75)[a]	148.8
Daily press (16 of 41)[a]	134.7
Weekly press (18 of 431)[a]	126.8
1964 Media Expenditure as a Percentage of 1954 Media Expenditure	
Democrats	1319.8%
Republicans	615.1

[a] Figures indicate number of responses and number of media outlets.

increased media spending. It is necessary to conclude that the increased expenditures for media advertising were not solely a result of displacing previous kinds of expenditures nor solely a consequence of increases in per unit media costs. Rather, politicians responded to media technology by purchasing larger amounts of media exposure at increased costs per unit while, at the same time, maintaining and expanding the previous level of other kinds of campaign activities. The development of media technology was therefore a spur to additional campaign spending, and it must be viewed as a major factor in the upward spiral in total political costs.

The increases in media spending by statewide party and candidate committees are matched by significant system-wide increases in media spending. While we do not have data on all media spending by all candidates and committees in the political system, the expenditures for radio and television have been detailed by the Federal Communications Commission. All Democratic political units at all levels in Wisconsin spent $34,373 in 1956 and $375,531 in 1964 for radio and television. Comparable figures for the Republicans were $89,774 and $434,160.

This amounted to a 1092.5 per cent radio and television spending increase for the Democrats and a 483.6 per cent increase for the Republicans. These media increases are substantially greater than the 324.2 per cent spending increase for all purposes recorded by the Democrats for the same period and the 371.9 per cent increase recorded by the Republicans. The increase in radio and television spending is also significantly more than the increase in per unit radio and television costs during the same period; an eight-station sample of television costs showed a 192.4 per cent price rise from 1956 to 1964 and an eight-station sample of radio costs showed a 148.8 per cent increase during the same period.[16]

Table 23

Increases in the Expenditures Per Vote for Radio and Television and for All Campaign Purposes, 1956–1966

Year	Radio-TV Cost Per Vote		Total Cost Per Vote	
	U.S.	Wisc.	U.S.	Wisc.
1956	$0.15	$0.08	$2.50	$1.21
1960	0.20	0.20	2.54	—[a]
1962	—	0.34	—	2.43
1964	0.34	0.48	2.83	2.91
1966	—	0.31	—	3.01

[a] Not analyzed (see p. 40).

The unusually large increases in system-wide expenditures for electronic media are confirmed by comparing the cost per vote of such expenditures in Wisconsin to the cost per vote of all campaign outlays. A further comparison shows that per vote media spending increased more rapidly in Wisconsin than in the nation. While this may have been partly in response to the rising intensity of electoral competition, it may also be related to the nature of the state's party system: as will be shown, the mass party system is ill suited to mounting traditional kinds of campaign efforts; this encourages politicians to rely more heavily on mass communications. Table 23 reports Wisconsin and nation-wide per vote expenditures for electronic media and for all campaign purposes from 1956 to 1966.

In media expenditures, as in general political spending in Wisconsin, the Republicans tend to outdistance the Democrats. A review of Table 21 shows that only in 1958 and 1964 did Democratic state level media expenditures exceed those of the Republicans. It has already been reported that in the former year the Republican state level campaign was weakened by the dissipation of resources in the 1957 special United States Senate election, by the defection of important conservative contributors, and by the unpopularity of the sitting Republican governor. In 1964, the very slight Democratic advantage in media spending was apparently related to Democratic incumbency in

Table 24

Percentage of Total Radio and Television Spending by All Candidates and Committees of Each Party: General Elections, 1956–1966.

Year	Total Radio-TV Spending	% by Democrats	% by Republicans
1956	$124,147	27.7	72.3
1960	352,734	46.8	53.2
1962	430,784	51.2	48.8
1964	809,686	46.4	53.6
1966	497,576	34.2	65.8

the United States Senate, the governorship, and the White House: both the statewide candidates and Democratic party headquarters were able to raise more money than usual for media campaigning. In the other elections, Republican media spending was greater than that of the competing Democrats by margins of 77 per cent to 23 per cent in 1954, 61 per cent to 39 per cent in 1956, 59.7 per cent to 40.3 per cent in 1962, and 55.5 per cent to 44.5 per cent in 1966.

An examination of total system-wide electronic media spending shows the same pattern of Republican superiority. Table 24 reports the disparity between the parties in general elections from 1956 to 1966. The slight Democratic advantage in 1962 is due mainly to the exclusion of the large pre-primary television expenditures on behalf of Republican gubernatorial candidate

Philip Kuehn. After spending so heavily in the primary, the Republicans either thought it unnecessary or could not afford to spend as heavily as usual in the general election. In addition, the re-election campaign of Senator Alexander Wiley was badly underfinanced, apparently because of his unpopularity with the conservative Republicans who dominated the state party organization in that year. Thus the temporary Democratic advantage in electronic media spending in 1962 was largely a consequence of Republican default in the general election.

Finally, it is useful to point out again that the allocation of funds to particular kinds of campaigning is a choice made by the

Table 25

Percentage of Total Electronic Media Spending Allocated to Each Media: Democrats and Republicans, 1960–1966

Year	Democrats		Republicans	
	TV	*Radio*	*TV*	*Radio*
1960[a]	75.5	24.4	64.3	35.7
1962	74.2	25.8	65.3	34.7
1964	78.2	21.8	72.2	27.8
1966	36.9	63.1	60.9	39.1

[a] General election only.

politicians. Table 25 reports the percentage of total electronic media expenditures which each party allocated to television and to radio. From 1960 to 1964 the Democrats put slightly more emphasis on television campaigning than did the Republicans. In part this occurred because the Republicans attempted to shift some media costs to local party units, particularly their Women's Federations. These groups prefer to concentrate their efforts in their local areas, and this ordinarily means that they pay for spot advertisements on local radio stations to aid the Republican state ticket. A second explanation is the traditional preference of Republican strategists for newspaper advertising, partly in response to the overwhelming editorial support for the Republican party among the state's daily and weekly press. Democratic county units had little money to spend for the statewide ticket so they were not a source of radio expenditures. At the state level, Democratic strategists were committed to the superiority of television as a result of their successes with that medium in the 1958, 1960, and 1962 campaigns. While this contributed to the greater Democratic preference for television campaigning, it may also explain why the Republicans moved gradually to a greater emphasis on television from 1960 to 1964. Defeated by the Democrats in those years, they increasingly adopted the same political techniques as their successful opponents.

In 1966, the pattern changed dramatically. The decrease in television allocations by both parties might be explained in part by the absence of a United States Senate campaign, for it is in statewide races for major offices that television is likely to be used effectively and to be within the campaign budget. In addition, both parties waged especially vigorous campaigns in key congressional and assembly districts. These areas are most efficiently reached by radio advertising because the shorter range of radio signals concentrates political advertising in compact geographical areas lying primarily within single districts.

These factors are only partial explanations, however. The strategic choices of politicians in both parties were significant in 1966. That the Republican decline in television allocations was so much smaller than that of the Democrats was due to a new enthusiasm among state Republican leaders for television advertising. Republican public relations planners had made excellent use of television in 1964, and this wiped away some of the stigma which had attached to television campaigning after the surprise defeat of their gubernatorial candidate in 1962, when the quality of the television spots was blamed by many Republicans for that defeat. Furthermore, Republican Governor Warren Knowles came across well on television and that medium was especially adaptable to his campaign.

On the Democratic side, the public relations people urged a change from the tested Democratic formula, dating back to the successful Proxmire campaign of 1957, of concentrating virtually all media efforts on television. It was argued that prime time television availabilities had become scarce in the Milwaukee metropolitan area where Democrats usually focused their efforts, that the change to newspaper advertising would give Democratic campaigning a new look which would draw attention, and that a newspaper campaign would more effectively reach that margin of voters in the upper socio-economic ranks whose defection to the Republicans had been a critical factor in the 1964 gubernatorial defeat. The ensuing decision to shift the media emphasis of the gubernatorial campaign from television to newspaper advertising accounts for the dramatic reversal in Democratic preferences for television and radio. While Democratic radio spending accelerated slightly at the local level, state level spending shifted from television to newspapers, leaving radio advertising the dominant use of electronic media.

The following sections will consider whether the increased emphasis by Wisconsin politicians on mass media campaigning was justified by the available evidence of its effectiveness in reaching voters. It is also important to consider the consequences for the political system both of the types of campaigning purchased by politicians and of the changes in their patterns of resource allocation—especially the increased reliance on media campaigning.

The Uses of Money: An Evaluation

The strategies of Wisconsin politicians have been shown to rest heavily on the use of campaign materials and especially on media advertising. Canvassing and similar activities by party organizations and candidate committees tend to be de-emphasized in the allocation of funds. On its face, this plan of resource allocation appears to ignore the considerable evidence that canvassing by party workers is one of the most effective of campaign techniques. Katz and Eldersveld reported that in 1956 Adlai Stevenson's vote in precincts with strong Democratic organizational activity was 5 per cent greater than could have been predicted by the demographic characteristics of the area; conversely, where there was strong Republican leadership and weak Democratic activity, the vote for Stevenson was 5.5 per cent less than expected.[17] As contrasted with this 10.5 per cent spread which might result from local party activity, Cutright and Rossi found a potential spread of about 5 per cent resulting from vigorous party efforts in precincts where the opposition was weak or inactive.[18] Wolfinger's study of New Haven, where party organization is quite strong, showed that the vote for a referendum proposition varied 25 per cent between wards where party leaders supported and wards where they opposed it.[19] This kind of test may be misleading, since voters probably care little and understand less about municipal referenda. On the other hand, these data may give some suggestion of the potential of canvassing in campaigns for those numerous offices which have low visibility, although in the case of such offices the party label provides a limitation on organizational impact that does not exist in referendum campaigning.

The choice of Wisconsin politicians to allocate their resources to campaign activities other than organization is not, despite the persuasive evidence of the effectiveness of canvassing, an unreasoned strategy. The mass membership parties in Wisconsin draw their followings mainly from the middle classes. Hence political activists of both parties live mainly in the well-off residential neighborhoods of urban communities.[20] For each party this concentration of party strength poses severe problems. Democrats, on the one hand, have been organizationally weak in the working class neighborhoods where their electoral potential is greatest. Republicans have, of course, had significant party strength in upper-income neighborhoods in the cities and suburbs, but since those of high socio-economic status generally have a high rate of voting participation, this Republican organizational strength may not have added many additional votes. On the other hand, Republicans have had little party machinery in the small cities and villages of the state which continue to provide the most significant base of Republican voting strength[21] and where strong organization might have significantly increased the size of the Republican vote. Basically, then, both parties have lacked muscle in locales where the existence of an effective organization might have made an appreciable difference in electoral outcomes.

The party machinery is further weakened by the almost

complete absence of patronage. Local governments are generally non-partisan in fact as well as by law. Civil service in both local and state governments encompasses virtually all public employees, including most part-time help. A governor, for instance, generally does not fill more than twenty-five salaried positions during his term in office. There is no network of political workers in Wisconsin whose jobs depend on party politics or who are able to devote their energies mainly to political organization. The party units are composed of, manned by, and led by volunteers who have more urgent time commitments to their jobs, their families, and perhaps other civic obligations. In sum, political machinery is quite weak in Wisconsin.

Finally, the orientation of Wisconsin political activists tends to be toward programs and issues, particularly national and state problems.[22] The mechanics of politics draw little attention from most party members, and steps to strengthen party organizations have frequently been attacked as immoral by party activists. For instance, the change from $25 per plate to $100 per plate for the annual Democratic Jefferson-Jackson Day Dinner in 1962 stirred a hornets' nest of opposition within the party despite explanations that additional funds were necessary to wage the 1962 campaign and that President Kennedy's acceptance of an invitation to be the guest speaker almost insured the dinner's success even at the higher price. For the intellectuals who were a substantial portion of the party's leadership, the $100 price was simply immoral. Similarly, party members are usually more willing to spend hours debating issues than a few minutes canvassing voters. Regardless of the many advantages attributed to an issue-oriented party system, the mass party organizations in Wisconsin are able to perform only weakly the mechanics of politics.

In these circumstances it is entirely reasonable for politicians to rely more heavily on mass media and certain kinds of campaign materials than on door-to-door canvassing. However, this line of reasoning should probably not be carried so far as to argue, with Leon D. Epstein, that "there is a serious doubt that the amateur clubs have any usefulness in fulfilling strictly electoral aims desired by party leaders and candidates."[23] It has been previously acknowledged that the strength of middle class membership parties is not strategically located for effective campaigning; and it must be recognized that these activists cannot be efficaciously shifted to other neighborhoods to perform canvassing chores inasmuch as those "well integrated into the social milieus of their precincts were the most effective workers for their parties."[24] This argument ought not be overdrawn, however, especially in the case of the Democrats. Warren Miller has discovered the so-called "breakage effect" by which the majority party in a one-party area tends to receive a larger share of the vote than the party identifications and the issue and candidate perceptions of the voters would make predictable.[25] "The minority party not only has fewer persons possessing or exhibiting motivations supporting it, and consequently fewer persons voting for its leading candidate than does the majority party, but also receives smaller dividends from its supporting motivations."[26] Although Miller draws the conclusion that party activity becomes more profitable where the party is dominant, he did not consider the possibility that the major base of recruitment for a party might be the very neighborhoods in which it is electorally weakest, as is the case for Wisconsin Democrats. But the existence of such potential strength, if coupled with campaign activity, may well have the effect of re-enforcing the motivations of those who lean to the Democrats, thus stemming the steady erosion of minority party vote strength. No one would argue that this is a better electoral strategy than being organizationally strong where one has electoral strength, but it suggests that the mass party's concentration in opposition neighborhoods is not completely useless in the hunt for votes.

There are also a great variety of other chores which can be done by middle class party activists working out of the party headquarters or in the precincts. Obvious examples are the preparation of mass mailings, door-to-door distributions of literature without canvassing, handing out campaign materials at plant gates and shopping centers, and the distribution of bumper stickers at appropriate locations. It is difficult to know how effective such activities are. The success of mail propaganda in getting out the vote among hard core apathetic voters has been mixed at best.[27] On the other hand, voters in Detroit had a very high recall of receiving literature from the two parties: 68 per cent recalled receiving Republican literature and 71 per cent recalled receiving Democratic propaganda.[28] There are no published data on the effectiveness of plant gate and shopping center handouts or on the value of bumper stickers. Politicians believe that such activities are valuable for establishing name identification for candidates for lesser office, for re-enforcing the commitments of party backers, and especially for providing information and campaign symbols to the opinion leaders who apparently are so important in conveying political preferences to the mass of the population. As a Democratic state chairman announced, "a man with a bumper sticker on his car is going to argue for our candidate in the factory, the local tavern and at home!"

There are other advantages in allocating resources for the building of party organization. One is that an expanded membership provides a larger list of people to whom the party and its candidates can go for contributions. The problem of identifying potential contributors is a difficult one, especially for the Democrats. Party members are more inclined than the ordinary party identifier to make contributions, as the evidence in Chapter 6 indicates. Another useful object of expenditure is the training of party workers and candidates. The turnover among party officers and among candidates, particularly in districts where the opposition is dominant, is high in Wisconsin. Most adults do not possess even the most minimal political skills, and money must therefore constantly be spent on the training of the activists and candidates. Such simple techniques as issuing press releases, canvassing, campaigning at plant gates and shopping centers, developing issues materials, recruiting new workers, running a headquarters, and filing the various financial reports required by law must all be taught to a continually changing body of partisans. To this end, both parties expend considerable sums on precinct schools, candidate seminars, organization manuals and materials, and other activities which seem useful to party leaders in developing the political competence of their party's cadres.

One of the most significant activities sponsored with money expended for organizational purposes is candidate recruitment. Although Wisconsin as a whole is closely competitive, many of its numerous legislative districts and counties are not so competitive. In opposition-dominated districts it is quite difficult for a party organization to find candidates who are willing to take an almost certain beating on election day. Yet both parties set considerable store in full slates. At a minimum, these local slates "provide visible social support and encouragement for the otherwise discouraged political minority."[29] Furthermore, political activity by a local ticket is commonly believed to attach some voters to the party's ticket at all levels. Friends, relatives, and co-workers of the local candidates, as well as some others who have contact with these campaigners, might be convinced to give their votes to the minority party ticket, thus aiding the state and congressional candidates whose races the party can reasonably hope to win.[30]

Candidate recruitment is an enormous task in Wisconsin, and more so for the Democrats than the Republicans. Every two years each party must field 724 candidates (725 in years when there is a United States Senate seat to be filled) for posts ranging from governor to county surveyor. A 1960 compilation showed that in 32 counties the average Republican vote for governor from 1948 to 1960 had been more than 60 per cent; in such counties Democratic contestants for local offices are unlikely to come forward willingly. There was only one county in which the Democrats had a record of such consistent and overwhelming strength, but the Republicans have no easy time finding local office candidates in such Democratic strongholds as Milwaukee, Racine, Kenosha, Forest, and Douglas counties.

The difficulty of recruiting candidates can perhaps be illustrated by the fact that Democrats contested fewer than half of the state's 576 courthouse offices in 1954, and after intensive recruiting efforts were able to challenge the Republicans for only 353 of these posts in 1960. The number of Democratic courthouse candidacies did not rise in the subsequent years despite vigorous recruitment campaigns. The Republicans ordinarily contested for between 500 and 525 courthouse offices during the years under study.

Both parties managed to field full statehouse and congressional slates, but each always defaulted a few legislative seats. The number of defaults sharply diminished, however, as Wisconsin politics became closely competitive at the state level and both party organizations allocated resources to candidate recruitment. Thus, before the advent of the Democratic Organizing Committee in 1949, the Democrats defaulted 9 of the 33 state senate seats filled in 1946 and 1948, and 15 of the 100 assembly seats filled in 1948, a year in which Mr. Truman won Wisconsin's electoral votes. In 1962 and 1964, Democrats failed to file candidates for only 2 of the state's 33 state senate seats and Republicans did not field a candidate in only 1 district. However, the Republicans did not contest 10 state assembly seats, primarily in urban centers, while the Democrats defaulted in no assembly districts. In 1966, the Republicans, under new party leadership, contested all state legislative districts. These figures show clearly that there is nothing automatic about filling party tickets. Assuring that the party will gain whatever benefits are connected with candidate activity requires vigorous and sometimes expensive effort by party leaders.

The cost of candidate recruitment is initially in the field work expenses of the state party organizations. Local party leaders and potential candidates are bombarded with calls and telegrams in the months preceding the filing deadlines. Gradually the pace steps up and party staffers are sent into the field to back up the local party recruitment efforts. One of the inducements to potential candidates is some assurance that part of their expenses will be defrayed. This puts the Republicans at somewhat of an advantage, since their local units can generally afford to budget money for courthouse and legislative candidates. In 1964 the Democrats finally organized a legislative campaign committee to help fund legislative campaigns, but most of its $9,300 budget was designated for close districts while ticket-fillers recruited in Republican-dominated districts were given nominal sums of $25 to $50. Wisconsin labor unions also allocate some funds to legislative races—between $6,000 and $7,000 in 1964. Labor's strategy was to contribute small sums to Democrats in "safe labor districts" to show labor's concern for their candidacies, but most labor funds were directed to close districts. Some labor units in Republican-dominated districts provided nominal contributions to Democratic candidates and may thus have aided the recruitment effort, but the state labor leadership seldom designated such districts for financial assistance. The Democratic state headquarters provided all of its legislative candidates with "mutual assistance literature" featuring the entire party ticket.

The need for campaign financing assistance as a recruitment device is more urgent as the constituency increases in size and population. Thus it is feasible to expect a local candidate to rely on extensive personal campaigning in which he must spend money only for campaign materials and perhaps for small amounts of media exposure in the last day or two before the election. Such activity may very well aid the ticket at the upper levels. However, candidates for Congress and state offices cannot easily substitute personal effort for other kinds of campaigning with any great usefulness to the party ticket. In 1964, for instance, the Democrats had considerable difficulty in recruiting a candidate to oppose Republican Melvin Laird in Wisconsin's Seventh Congressional District; and although candidates came forward, Democratic prospects were also viewed as quite dim against incumbent Republicans John Byrnes in the Eighth District and William Van Pelt in the Sixth District. In all three districts labor and party funds accounted for virtually the total sums available to the Democratic candidates. In scoring an upset victory in the Sixth District, Democrat John Race received a total of $5,143, of which $2,386 was from labor and another $1,400 was from the Democratic party. In their losing campaigns in the Seventh and Eighth Districts, respectively, Democrat Thomas Martin received $3,795 of his $7,240 from labor and about $1,000 from the Democratic party while Democrat Cletus Johnson received $2,392 of his $3,392 from labor and the remainder from the Democratic party.[31] Without this assistance none of these Democratic congressional candidates could have been expected to run. It is somewhat more difficult to know the impact of party organization on candidate recruitment within the Republican party, but there is no doubt that Republican candidates in heavily Democratic congressional districts such as those in Milwaukee and in close districts in other sections of the state can rely heavily on party funds, thus making candidacy for office a reasonable course even when the prospects for victory are not certain.

The foregoing paragraphs have attempted to point out the importance of organizational spending for candidate recruitment. Finding candidates and getting them on the ballot requires a major effort by both parties and accounts for an important portion of each party's organizational expenses. Beyond those expenses, there is the additional cost of providing, whenever possible, some support in the form of money or materials or services to the candidates who are induced to file. Few politicians or political commentators would view such expenditures as wasteful. Indeed, there is probably a good argument that too few resources rather than too many are devoted to this purpose.

Party and candidate organizational activity accounted for only 13 per cent of total spending by state level Democratic party and candidate committees. The Republicans probably spent a somewhat larger proportion of their funds for such purposes. Another 2.8 per cent of Democratic expenditures was devoted to candidate travel expenses. There is little evidence on the value of personal campaigning by candidates. However, politicians believe that candidate travel and speech-making are essential for news coverage in the media. Ordinarily a candidate for high state office can count on significant coverage in the press and electronic media in the area in which he campaigns. In addition, stumping creates the opportunity for the issuance of press releases tied to real political events, the latter qualification being an important condition for coverage in Wisconsin's metropolitan papers.

A few Wisconsin politicians have engaged in personal campaigning on a scale that makes the contact itself a meaningful campaign technique. Senator William Proxmire is renowned for his prodigious personal campaigning at plant gates, shopping centers, sports events, parades, and other places where crowds gather. He has engaged in such campaigning from his first campaign for governor in 1952 to the present time, and by his own estimate has met, at least once, more than 1.5 of Wisconsin's 2.2 million eligible voters. Proxmire's campaign techniques have created certain expectations, particularly among Democratic activists, about candidate campaigning, and other candidates have undertaken, sometimes reluctantly, extensive personal campaigning. As a result there is probably much more voter contact with state level candidates in Wisconsin than elsewhere. A study of Detroit area voters found that only 1 per cent of Republicans and 7 per cent of Democrats recalled meeting a gubernatorial candidate in 1956 and even fewer recalled contacts with other state office candidates and congressional aspirants.[32]

As previously pointed out, personal contact with voters by party workers has been proven quite valuable in campaigning. Contact with candidates, particularly those running for highly visible offices or who are well known as incumbents, is likely to activate a voter, either by increasing his interest in the campaign, by moving him to vote or, in a few cases, by changing his voting preference. A recent study of a non-partisan local election suggested a considerable increment in voter turnout among those contacted by or on behalf of candidates in a situation where more than 77 per cent of such contacts were made by candidates themselves.[33]

A final effect of candidate campaigning is probably to inspire party activists to greater campaign efforts of all kinds, including financial giving. In a party system without significant patronage, personal contact with candidates for high office provides an important incentive to political workers. Similarly, the opportunity to campaign with the gubernatorial or senatorial candidate undoubtedly creates momentum in the campaigns of candidates for lesser office, particularly those running in districts dominated by the opposition.

Although the sum of the evidence on the significance of candidate campaigning is slight, it seems quite likely that the small sums spent for this purpose are justified in terms of the effects on party activists and on voters, but especially in terms of the publicity benefits which a candidate can gain from stumping. A contrary case might be made, however, by arguing that a candidate's time is a resource which he can most effectively use to raise money for the purchase of a greater volume of more easily controlled contact with the public through the mass media. This may well depend on the candidate's own fund-raising abilities and the availability of a corps of competent fund raisers who make the candidate's participation in such activities of only marginal value. Others can perform the fund-raising task, but no one else can perform the stumping chore with nearly the effectiveness of the candidate.

Whatever may be said about the usefulness of spending for organization and candidate campaigning, the fact remains that in Wisconsin to a larger extent than elsewhere campaigns are conducted through the mass media, particularly through television broadcasting. Since party organizations in Wisconsin are not of the type which can engage in the most effective campaign technique—door-to-door canvassing by neighborhood people —the decision to engage in media campaigning may be a necessary alternative. But the value of media campaigning need not be based purely on the notion that it is merely an alternative to something inherently better. Leon D. Epstein has argued that the expansion of mass media audiences and the development of television, along with "increased formal education and a pervasive home-centered middle-class life style make for a large audience that is responsive to direct appeals about politics as about everything else."[34] Indeed, the fact apparently is that, whatever the effectiveness of canvassing, most Americans now gain political information through the media. In 1964, only 26 per cent of the adult public reported being contacted in person or by phone by campaign workers. On the other hand, 12.4 per cent reported "a good many exposures" to the campaign through radio, 9.8 per cent through magazines, 39.7 per cent through newspapers, and 41.3 per cent through television. Fully 56.5 per cent thought that the largest quantity of their exposure to the campaign came from television.[35]

We have previously pointed out that Wisconsin politicians have relied increasingly on television as a method of getting their messages across. Their strategy is consistent with these data that most Americans get their greatest media exposure to campaigns through the television. In 1963, for the first time, more Americans reported that television rather than the newspapers was their major news source. That pattern has continued to prevail. Furthermore, polls show that television is the medium most likely to be believed by the public: asked which medium they would be least inclined to believe, 28 per cent of respondents named the newspapers, 24 per cent magazines, 11 per cent radio, and only 6 per cent television.[36]

There are some differences in media use for following politics at various levels of government. Thus newspapers are rated highest for following local affairs, with television second. State level campaigns were reported in June, 1964, to be followed more extensively through the newspapers—52 per cent of the public named newspapers, and 49 per cent named television, some respondents naming several media. But by November, 43 per cent of respondents reported they relied most heavily on television, and 41 per cent named newspapers.[37] Not only do the largest number of people rely on television for information, they apparently recall better the content of television messages than those received via radio or newspapers.[38]

Wisconsin politicians, as previously noted, have relied increasingly on television to get their messages across. This is consistent with the evidence that media are increasingly important for political communication and that television is the most effective of the media. Avery Leiserson has argued that insofar as a person "looks to the newspaper or other mass media for his information about the world of public events, forms his opinions from them, and takes his cues for action in voting and expressing his views on public policy from them, the influence of party affiliation or identification is seriously weakened."[39] Mass media thus become a competitor and alternative to parties in performing certain political functions. To the extent, however, that politicians have money to purchase a segment of the media's impact, parties can use the media to strengthen their efforts. Thus, the heavy concentration of spending in media may be essential for parties to convey their messages and to maintain their followings against the blandishments of other centers of political leadership and information.

Despite the advantages which can be attributed to mass media campaigning, it is not, in its direct effects, the most important factor in conveying political sentiment. A large number of studies report that opinion leaders perform this function. Opinion leadership is difficult to define, but it apparently consists of giving opinions on political subjects, and in being asked by others for opinions.[40] Opinion leaders discuss politics much more frequently than others, and they are more interested in the campaign.[41] They are characterized by particular competence in politics; they are better informed than most persons. They possess strategic social locations: generally they are in the same social and economic stratum as those they lead but in somewhat higher positions within that broad stratum, and they tend to be members of more organizations than the average and thus in a position to influence a larger number of people.[42] To a slight degree they are better educated than those who rely on them for political opinions. Opinion leaders are found in substantial numbers in all socio-economic groups in the community.[43]

The influence of opinion leaders is far-reaching. A study of the 1940 election reports that 75 per cent of those who did not expect to vote but finally did, mentioned personal influence of others as the key factor.[44] Similarly, a study of the 1948 election reports that vote decisions were affected by the persons to whom a voter talked. Those who discussed politics with persons of the same party tended to be re-enforced in their allegiance, but those who talked politics with people committed to the opposition party tended in a larger proportion than the average to change their votes.[45] However, most political discussion tends to be among people who agree with one another. This is not surprising, since most political discussion takes place with family members and co-workers; thus it occurs with people of similar social and economic background and of similar political predispositions. The opinion leaders tend to give cues to people who would ordinarily be disposed toward the same party, and the main effect of opinion leadership is to re-enforce the allegiances of those with whom opinion leaders talk, or to "reconvert" them by bringing them back into line with previous allegiances if they have strayed from their ordinary party disposition in the inter-election period. This reconversion was shown to be extremely important in 1948 when the Democrats regained 11 per cent of their 1944 voters during the campaign;[46] apparently the inter-election period is characterized by considerable diminishing of party regularity and the election period by "reconversion" to prior party loyalties. In this process opinion leaders play a key role.

A vital characteristic of opinion leaders is their heavy reliance on media for information. V. O. Key, Jr., has shown that those people who try to persuade others to vote for a candidate or party are much more highly exposed to all four major media than are those who are not "convincers."[47] The authors of the 1940 presidential election study suggested that there is a "two-step flow of communications," with ideas flowing from media to opinion leaders and from opinion leaders to less interested sections of the population. This theory has been modified by recent writers who have found that opinion leaders not only pay more attention to media and give more advice, but they also ask more advice as well. Thus there is a multi-step process of communication in which media pump ideas into the political system where they are picked up by opinion leaders, either directly or through their contacts with others who are intensively exposed to media, and these opinion leaders convey ideas and viewpoints to others in the community.[48]

It is also true that opinion leaders tend to be quite fixed in their partisan commitments. They are not "converted" to candidates and parties by the information they receive from the media or from personal discussions. They are, to an even greater extent than the rest of the population, selective in their perceptions. They pay attention to communications which agree

with their commitments and they tend to disregard or reinter-
pret communications which disagree with their prior leanings.

For politicians, the implications of these data on media flow
are clear. They can attempt to reach voters individually through
the media, and in some degree they can be successful. Indeed,
there is good evidence that the more exposed a person is to
media, the more correctly he perceives the issues and correctly
relates issue positions to candidates.[49] As politicians purchase
larger segments of the media, they gain this kind of exposure to
that large share of the public which is attending the media. But
the more important channel of communication for political
influence is to opinion leaders, either directly through the media
or indirectly through other opinion leaders who are exposed to
the media, and from opinion leaders to the broader public. The
opinion leader performs some of the tasks which are commonly
associated with the canvasser. He discusses politics with people
in his immediate vicinity, and his standing permits him to do so
effectively. The non-purposiveness of his contacts with those
whom he advises aids his effectiveness.[50] For the politician, the
desired impact of media campaigning, whether it reaches the
voter directly or through opinion leaders, is to activate interest
in the campaign and to motivate voting, to re-enforce the commitments of those who ordinarily support his party or candidate, and to convert whatever portion of the opposition and
independent voters is open to persuasion.

It is important to remember, however, that these are the
desired effects. There are powerful countervailing forces which
prevent the politician from pursuing successfully these strategies
simply by expanding his purchases of mass media and his other
campaign efforts. The process of campaigning operates within
severe limitations. Most Americans—perhaps as many as 75 per
cent—have quite firm partisan commitments,[51] and Greenstein
reported that prior to the massive Republican defections of
1964 fully 50 per cent claimed that they had always voted for
the same party.[52] His subsequent research shows that, even
taking account of the 1964 defections, more than 40 per cent of
respondents claimed such election-day consistency. Large num-

bers of voters are not, therefore, subject to the process of conversion. Furthermore, voting decisions may be made before the campaign begins. A 1952 study, for instance, showed that 31 per cent of those sampled had made up their minds prior to the national party conventions and an additional 34 per cent decided at convention time.[53] Also, those who make late voting decisions, and thus are theoretically susceptible to the campaign, are generally those who are least interested in and least informed about politics. They are most likely to ignore the media messages sponsored by politicians, but they might be influenced indirectly by such messages via opinion leaders. Finally, the media campaigning of each party is largely matched by similar efforts by the opposition. Neither party, therefore, has a clear field for its media messages to take effect, although in part the process of selective perception by those who are exposed to such messages gives each party an advantage in putting across its pleas to those predisposed to it. In sum, while the spending strategies of Wisconsin politicians, with their heavy emphasis on mass media campaigning, are consistent with the nature of party organization in the state and the available data on the effectiveness of non-organization campaign techniques, these strategies operate within a context of countervailing forces which diminish the effectiveness of campaigning.

This evaluation of the campaign strategies of Wisconsin politicians is necessarily incomplete because it focuses on the use of their financial resources, and because of the limited social science data on the effects of various types of campaigning on voters, which makes it impossible to link particular campaign strategies with specific campaign results. This evaluation, therefore, is one based on the tying together of financial inputs, campaign outputs, and voter responses without sufficient data to establish the existence of causal links.

The campaign process is incredibly complex. There is no sure cost-effectiveness ratio for measuring the relative value of the various kinds of expenditures. But politicians seem to spend their money for kinds of campaigning which, within the particular Wisconsin political environment, are likely to yield the greatest results. If their conduct is susceptible to any criticism, it is that they do not spend more money for each of the major campaign activities, since the crude measures available do not indicate that campaigners have reached the point of diminishing returns in any of them.

The Uses of Money: Two Gubernatorial Campaigns

The discussion in this chapter has so far been aimed at describing the allocation of money between various campaign activities and at evaluating this allocation by employing the available social science data on their effectiveness. In addition, the relation of the Wisconsin party system to the campaign techniques used by politicians has been considered as have a number of the counterforces which limit the effectiveness of campaigning. The present section describes the 1962 and 1964 gubernatorial campaigns, each of which is interesting enough to merit a book of its own. The present purpose is to examine the uses to which politicians put their financial resources in specific political situations. The materials for this enterprise are better than those ordinarily available for non-presidential campaign studies, but they are not so complete as to permit analysis with the degree of certainty that has been the standard in the presidential election studies. The professional opinion polls used by the Democrats in both years are available, as are the data from the Wisconsin Survey Research Laboratory's post-election studies. In addition, we have several published sources which are pertinent[54] and a large collection of materials used in these campaigns.

The 1962 gubernatorial campaign pitted Republican Philip Kuehn against Democrat John Reynolds. Kuehn had served as Republican state chairman and had been the Republican gubernatorial candidate in 1960. His strong showing—48 per cent of the two-party vote—in that election surprised veteran politicians who had conceded an easy win to incumbent Democrat Gaylord Nelson. In 1962, Kuehn was endorsed by the Republican convention but was forced to fight a bruising primary battle with Wilbur Renk, a leader of the more liberal wing of the Republican party. Kuehn won the nomination by a vote of

250,000 to 199,000 only after considerable sums had been spent for television and newspaper advertising by his own backers and by the Republican headquarters. Nonetheless, a Kuehn victory in November was expected by virtually all Wisconsin politicians, including most Democratic leaders.

John Reynolds was serving his second term as attorney general in 1962. He had been elected by a substantial margin of 84,000 (54 per cent) in 1958, but had barely managed re-election in 1960 with a margin of 29,000 (51 per cent). Reynolds had run unsuccessfully for Congress from the Eighth District and had served in a variety of Democratic party positions at the state and local levels. In 1962, he was embroiled in a series of governmental and party controversies. He had supported John F. Kennedy in the bitter 1960 presidential primary and had backed State Chairman Patrick J. Lucey against Governor Gaylord Nelson in an intraparty fight in 1961. He had drawn criticism for refusing to act as legal counsel for state agencies engaged in conduct which he deemed wrong, and he several times filed as *amicus curiae* on behalf of individual citizens litigating against such agencies. He had begun reapportionment litigation against the state legislature before the United States Supreme Court handed down *Baker v. Carr,* 369 U.S. 186 (1962), and had been roundly criticized at the time for his "illegal lawsuit."

Despite the extensive political activity of both candidates, neither was widely known in September, 1962. A Louis Harris poll taken on behalf of the Democrats showed that only 55 per cent of a statewide sample of 861 voters could identify Kuehn and only 56 per cent knew Reynolds; 44 per cent of the sample preferred Kuehn, 40 per cent favored Reynolds, and 16 per cent were undecided. At the same time, the Democratic United States Senate candidate, Governor Gaylord Nelson, was trailing Republican Senator Alexander Wiley by only 1 percentage point, 48 per cent to 47 per cent with 5 per cent undecided. The Harris poll showed Reynolds running behind Nelson in Milwaukee County, among women, and among union families. Only 37 per cent of the respondents had any idea of Reynolds' record as attorney general, and on balance they viewed his record negatively. The comments about Kuehn were a good deal more favorable.

By the time this poll was taken, Reynolds had made an important move toward establishing his campaign theme. Throughout the 1950's the Democratic party had been vociferous in its opposition to a state sales tax, mainly on the ground that such a tax was "regressive." This was in the La Follette Progressive tradition, from which many of the Democratic activists, including Reynolds, had come. In the 1961 session of the legislature, the Republican majority had rejected Governor Nelson's attempt to meet rising state costs by instituting the withholding method of collecting the income tax, an increase in the existing income tax rate, and certain additional excise and bank taxes. The Republicans passed instead a general sales tax with a limited income tax credit designed to offset the sales tax payments on food, clothing and certain other necessities. After protracted negotiations, a compromise tax bill was passed which included some sales taxes and a small income tax increase coupled with the withholding system. Reynolds had been one of the most outspoken of the anti-sales-tax Democrats. At the state Democratic convention on June 22–23, 1962, Reynolds and his supporters obtained a platform plank pledging repeal of the "Republican sales tax."[55]

Although the Republican state convention pledged itself only to "a tax reform program that is equitable, easy to administer, and provides adequate revenue," Kuehn insisted that the party's statutory convention on October 2 specifically endorse a sales tax with a credit refund provision.[56] Kuehn took a generally conservative position on a wide range of other issues, including a comparison of welfare programs to the feeding of ducks in the Milwaukee lagoon: both deprived the recipients of their independence. But the campaign was waged basically on the tax issue. Kuehn charged that Reynolds' sales tax position was "a hypocritical hoax . . . a facade of deception built on flimsy foundation of grossly inaccurate statistics."[57]

The Kuehn media campaign, however, was based on his belief that he was well ahead and that if he could rally the Republican voters he would be victorious. His main television

effort was an especially effective musical spot which identified
Kuehn and identified him as a Republican. His newspaper ads
stressed the previously mentioned conservative theme of "independence" by comparing lagoon-fed ducks to soaring American
eagles.

The Reynolds media effort was concentrated in the last ten
days of the campaign. The major thrust was on television. A
series of spot announcements were screened which portrayed
items of food and clothing and which urged a "vote against a
sales tax on your children's milk [clothing] [diapers] . . . a
Republican victory would mean a tax on every morsel of food
you eat."[58] Small newspaper ads were scattered throughout the
pages of the daily press in the closing days; they featured the
message "beat the Republican sales tax on bakery [fish]
[groceries] [children's toys]." Only in the last days did Kuehn
respond to this issue through media. He appeared in a series of
spot television announcements explaining that the Reynolds tax
program would mean an increase in the income tax and would
take more from the budget of a family of four than would the
Kuehn tax program. The Harris poll suggested that Kuehn had
the more popular side of the issue. Seventy-three per cent of the
respondents had opposed raising the state income tax while only
19 per cent favored it; this contrasted with 40 per cent who
preferred to raise the state sales tax and 53 per cent who
opposed it. Kuehn was, however, late in developing his response
to the Reynolds position of simply opposing the sales tax.

On election day, Reynolds was elected governor by a few
more than 11,000 votes, only 50.5 per cent. In a subsequent
study of the campaign, Leon D. Epstein has shown that the tax
issue was named by more respondents than any other in explaining their gubernatorial vote. Of these tax-concerned voters,
47 per cent favored increasing the sales tax and 49 per cent
favored increasing the income tax. Furthermore, their correct
perceptions of party positions were high: 80 per cent knew that
the Republican party was for the sales tax and 71 per cent knew
that the Democratic party was for the income tax. Among all
voters these perceptions of party stands on the tax issue were a
respectably high 63 per cent and 52 per cent. The tax-con-

cerned voters constituted more than 25 per cent of the respondents. Correctly perceiving the tax positions of the two parties,
they voted 58 per cent for Reynolds and 42 per cent for Kuehn.
However, almost two-thirds of Kuehn's tax-oriented votes came
from usual Republican voters and 57 per cent of Reynolds'
tax-concerned ballots came from usual Democratic voters.[59]
Thus, Reynolds made a net gain on the tax issue.

Epstein cautions that the number of respondents is too small
for certainty, but he finds confirming evidence in an examination of the small number of voters who reported that they cast
ballots on the anti-sales tax issue. A third of this small sample
were not Democrats, but voted for Reynolds on the tax issue.[60]
Finally, Epstein points out that the Democratic gubernatorial
electorate, as compared to the senatorial electorate, was more
heavily composed of "usual Democrats and those with little
formal education, which groups also happen to have been
against the sales tax."[61] On the basis of several pieces of evidence, then, it seems plausible that voters who were influenced
by correct perceptions of the tax positions of the two gubernatorial candidates gave Reynolds his narrow margin of victory.

The political strategists in the Reynolds camp devoted more
than 75 per cent of their limited budget of approximately
$123,000 to mass media. All but a tiny fraction of the media
budget was devoted to the tax issue. In addition, campaign
materials purchased from the remaining share of the campaign's
financial resources emphasized the tax issue. It is not possible to
know whether the large amount of correct perception on the tax
issue in the population was related to the television and newspaper campaign waged by Reynolds. This would not be an unrea-
sonable assumption, however, since the events of the preceding
two years, including Nelson's approval of a compromise measure including sales taxes, did not highlight the differences between the parties on this issue. It appears that the Reynolds
campaign strategy re-enforced the loyalties of many normal
Democratic voters and perhaps converted a small but crucial
margin on the tax issue. The Kuehn campaign used its financial
resources to re-enforce the lead that Kuehn had in the early
polls; it was aimed primarily at Republicans. It did not antici-

pate that the Reynolds campaign would convert some of those who had earlier preferred Kuehn. In short, each candidate allocated his resources to effective campaign techniques and each followed a strategy which seemed suited to his circumstances as he understood them. But there can be little doubt that the effective use of campaign resources gave Reynolds his narrow margin of victory.

The 1964 gubernatorial election presents a much more complicated political situation. It occurred against a background which largely determined the strategies of the candidates. Although Reynolds had been successful in 1962, the Republicans captured both houses of the state legislature. The legislature refused to provide a state budget until there was agreement on a tax plan, and the Republican majority in each house insisted that revenue should be raised from an extension of the sales tax. The Republicans passed a general sales tax with a credit refund. Reynolds vetoed the bill. He called the Republican refusal to pass a budget "blackmail" and insisted: "I will not go back on my commitment to fair taxation." He introduced his own revenue measure, relying primarily on income taxation, but the Republicans killed it immediately. Finally, after the state was apparently headed for a severe reduction in state services because no budget had been passed by the beginning of the fiscal year, a compromise was reached which included extension of the sales tax and an increase in the income tax.[62] Accused of violating his 1962 campaign pledge, Reynolds told Democratic legislators "What can I do? . . . We have to have the budget."[63]

Also in the background of the 1964 election were controversies over highways, appointments, and reapportionment. In each area the governor and legislature deadlocked. Reynolds' proposal to bond for the acceleration of the state's highway construction program and to increase gasoline taxes was referred by the Republicans to a referendum where it was overwhelmingly defeated. The Republican majority in the state senate refused to consider his nominations to fill a number of important state positions. In ensuing litigation, the state supreme court, while seating some Reynolds' appointees, handed down a decision which was generally viewed as a defeat for the governor. A congressional reapportionment plan was agreed on, but legislative reapportionment also went to the supreme court after the governor and legislature could not agree. Again, the court's decision did not give the governor a victory, although the decision was not viewed as a clear-cut defeat either. In April, 1964, George Wallace entered Wisconsin's presidential primary and Reynolds filed as the Democratic party's favorite son, pledged to President Johnson. Although Reynolds declared that more than 100,000 votes for Wallace would be a disgrace to the state, the Alabama governor received 266,000. This was widely taken as an anti-Reynolds vote, even though the governor's total of 522,000 was the highest ever received by any Democratic presidential candidate in the Wisconsin primary.

As Reynolds embarked on his re-election campaign in the late spring of 1964, he was able to claim that he had held off a sales tax on food, clothing and other "necessities." He took credit for the passage of programs of medical care and property tax relief for the elderly; and he pointed out that the budget he had insisted on had provided an improved level of public services in the areas of higher education, care of the mentally ill and retarded, and other welfare activities. The Republican convention endorsed Warren Knowles, a former lieutenant governor. Both Reynolds and Knowles faced nominal opponents in their respective party primaries, but both won by substantial margins.

At the outset of the campaign, a poll taken by Oliver Quayle and Company for the Democrats showed Knowles with 52 per cent of the vote to 33 per cent for Reynolds and 15 per cent undecided. Knowles was shown to be leading by 44 per cent to 40 per cent in the city of Milwaukee, a Democratic stronghold, and by even wider margins in such normally Democratic industrial centers as Racine and Kenosha. The poll gave Reynolds a highly unfavorable rating on bread-and-butter issues such as attracting new industry and providing new jobs. Eighty-two per cent of the respondents rated him unfavorably on tax reform and 76 per cent scored Reynolds for not keeping his promises. Sixty-four per cent of the people believed he had improved the state's university system and its secondary and elementary schools. Fifty-eight per cent responded favorably to his programs for mental illness and retardation, and 56 per cent thought well of him on highway improvement and highway safety. Only 4 per cent of the voters did not feel familiar enough with Reynolds to rate him on any of a list of state issues about which they were asked. By contrast, 56 per cent were not familiar enough with Knowles to make any comment about his personal attributes or his past record in public life. Democrats attributed Knowles' large lead in the poll to anti-Reynolds sentiment.

Two months after this initial poll, the Democrats commissioned a second poll—this one conducted in ten major Wisconsin cities. The poll showed Reynolds ahead by a single percentage point; he had 37 per cent to Knowles' 36 per cent with 27 per cent undecided. This poll, since it was taken in the locations of usual Democratic strength, confirmed the enormous Knowles lead in the campaign. Reynolds' 37 per cent of the vote in these cities contrasted sharply with Senator Proxmire's 54 per cent and President Johnson's 58 per cent. Reynolds, in other words, was trailing his ticket mates by 17 and 21 percentage points in the urban centers. Open-ended questions permitting respondents to mention state issues of importance to them showed that taxation and the state's economy were mentioned most often. Reynolds was rated negatively by a margin of 4 to 1 on taxes and by a narrow margin on the state's economy. He again drew favorable comments in the areas of education and welfare. The pollsters discovered in a series of direct-issue questions that a large number of people agreed with such programs as property tax relief for the aged (85 per cent) and medical care for the aged (73 per cent), but few knew Reynolds' record on these issues (41 and 35 per cent respectively).

It was against this background of popular sentiment that the two parties launched their campaigns. The Democrats began their formal campaign activities somewhat early, apparently in response to the governor's unpopularity. Reynolds insisted that an elaborate 16-page tabloid be prepared to explain in detail his record on every issue. This expensive campaign document was circulated to the 26,000 Democratic party members, to the state's union leaders, to the officers of friendly farm groups, and to the statewide circulation of the Madison *Capital Times,* the former Progressive party house organ which leaned editorially to the Democrats. Reynolds explained this use of money as an attempt to get his record into the hands of liberal opinion leaders; he viewed the cost as justified on these grounds.

Most of the Democratic effort was concentrated on television, with a secondary campaign in the press. The basic campaign weapon was a five-minute documentary film showing the governor with his family and the governor on his well-known budget tour to state education and welfare institutions. He had used the tour to generate public support for sharp increases in spending for these programs. The film stressed his education and welfare record. It also showed him with elderly citizens and tried to explain his tax relief and medical care programs for the elderly. It reported that he had blocked the Republican attempt to extend the sales tax to food, clothing, and other necessities. Finally, it closed with a message supporting Reynolds which had been prepared by President Kennedy in the fall of 1963 and had not been previously used in Wisconsin. From the basic five-minute documentary came a series of one-minute and twenty-second spin-offs which merely repeated the same film segments and audio arguments but included opening and closing sections urging voters to retain Reynolds on his record.

The Reynolds newspaper campaign consisted of a series which his aides called the "thanks to . . ." ads. Each advertisement pictured Reynolds with representatives of a well-recognized group and carried a caption stating the improvement in state programs for them "thanks to Governor Reynolds." Thus a picture of Reynolds with elderly citizens carried the slogan, "tax relief for the elderly—thanks to Governor Reynolds." These newspaper presentations followed the same themes set in the five-minute documentary television film and its spin-off spots.

The Republican campaign, like the Democratic campaign, zeroed in on Reynolds. Its focus however was quite different. One series of twenty-second television spots consisted of rapidly alternating words: "Reynolds! Taxes! Reynolds! Taxes! . . ."

Radio spots hammered home the point that Reynolds had "fooled the people last time" and was trying to do it again. A different series of television spots featured Knowles answering questions; his emphasis was on the state's economy and on taxes. He argued that new taxes "could be avoided by an expected growth in the state's economy. . . ." He did acknowledge, however, in late September that "necessary increases in tax revenues might have to come from an expansion of the state sales tax."[64]

A newspaper series sponsored by the Knowles campaign committee cited "Six Failures of Governor Reynolds' Administration!" These ads stressed Reynolds signing of the sales tax after pledging to block it, the large vote piled up by Wallace in his primary against Reynolds, the repudiation of the Reynolds highway program in the April referendum, and other setbacks which the governor had suffered. A second series of newspaper pieces were headlined "Had Enough?" Beneath the headline were the major criticisms which the Knowles campaign was making of Reynolds: "broken promises . . . high taxes . . . job losses . . . industry moving out. . . ." The advertisements urged electors to "vote for the man you can rely on to *do* what he says. . . ." And, they included favorable comment on Knowles from a number of daily newspapers.

Unlike 1962, both campaigns had flexible strategies. The Republicans responded to the "thanks to Governor Reynolds" series with a "straight talk" series. For example, they pointed out that tax relief for the elderly had been "recommended by Commission on Aging, introduced by nine Republicans, passed by a Republican legislature, *no thanks to Governor Reynolds. For Straight Talk, Wisconsin Needs Knowles.*" Democrats answered the Republican hammering on the sales tax issue with a one-minute television cartoon which pictured Republican legislators battering down the doors of the capitol to get "a general sales tax on food and clothing and necessities of life." Reynolds was portrayed as slamming the door in their faces. In the closing days of the campaign, the Republicans sponsored television spots which opened with a cascade of peanuts and warned that present taxes would be peanuts if Reynolds was re-elected—he would "increase income taxes by $150 million."

Each side spent heavily on media. The Reynolds media effort apparently cost in the neighborhood of $194,000, 71 per cent for television. The Knowles media campaign cost somewhat more. Each side stressed the issues on which it was strongest. Reynolds emphasized education, welfare, his stand against the general sales tax, and his programs for the elderly. Knowles emphasized Reynolds' default on his promises on taxes, the increase in state taxes, and the condition of the state's economy. Each camp was also prepared to counter the claims of the other and did. The initial strategy of each side followed the pattern found in other campaigns: "the opposing candidates tended to 'talk past each other.' . . . Each candidate stressed the matters considered most strategic and effective in his own propaganda."[65] Each party recognized that voters perceived a large number of issues; many of those who criticized Reynolds on taxes also praised him on education and welfare. Each therefore sought to "affect the priorities and weights [the voters] give to subpreferences bearing on the [voting] decision."[66] Both campaigns tried to increase the salience of their strong issues and the intensity of voter opinion about them. Finally, however, each party also responded to the opposition by seeking to discredit its strongest arguments.

On November 3, 1964, Warren Knowles was elected governor by a margin of 18,000 votes; he received 50.6 per cent of the two-party vote for governor. It is difficult to know what factors diminished Knowles' early lead. The strength of the Democratic presidential trend may have been influential. Reynolds, who had trailed Johnson by 20 percentage points in the early Quayle rating was actually behind Johnson on election day by 13 percentage points. He managed to pull even with his own 1962 percentages in Milwaukee and Winnebago counties and to gain a percentage point in Marathon and Eau Claire. However, in the other 6 urban areas, he was off 1 percentage point in 4, off 3 points in another, and off 5 in the sixth. Nonetheless, Reynolds apparently gained back a substantial share of the urban voters who had reported defecting from him in the summer.

In order to evaluate the effects of the campaign on the vote, data made available by the Survey Research Laboratory of the University of Wisconsin were examined. This post-election survey does not provide the exact data that would be most useful for the specific purpose of this inquiry, but it does include some materials which are helpful in suggesting the impact of the 1964 gubernatorial campaign strategies.

The available poll consists of a sample of 702 Wisconsin adults, of whom 544 reported voting for the major party candi-

Table 26

Percentage of the Vote for Democratic Gubernatorial and Senatorial Candidates According to the Usual Preferences of the Voters, 1962 and 1964

Usual Vote Preference	Reynolds % 1962[a]	Reynolds % 1964	Nelson % 1962[2]	Proxmire % 1964
Republican	13	4	19	21
"Depends"	57	46	65	66
Democratic	87	76	86	90

[a] A recomputation of data in Leon D. Epstein, *Votes and Taxes* (Madison: Institute of Governmental Affairs, 1964), p. 75.

dates for governor and United States senator. A combination of sampling error and the "halo effect" tends to exaggerate the percentage of the vote received by the winners, and this is most pronounced in the senatorial contest between Republican Wilbur Renk and Democratic incumbent William Proxmire.

It was first desirable to test whether there was a sharp defection from Reynolds among Democratic voters as suggested by the early polls. Table 26 shows the percentage of the vote won by 1962 and 1964 Democratic candidates among groups of voters who identified how they "usually voted for statewide and county offices." These data reflect the fact that Reynolds was weaker, even in his successful 1962 campaign, than both Nelson and Proxmire. While managing in 1962 to run about as well as they among Democrats, he lagged substantially behind among Republicans and independents. In 1964, Reynolds was about 11 percentage points off his 1962 vote among each group of voters, irrespective of their usual preferences. His defeat in 1964 cannot therefore be attributed to a particular defection among Democrats.

A somewhat different thesis is that the attrition of Reynolds' strength occurred among those voters who were disturbed about the large increase in state spending and the concomitant increase in taxes. This would be especially true among those voters who opposed the sales tax. Such voters would perceive Reynolds as having broken his campaign pledge. These were, of course, exactly the issues on which Reynolds had drawn a negative response in the two opinion polls taken by the Democrats. They were also the themes which Knowles developed in his campaign, and to which he tied the economic growth issue by arguing that such growth would bring in more tax revenue without increasing tax rates.

Epstein found that in 1962 attitudes toward spending and taxes were highly related to the voter's educational background. Those with elementary and secondary educations overwhelmingly believed that the state should "get along with the money it now has," while the college educated tended to believe that "Wisconsin needs to raise more money by some kind of new or increased taxes."[67] The same pattern prevailed on tax preferences. Those who had elementary and secondary education believed that "as a matter of principle" the income tax was "most fair to everybody," while the college educated by a slight margin believed that the sales tax was more equitable. If more revenue was absolutely needed, the less-educated groups preferred an increase in the income tax; the college educated by a large margin preferred a sales tax increase.[68]

Thus, if voters rejected Reynolds in 1964 on the set of issues which clustered around taxation and spending, his losses should have been most pronounced among those voters who were not educated beyond grade and high school. Table 27 indicates that Reynolds' share of the vote dropped most sharply among the

high school educated. He suffered a 3 per cent loss among the
grade school educated but stayed almost even with his 1962
showing among the college educated. The congruence between
Proxmire's vote in 1964 among the grade and high school
educated and Reynolds' vote among those same groups in 1962
is striking. It suggests that those percentages are necessary for a
Democrat to win in Wisconsin, even if he is weak among the
college educated as Reynolds was in 1962. It was Reynolds'
failure to hold the necessary vote among the grade and high
school educated that apparently cost him the 1964 election.

Table 27

Vote for Reynolds According to the Educational
Background of Voters, 1962 and 1964

Voter's Education	Reynolds % 1962[a]	Reynolds % 1964	Proxmire % 1964
Elementary	59	56	60
Secondary[b]	54	48	55
College[c]	28	27	39

[a] Reported in Leon D. Epstein, *Votes and Taxes*,
p. 64.
[b] Includes those with vocational training.
[c] Includes those with graduate training.

These data seem to raise a reasonable inference that the 1964
election was decided by the shift of a small but decisive percentage of voters in those groups which opposed increased spending
and the sales tax. This is not evidence, however, that they
shifted because of those issues. Although the numbers are small
and do not lend themselves to the kind of further cross-tabula-
tions necessary for verification, a substantial percentage of the
respondents who reported splitting their tickets for Proxmire
and Knowles also reported disliking Reynolds for reasons similar to those stressed by Knowles in his campaign. Four major
categories of replies to an open-ended question seem so related:
that Reynolds was weak and lacked leadership; that he was
insincere and broke his tax pledge; that his tax program was

wrong; that his economic policies were inadequate. Of the 336 respondents who reported voting for Proxmire, 22.9 per cent (77) mentioned these themes and of this small group, 44.2 per cent (34) voted for Knowles. They constituted 11.7 per cent of the 291 respondents who reported voting for Knowles. Among these 34 Proxmire-Knowles split-ticket voters who disliked Reynolds for reasons emphasized by Knowles during the campaign, 18 identified themselves as Democrats and 6 said they were independents. They were respectively 5.3 per cent and 1.7 per cent of Knowles' total voters.

The survey data do not show whether this group of Proxmire-Knowles split-ticket voters who registered concern about these issues said that they voted for Knowles because of them. Also, these voters were not the only ones who split their tickets between Proxmire and Knowles; indeed they were only about a third of all the split-ticket voters. A reasonable inference is, however, that the Knowles campaign either raised these issues for this group of voters or, more probably, it re-enforced their pre-existing discontent with Reynolds on these issues. In the instances of the Democratic split-ticket voters, this required sufficient re-enforcement to offset their ordinary partisan tendencies in a year when Democratic re-enforcement at the national level was great and when the state level Democratic campaign was making a vigorous effort to overcome the tax and spending issues by raising other aspects of Reynolds' record. In short, the Knowles campaign may have achieved for these and other voters a sufficient re-enforcement effect to overcome strong forces operating to win their votes for Reynolds. And if the limited number of cases examined above are representative, there is a fair implication that the Knowles campaign was crucial to his narrow election victory.

No indisputable conclusions can be drawn from this study of the 1962 and 1964 Wisconsin gubernatorial campaigns. Especially in the latter campaign our data are insufficient, both because some crucial questions were not included in the survey and because the number of cases available in some of the analytic categories is small. It seems, however, that to a surprisingly large extent Wisconsin politicians use their money effectively. They consistently employ the mass media as a major campaign device, and they tend to rely heavily on the most effective of the media. Their selection of media as a campaign device is consistent with the lack of party organization in crucial locales. Finally, they select the issues on which they appear to be strongest and they seek to increase the salience of those issues for the public and the intensity of feeling about them.

In 1962, the sales tax issue apparently won John Reynolds a small but significant bloc of Republican votes which permitted him a narrow victory. In 1964, Reynolds' campaign apparently served well to repair his battered image among the urban Democratic vote base. But the Knowles campaign stressed Reynolds' weak points in such a way as to encourage voters who cast ballots for his senatorial running mate to desert Reynolds. At the very least the Knowles campaign re-enforced the anti-Reynolds sentiments of a small group of voters, including those who usually voted Democratic. Their votes may have been determinative in an election decided by 0.6 per cent. Both of the campaigns used their financial resources quite effectively in raising issues and communicating them through effective media. Every dollar was not of course spent for these purposes. Even the money which went for candidate stumping and for organizational efforts seems to have been reasonably well spent when it is recognized that candidate speeches and press releases as well as the materials distributed to and by party activists tended to stress the same messages that were developed in the media campaigns. In contrast to the usual view that money is badly managed by politicians, who engage in irrational types of campaigning,[69] the perspective one gains from these two gubernatorial campaigns is that, on the whole, politicians use their financial resources with surprising effectiveness.

The Uses of Money: Systemic Consequences

Although politicians use their resources to pursue self-promoting objectives, the political activities which they sponsor with these resources may have other, unintended consequences for the political system. Chapter 1 reviewed the systemic "functions" whose performance is commonly attributed at least in part to political parties. The present discussion is directed at assessing the possible systemic consequences of the activities which were found in previous sections to be the objects of political spending. In this way it is possible to make some appraisal of the role of money in the political system.

In recent decades a number of political thinkers have argued that the only reasonable role which voters might play in a modern democratic political system is to choose between rival groups of political leaders.[70] Issues are so complex and time so limited, the argument runs, that voters in large numbers cannot hope to mandate policies at the polls. Even this limited citizen participation in the democratic system cannot be achieved, however, unless alternate sets of leaders are available. The expense of the substantial efforts which politicians make to file full slates of candidates has already been noted. They do so, of course, to win office, either by electing the candidates filed or, in one-party districts, by attracting to the whole ticket additional votes which may be helpful to those running in larger and more competitive constituencies.

The magnitude of this recruiting effort has been discussed previously, but it may be helpful to add that 86 per cent of Wisconsin party officers reported in the mid-1950's that they had sought, encouraged, or persuaded candidates to run for legislative office; the efforts made to recruit candidates for county offices were probably at least as great.[71] It cannot be argued that such candidate recruitment is unnecessary in one-party districts on the ground that primaries provide the electorate a choice: Julius Turner has pointed out that primary competition occurred in only 50 per cent of the one-party congressional districts in the four elections from 1944–1950.[72] While a few other agencies in the society engage in candidate recruitment, their activity is minimal compared to the expense and effort in this direction by political parties. It must be concluded then that political spending for candidate recruitment has a vital consequence for democratic politics: it helps provide opposition candidates who make effective the opportunity for voters to choose their leaders.

A somewhat different aspect of the recruitment process is the enlisting of party activists. It is now argued that every citizen need not be active in politics, and indeed that too widespread activism would jeopardize the system both by making politics inflexible and by unduly straining consensus.[73] However, it is recognized that some body of activists is essential to perform the functions of vigil and criticism that the larger public does not ordinarily perform.[74] In addition, the recruitment process is a first step toward training some citizens in the specialized tasks of operating the electoral system and political campaigns. Effective opportunities for choice are unlikely without some group which understands these tasks and performs them. There is also some evidence that "participation in politics builds a commitment to democratic values and that elites are much more likely to understand and adhere to specific applications of general democratic principles than are average citizens."[75] Essential democratic political values are of course disseminated through a wide range of outlets in the system, but parties are one of the significant agencies which perform this function.

The significance of the mass party system's recruitment efforts can perhaps be indicated by the contrast between the 4 per cent of a national survey sample who responded in 1964 that they were members of a political party, and the 7.7 per cent who so responded in Wisconsin.[76] In the present American context, the concern is clearly not too much activism, but too little. Money spent for maintaining party membership, recruiting new activists, and training party cadres must therefore be viewed as strengthening the political system through its consequences in promoting electoral alternatives and expanding adherence to democratic values.

A few writers take a more optimistic view of the role of voters in the democratic system than the previously cited idea that electors can effectively do no more than choose between competing sets of leaders. V. O. Key, Jr., for instance, has pointed out that the "shifting voters" in elections from 1940 to 1960 were in large measure those whose views on highly visible campaign issues were the same as those of the party to which they shifted.[77] This also appeared to be the case in the 1962 gubernatorial election in Wisconsin, and perhaps in the 1964 contest as well. Furthermore, there is a high congruence between the issue positions of voters on domestic social welfare activity by the federal government and their identification with the national political party whose position (as expressed in congressional voting) is closest to their own.[78]

Whichever of these views of democracy one holds, the political campaign seems to have an important role in permitting voters to operate the system. The condition precedent in either case is that information should be available to those voters who are willing to be exposed to it, even though they are not willing to devote any substantial time or energy to obtaining it. Most campaign money buys campaign materials, publicity, and mass media exposure.

At the minimum level, these types of campaigning provide name identification of the candidates. The need for such activity is demonstrated by the fact that sports, entertainment, and cartoon personalities are better known by the public than many national political leaders.[79] There is even less candidate identification in contests for lesser offices, as the previously reported post-primary election data on public recognition of the 1962 Wisconsin gubernatorial candidates revealed. Confirming evidence is found in the 1964 post-election survey in Wisconsin, which showed that only 31 per cent of respondents could name their congressman and only 18 per cent could name the unsuccessful candidate in their district. In other states, substantial numbers of those interviewed were unable to identify various state offices, their incumbents, and the methods of selecting those officials.[80]

For those who believe that elections ought to influence policy in a democratic polity, it is clear that campaigning helps make easily accessible to voters the issue positions of candidates and parties. As noted earlier, people have a relatively high recall of campaign propaganda, and, up to some saturation point, the more messages are available through the media the more likely people are to take notice of them, and "the more reading and listening people do on campaign matters, the more likely they are to come to recognize the positions the candidates take on major issues."[81] At the very least, mass media reach the influentials who then convince or advise others on political matters.[82] Since media are the largest object of political expenditure in Wisconsin, the self-promoting conduct of politicians also strengthens the democratic political system insofar as it expands the understanding of the candidate and policy choices available to the electorate.

This argument cannot be made without qualification. There are other available sources of information in the community. The flow of information from these sources may, however, be quite inadequate, especially for offices with low visibility. Furthermore, campaigning not only increases the volume of available political information, it also conveys the messages as politicians conceive them rather than through the interpretive process of other channels of communication. Campaigning provides a direct information link between candidates and voters to add to the indirect links provided by media news reporting. At a time when mass media are increasingly influential in shaping opinion, it is important that those who own and operate the media should not be the arbiters of all the messages which are transmitted. Advertising is not subject to this distortion; it will, of course, reflect the biases of those who pay for it, and it will not necessarily be informative on issues. The point, however, is not that politician-sponsored media campaigning is a superior source of information, but rather that it is an additional source both in volume and in bias. In this way campaign expenditures increase the information available to voters, thus expanding their opportunity to make an effective choice.

It should be noted also that party canvassing as well as expenditures for media may have the potential for strengthening democracy by increasing the flow of information available to the voters. But canvassing is apparently on the decline. Only a small percentage of survey respondents indicated they had been directly contacted by party workers. The patronage incentives which once maintained the network of efficient precinct workers are no longer operative, both because of the decline in the number of such jobs and the decline in their desirability. Furthermore, expanded education and media attentiveness have probably diminished the effectiveness of canvassing even where it still exists, except perhaps with regard to low visibility issues and offices. In these circumstances it is difficult to argue that money spent for organization has significant systemic consequences as a side effect of door-to-door canvassing.

Three other consequences or "functions" which are commonly attributed to parties can be considered more summarily. It is generally argued that parties organize the government by filling the critical posts with men of like minds on policy; the separation of powers is "bridged" by party, thus permitting unified policy. Arguments are made that this increases the effectiveness of government, or at least does not diminish public confidence in a government deadlocked by party conflict; in either case this is allegedly an aid to maintaining the system. Regardless of whether this organizing "function" actually has systemic consequences and whether in practice parties have unified separated governmental institutions, it seems fairly clear that any relationship of political finance to this "function" is so remote and peripheral as not to warrant further discussion.

Similarly, the argument that parties are a symbol which draw the allegiance of people to the political system, thus maintaining stability, ought to be by-passed. A recent study of mass attitudes toward parties suggests that party has mixed value connotations at best: there is not the kind of overwhelming confidence in parties that would permit them to transfer legitimacy to the political regime.[83] Furthermore, it is difficult to see that campaign finance, except as money is used to publicize the party, aids in the development of popular allegiance.

Finally, the argument is made that campaign activity increases vote turnout. The evidence seems to suggest that canvassing is highly correlated to getting out the vote. In Wisconsin large sums are spent on a substitute for personal canvassing, the phone canvass. Furthermore, mass media campaigning may have a similar effect: "the heavier the flow of propaganda, the higher the voting turnout."[84] Participation is also increased where the choices are made clear, as where campaigns emphasize sharp differences between parties or candidates.[85] However, it is also true that the largest proportion of the well informed tend to vote even in the absence of these stimuli. Thus, these activities bring into the system the ordinarily disinterested voter. His conduct is unlikely to meet a model of the rational voter.

The argument made for the importance of participation is not, however, that voters brought into the system will meet some model of rationality; rather it stresses the "importance of voting for the political system generally, as a means of building or maintaining individual allegiance, i.e., voluntary acceptance of the constitutional arrangements and specific regulations of a regime."[86] Very limited data from Great Britain show that voters justify allegiance to the constitutional structure and obedience to the law on the ground that these were ordained at the polls.[87] However, the data also show that those voters most aware of the role of government in the society more often justify allegiance on the basis of electoral endorsement. This suggests that increased participation which brings the less informed to the polls may not increase the sense of allegiance through the medium of casting a vote. That is, it may be interest and understanding coupled with voting that generate a feeling of loyalty to institutions and laws.

It is necessary to conclude that the most likely systemic consequences of political expenditures result from the recruitment and propagandizing efforts financed by political parties. Recruitment of candidates helps assure that an alternate set of leaders will be on hand if the public seeks to change its governors. The recruitment of activists helps provide a corps of specialists who can manage the election machinery and campaigns; to a lesser extent, it brings people into circumstances where they are exposed to democratic values. The other major consequence of political expenditures is to increase the flow of information so that the democratic electorate is better able to make its vote effective. The relationship between campaigning and voter turnout is not so clear, but mobilizing the vote may be a third major consequence of the campaign efforts which money buys. The degree to which any of these efforts are carried on is dependent to a significant extent upon the availability of financial resources to support them. Politicians' expenditures for self-promoting political activities thus have systemic consequences. They are probably not alone essential to the continued operation of the system, but the failure of politicians to finance these activities would clearly diminish in a significant way the total of such system-maintaining functions performed within the political system.

Financing the Political System

Estimating Political Receipts

It is a good deal more difficult to tabulate the receipts of Wisconsin political committees than to ascertain the level of expenditures. One problem is that receipts received in prior years and retained for use during the campaign year are not reported as receipts in the official filings for that year; as previously indicated, testimonial dinners and other devices are often used to build up party treasuries in the inter-election period. The statement of receipts filed in the election year statement, therefore, errs substantially on the low side.

Inasmuch as the methods used in Chapter 3 to tabulate total costs are not appropriate to the calculation of total receipts, an alternate method has been used here. Total receipts can be estimated by subtracting the reported or estimated debts of political committees from their total expenditures, on the simple premise that any expenditure not accounted for by debt must have been made in cash which was received from some form of contribution. It was possible to make such calculations for statewide party committees and the campaigns for governor and United States senator in 1964; the filed reports were accessible in Madison and were of fairly good quality. It was not possible to make detailed calculations of debt for campaigns for other offices because the reports were scattered in many county courthouses, because help in developing estimates could not be obtained from political leaders so widely dispersed, and because the quality of local level reporting is, as previously pointed out, quite poor. It was quite difficult to calculate total receipts for even statewide campaigns in the years prior to 1964 because the personal recollections of political leaders were not as clear for those years and there was, therefore, no way to affirm the filed reports with interview evidence. Preliminary evidence on total receipts by state party and gubernatorial campaign committees were available for 1966. It should be noted that, while the reported expenditures are used as a base for calculating receipts here, the use of estimated expenditures for that purpose would increase the figures by 10 to 20 per cent for the same reasons as stated in Chapter 2 (pp. 37–40).

In 1964, the total reported spending by the Republican Party of Wisconsin, the Republican gubernatorial campaign, and the Republican senatorial campaign was approximately $1,170,000, after the elimination of transfer payments among the committees involved. The total Republican deficit of $80,000 would put receipts to cover this level of expenditure at about $1,090,000. Similarly, Democratic expenditures by the corresponding committees were approximately $746,000. Deficits were about $40,000, which would peg the level of receipts at about $706,000. In 1966, total expenditures by the Democratic state headquarters and the Lucey campaign were $387,092, and an additional $50,000 in debts was reported. Of the expenditures, $384,479 was accounted for by income reported during the seventeen-month period covered by the 1966 reports. The Republican state headquarters and the Knowles campaign reported spending $797,950, and there was an additional $96,483 of reported debt. However, fully $105,282 of the receipts needed to cover the direct expenditures were not detailed on the official financial statements for the seventeen months preceding the election and must therefore have been collected prior to that time.

In 1964, Democratic receipts were about 6 per cent less than the amounts expended by the gubernatorial and United States Senate campaigns and the party headquarters. Republican receipts were 7 per cent less than the spending by the comparable committees. In 1966, receipts were 11 per cent less than expenditures for both parties; proportionally each had run up larger debts than in 1964. If simple straightline projections are made onto the total reported expenditures in Tables 13 and 14, total system-wide receipts for each party can be estimated: total Democratic receipts in 1964 would be $1,217,770, or 6 per cent less than total spending; total Republican receipts that year would be $1,857,582. In 1966, each party's total receipts would be 11 per cent less than total system-wide expenditures, thus putting Democratic receipts at $995,821 and Republican income at $1,508,461. If these figures are at all representative, one might estimate that total receipts would be from 5 to 15 per cent less than total expenditures in the prior years under study.

The projections of system-wide receipts may be subject to question if local level political organizations are less willing to incur debts than state level groups because they do not have the potential fund-raising capacity that state level committees have. The successful election of a district attorney or county clerk does not yield the local organization the fund-raising advantages that the successful election of a governor may yield at the state level, and local organizations may therefore be less willing to amass debts in order to win elections. Furthermore, the most effective fund raisers are generally tied to the state political level, either as part of the Republican state finance organization or the *ad hoc* Democratic fund-raising committees which surround the various centers of influence within that party. Local party leaders may therefore see less prospect for raising funds to pay off obligations which are run up during a campaign than do their state level counterparts. On the other hand, local candidates may be willing to put their personal credit behind a certain number of campaign debts, which is a practice unusual at the state level. Furthermore, the local tickets are longer than the state ticket and there are, as a consequence, more committees and candidates to incur political debts. In sum, then, these projections of total political receipts are as good an estimate as can be made, even considering the factors which may cast a shadow on their accuracy. Unlike state party, gubernatorial, and senatorial committee estimates, these system-wide estimates cannot be tested by actually retabulating the reported receipts because of the vast number of committees involved in the host of local primary and general election contests and because of the inadequacies of the financial reports filed by local level candidates and committees.

Raising Political Money

Analyses of political money indicate that there is a wide range of fund-raising methods and financial sources. For the present study there is established a series of simple categories into which the various kinds of receipts can be grouped for comparative purposes, both between the parties and over the time period from 1950 to 1964. These categories tell more about the methods of raising political money than about the sources from which such funds are raised; that problem is discussed below.

The data for analysis are limited to the state party committee of each party and the statewide committees which filed in behalf of the candidates for governor and United States senator for each party during the seven elections under study here. In most elections these political units made more than half the expenditures in the total Wisconsin political system. Some mention will be made of possible differences between the fund-raising methods at the state level of operation and at the local and district levels. However, financial statements for local and district candidates and committees were, for the most part, filed at local courthouses and not in the state capitol; and they were not therefore generally accessible for this study. Nor were they often of a quality which permitted the kind of detailed analysis that was made of the state level receipts. This is, of course, in keeping with previous discussions indicating that amateur political activists, where not under the close scrutiny of a politically conscious press corps or the direction of paid staff members, simply do not have the time, inclination, or understanding to file the kinds of detailed financial statements contemplated by the state's corrupt practices laws.

The receipts of these various statewide political committees were grouped into ten well-defined categories and an eleventh catch-all to cover odd receipts not reasonably encompassed in the other categories. The amounts assigned to this miscellaneous category were never significant enough to cast any reasonable doubt upon the validity of the general pattern of receipts; they reached a high of 8 per cent in the Democratic receipt pattern of 1966 because of large sums raised from the sale of campaign materials and transferred from a party savings account to the regular campaign fund, but otherwise they seldom reached a level of 2 per cent of total receipts.

Five of the ten categories describe various kinds of individual contributions. Wisconsin's party organizations have been of the "club system" variety which is characterized by "largely nonpatronage . . . regularized, often dues-paying, mass membership."[1] This kind of party organization is, of course, more familiar in Britain and continental Europe than in the United States, although it has developed extensively in the upper midwest and in California and some parts of New York. One source of funds in such a political system is likely to be membership dues. In Wisconsin the Democratic party collects its dues at the state level and rebates a certain amount to the local units. The Republican party does not have a uniform membership system, but in recent years a growing number of county organizations have adopted formal membership procedures: dues are collected locally and membership information is then reported to the state headquarters. The result of this practice is that dues are not a source of state-level financial support, although some portion of those dues paid at the local level may flow upward to the state committee in the form of payments made by each county toward its state fund quota.

A second source of funds, related closely to the first, is subscription to party publications. This form of income was more common in the early 1950's when the Democrats attempted to make their party organ financially self-sufficient. Two other kinds of individual giving involve money raised by selling various items for profit, and selling tickets or admissions to political events. In Wisconsin the parties have sold phonograph records of political speeches, campaign buttons, jewelry with political insignia, items of clothing (including "I Love Gaylord" sweatshirts to further the candidacy of Senator Nelson), and a wide range of other such items. Similarly, tickets to certain kinds of political events, including registration fees at state party conventions, have been used to raise funds.

The most important category of individual receipts is direct individual contributions. This category may overlap some of the others, depending upon the methods of reporting used by the various committees. Each individual ticket to a fund-raising dinner or other political event may be reported as an individual contribution or the total receipts may be lumped together and reported as one sum. This is also true of the sales of various items described above. Since the statutes apparently contemplate the first form of reporting, most contributions are listed as gifts from specific individuals, regardless of the fund-raising method used to solicit them. In this study all contributions listed as gifts from individuals were categorized as "individual contributions," even though a substantial number of them must have been made in connection with fund-raising dinners and drives to sell various novelties. Only when a committee reported a lump sum as a sale of tickets or items was it categorized in this way in our analysis.

Five additional categories of receipts were established to cover contributions from organizations. One category involves receipts from party organizations, national or state or local. For this study, contributions from the state party organizations to senatorial or gubernatorial campaigns were eliminated because they constituted a transfer payment among the committees here being analyzed and would have improperly inflated the total receipts. A second category involves receipts from committees supporting other candidates, and again transfers among the committees analyzed here were eliminated to avoid exaggeration of the actual level of receipts. A third category encompasses receipts from "other associations." This includes contributions from organizations such as the National Committee for an

Effective Congress or the American Medical Association's Wisconsin Political Action Committee (WISPAC). A fourth category is labor's political contributions, which are considered separately because of their importance in the political system.

Finally a separate category was established to include the receipts from the sale of advertising in program booklets or other political publications. The two parties differed substantially in their handling of such funds. The money received from advertising was not regarded by either as a contribution, but rather as a receipt from a sale of something of value. This was necessary in order to permit the purchasers to deduct the cost of advertising as a business expense and to avoid violating Wisconsin's Corrupt Practices Act, which prohibits contributions by corporations.[2] If receipts from such advertising were not contributions, then it appeared that they should not be included in candidate and committee financial statements since the law only requires the reporting of "contributions."[3]

The Democrats apparently decided that they would report receipts from advertising in lump sum amounts, but would not list individual purchasers. This was an attempt to reconcile full disclosure of sources with the stance that purchasing of advertising was not a political contribution. The Republicans, except in one instance, did not report advertising receipts at all. It was therefore a simple matter to calculate the Democratic income from this source, but somewhat more difficult to determine Republican reliance upon the sale of advertising. Interviewing revealed that the Republicans had not used this fund-raising method in 1962, but had used it extensively in 1964. The 1964 publications in which advertising was sold were obtained and the total value of the advertisements in each publication was determined, using a rate of $1,000 per page and proportional amounts for smaller ads. (There is some evidence that the rates did not decline at a precisely proportional rate, but an exact rate card could not be obtained.) The estimated amount of program book receipts was then added to the contributions reported at the Secretary of State's office to obtain a full picture of Republican party receipts.

The pattern of Democratic party receipts in Table 28 indicates at the outset that dues collections alone have not played a substantial role in financing liberal campaigns in Wisconsin. The largest percentages of receipts attributable to membership dues were 7.2 per cent in 1958 and 7.6 per cent in 1966. The Republican cause at the state level received no support whatsoever from membership dues, although in recent years membership fees have become more significant at the local level, particularly in Republican clubs in suburban areas.

A second important aspect of the pattern of receipts is the close and continuing alliance between the labor movement and the liberal political party. Generally labor's participation in financing the Democratic cause at the state level has been greater than any other single interest or group. Table 28 indicates that 1956 was an exception to this rule and that labor's money accounted for only 7.4 per cent of the statewide financial effort. In that year labor's efforts were constrained by the so-called Catlin Act, which prohibited unions from contributing to political committees and candidates. The law had been passed in the wake of William Proxmire's near upset of the incumbent Republican governor in 1954, when Proxmire's 49 per cent of the vote was the most competitive Democratic showing since 1932. The overall statewide effort in 1954 had relied to the extent of 36.2 per cent on labor's money and the Proxmire campaign effort, considered alone, was financed 55 per cent by union contributions.

Labor's role was proportionally more significant in the earlier years under study when the newly born Democratic party had no other allies and few other sources of funds. In those years, labor's support of the Democratic cause always amounted to at least 20 per cent of the total financial resources. In 1962 and 1964, labor's proportional financial role was below 20 per cent, although its actual dollar contributions rose substantially in each election. In 1966, union contributions to statewide Democratic committees fell sharply. The decline in labor's significance in the overall Democratic financial constituency is probably related to the maturing of the Democratic party. As the Democrats demonstrated that they were serious competitors for power, by winning some major contests and making impressive electoral

Table 28

Receipts by State Party, Gubernatorial, and Senatorial

| | 1950 | | 1954 | | 1956 | |
	Amount	%	Amount	%	Amount	%
DEMOCRATS						
Dues	$ 3,478	4.0	$ 3,507	2.5	$ 4,026	4.2
Subscriptions	—	—	7,062	5.0	9,760	10.3
Sales	—	—	—	—	6,231	6.6
Political events	—	—	3,666	2.6	1,993	2.1
Direct individual contributions	11,085	12.8	71,841	51.2	54,496	57.4
Party units	44,088	50.8	1,260	0.9	1,015	1.1
Candidate committees	4,516	5.2	—	—	8,503	9.0
Other assns.	—	—	—	—	594	0.6
Labor	23,702	27.3	50,901	36.2	6,997	7.4
Advertising receipts	—	—	—	—	—	—
Other receipts	—	—	2,211	1.6	1,283	1.4
Totals	*$86,869*	100.1ᵉ	*$140,448*	100.0	*$94,898*	100.1ᵉ
REPUBLICANS						
Dues	$ —	—	$ —	—	$ —	—
Subscriptions	—	—	—	—	—	—
Sales	—	—	—	—	855	0.2
Political events	4,361	1.6	6,832	2.1	6,971	1.5
Direct individual contributions	251,140	89.9	255,379	78.9	402,434	85.4
Party units	23,570	8.4	59,834	18.5	59,811	12.7
Candidate committees	—	—	9	—ᵇ	500	0.1
Other assns.	—	—	—	—	—	—
Labor	—	—	—	—	—	—
Advertising receipts	—	—	—	—	—	—
Other receipts	333	0.1	1,815	0.6	800	0.2
Totals	*$279,404*	100.0	*$323,869*	100.1ᵉ	*$471,371*	100.1ᵉ

ᵃ 1952 and 1960 omitted (see p. 40). Unless otherwise identified, a dash

ᵇ Less than one-tenth of one per cent.

ᵉ The result of rounding of figures.

showings in others, Democratic fund raisers were able to increase the number of contributors and the average amount that they contributed. In this rapidly expanding financial constituency, labor's contributions, although increasing in absolute

Committees by Fund-Raising Categories, 1950–1966[a]

1958 Amount	%	1962 Amount	%	1964 Amount	%	1966 Amount	%
$ 15,167	7.2	$ 31,950	5.8	$ 40,584	5.8	$ 29,177	7.6
—	—	—	—	729	0.1	—	—
6,203	2.9	—	—	—	—	—	—
7,910	3.7	8,710	1.6	259	—[b]	15,876	4.1
96,735	46.0	308,509	56.1	252,026	35.8	218,951	56.9
22,011	10.4	29,956	5.4	48,500	6.9	6,506	1.7
12,836	6.1	3,037	0.6	2,215	0.3	—	—
4,030	1.9	365	0.1	5,256	0.7	—	—
45,704	21.7	94,734	17.2	127,617	18.2	39,530	10.3
—	—	70,595	12.8	191,441	27.2	43,727	11.4
498	0.2	2,200	0.4	35,348	5.0	30,712	8.0
$211,094	100.1[c]	$550,056	100.0	$703,975	100.0	$384,479	100.0
$ —	—	$ —	—	$ —	—	$ —	—
—	—	—	—	—	—	—	—
—	—	11,985	2.0	13,941	1.2	6,748	0.9
219,200	76.9	426,299	71.6	576,483	53.8	468,719	67.6
58,840	20.6	122,533	20.6	293,491	27.4	170,667	24.6
2,580	0.9	—	—	145	—[b]	14,528	2.1
689	0.2	6,750	1.1	6,700	0.6	—	—
—	—	—	—	1,000	0.1	1,000	0.1
—	—	—	—	179,750	16.7	32,000	4.6
4,237	1.5	28,089	4.7	1,748	0.1	—	—
$285,546	100.1[c]	$595,656	100.0	$1,073,258	99.9[c]	$693,662	99.9[c]

means that there were no receipts in this category.

sums, were not so large a percentage of total Democratic receipts. The 1966 drop in labor funds to the Democratic state level effort reflects two additional factors: the absence from the ballot of a United States Senate seat, an office which has traditionally occupied labor's special attention, and labor's deliberate choice to concentrate its efforts on marginal congressional and state legislative contests. Nonetheless, labor remained the largest single interest group source of Democratic financial support.

Labor's significance in campaign finance must be seen not only in terms of the amount of its contribution, but also in terms of its almost complete commitment to Democratic candidates. Only in 1964 did the Republican statewide effort finally receive as much as a single dollar from labor, and then only $1,000 from a faction within the Teamsters Union which was attempting to punish Robert F. Kennedy by contributing to the defeat of his Wisconsin ally, Governor John W. Reynolds. In 1966, the Republicans received a similar sum from labor. Of all labor spending at the state and congressional levels in 1964, nearly 93 per cent went to Democrats, and the percentage would have been larger had not labor contributed so generously ($13,950) to the re-election campaign of liberal Republican Alvin O'Konski in Wisconsin's Tenth Congressional District.[4] Data for 1966 show that labor gave only $4,150 (3.1 per cent) of its $133,737 in candidate contributions to Republican candidates for state and congressional office and for the 16 state senate and 32 state assembly seats for which data are available. Again Representative O'Konski received the lion's share ($2,150).

A further aspect of labor's aid to Democratic campaigns was its direct political efforts, whose costs have been estimated in Chapter 3 as starting at about $50,000 and rising to $100,000 or more in the 1960's. These expenditures paid for phone banks to get out the vote, special endorsement cards to be handed out at plant gates, a special supplement in the *Milwaukee Journal* featuring labor's endorsed candidates, salaries of certain personnel working on political projects, and voter registration.[5] In a very real sense, these expenditures were a form of contribution to the Democratic cause, although neither the money nor the activities were found within the party or candidate committee structures. Thus even the substantial amounts reported in Table 28 understate labor's contribution to the Democratic cause.

The importance of advertising receipts to both political parties during the 1964 campaign must also be briefly considered at this point. The advantages of the system of selling advertising, instead of soliciting contributions, accrued to both parties. It allowed the Republicans to obtain larger sums from an already friendly business community by permitting corporations to take tax deductions for doing what came naturally. The Democrats obtained not only the advantage of pointing out that advertising was tax deductible, but also the opportunity to approach Republican-oriented firms with the argument that their customers and stockholders undoubtedly included a large proportion of Democrats who would certainly want their party to receive some of the same consideration as the Republicans. Such an argument could not be logically directed to the personal solicitation of corporate officers and directors. Thus a substantial portion of the advertising receipts represented for the Democrats a source of income which could not otherwise be reached. It is clear that in 1966 advertising receipts dropped sharply for both parties. Indeed, that any revenue at all came from this source is due only to the hurried staging of fund-raising affairs with the usual advertising booklets before the date on which an act of Congress eliminated tax deductibility for such advertising. It seems almost certain that this action has hurt the Democrats more than the Republicans: in 1966 State Democratic Chairman, J. Louis Hanson, estimated that 30 per cent of campaign funds (as opposed to all costs of running the party) had been derived from advertising receipts and declared bluntly that "we are going to be hurt much more than the Republicans. These corporations will continue to contribute to the Republican Party through individual executives, while we can no longer call on them for advertisements."[6]

A final facet of the pattern of receipts which must be considered here is the portion of income derived from other party units. Democratic receipts from other party units have generally not been much more than 10 per cent of total income, except in 1950. In that year the party was one year old, had virtually no membership, few financial sources, and no corps of fund raisers. The New Deal-Fair Deal elements had just triumphed, both within the party structure and in the primary elections, over the more conservative elements which had held sway in the Democracy throughout the three-party era. The national administration determined to pour funds into Wisconsin in order to strengthen the hands of its allies as well as to build up the fledgling party to the momentous task of challenging Senator Joseph R. McCarthy in the 1952 election. Of the $44,088 received from party units in 1950, $43,540 was received from the national Democratic party. This continued to be the pattern, with the national party accounting for the bulk of inter-committee receipts in any year in which the Democrats obtained more than nominal income from such sources. In 1962, for instance, when these gifts constituted 10.2 per cent of total receipts, the various national party agencies contributed $20,000, while local party units gave $9,956. In 1964, the national party transferred $39,349 to the state campaign, while local units contributed $9,151; but in 1966, when no United States Senate seat was contested, Wisconsin Democrats received no aid from the national party.

The Republican transfers present a considerably different picture. Transfer payments to the state level committees constituted a substantially larger share of Republican income than of Democratic receipts; thus the state level Republicans usually counted on about 20 per cent of their money coming from other party committees, while the Democrats looked for less than 10 per cent from such sources. Furthermore, while the significant Democratic transfers originated at the national level, the major Republican transfers were received from local party organizations. The closest ratio was in 1958, when national transfers totaled $21,578 and local transfers $37,262. The more usual pattern, however, has been for the national Republican party to send $5,000 to $10,000 to aid the United States Senate candidate, with all other party organization transfers received from local units. In 1964, national Republican sources provided $5,000 of the transferred funds, contrasted to the $288,491 provided by local sources. The pattern was somewhat different in 1966 when $18,824 of $170,167 of transfers was from the national party; this sum was apparently channelled through Republican state headquarters to critical congressional races. It should be additionally noted that in most years both national parties made some subventions directly to congressional district campaigners.

It is useful to recall here that local Republican organizations have traditionally been financially stronger than their Democratic counterparts. Not only have the county and ward Republican committees waged well-financed efforts for local Republican tickets, but they have substantially supported the state ticket efforts as well. The Democratic under-structure, by comparison, seldom has had financial strength beyond the local shares of the dues (about 35 per cent) and of Jefferson-Jackson Dinner ticket sales (about 15 per cent) which were returned to the counties quarterly from state headquarters. If the financial structure of a party provides a significant clue to the distribution of internal power, then the Republican local units have wielded substantial influence within the party structure because they have been both the centers of membership affiliation and a significant force in financially supporting the campaign efforts of the center. By contrast, Democratic members have been directly affiliated with the state headquarters, and local party units raised and spent only small sums, while the state headquarters and candidate committees either raised or directed the raising of most Democratic money.[7]

The Membership Party and Political Finance

The party organizations in Wisconsin are quite different from those found in most of the American states. They more nearly resemble the mass parties of Great Britain and Western Europe than the usual state and local party machinery in all but a handful of American jurisdictions. First, both parties in Wisconsin have had some system of formal membership. The Democrats use a membership application and card to recruit and identify members. The Republicans have been less consistent in this practice—sometimes denoting all sympathizers included on extensive mailing lists as members—but in recent years the state leadership has urged local units to convert to a more formal system of membership affiliation. Second, both parties have collected dues as a part of the membership process. In 1966

Democratic dues were $2 for a single person and $3 for a man and wife; in the 1960's the Democrats adopted some additional membership fee scales, ranging from $12 to $100, for those who wished to make more substantial contributions. The Republican membership fee is not set at the state level, but is left to the discretion of local units. Several have set $5 for membership, while others seek larger sums. Third, both parties have been composed mainly of middle class people whose involvement in politics is primarily related to the advancement of political programs in which they believe rather than to patronage or favors. Finally, the parties have tended to be sharply divided along liberal-conservative lines as those terms are generally understood in the United States.[8]

The development of these mass membership parties has generally been attributed to a desire by issue-oriented activists to make the two parties responsible. This requires some control over nominations by those activists who develop platforms, campaign for candidates, and finance the political movements. The party organizations established by statute permit no such activity, and those interested in programmatic politics have thus taken refuge in the extra-legal, mass-membership party.[9] A secondary purpose has been to evade the state's strict election expenditures law, whose limitations on spending are unreasonably low. In addition, the collection of dues—especially for the Democrats—was intended to finance political activity on a mass basis.

The Wisconsin parties resemble to some extent the mass parties defined by Maurice Duverger, who argues that the political and financial base of a mass party is a large membership of individuals who subscribe to the party's ideology, enroll as members, pay dues, and work for the party's candidates and programs. Thus the mass party is theoretically dependent in every respect upon its members. The other model of party organization is the party of notables: ". . . influential persons in the first place, whose name, prestige, or connections can provide a backing for the candidate and secure him votes; experts, in the second place, who know how to handle the electors and how to organize a campaign; last of all financiers, who can bring the sinews of war."[10] These cadre parties may attempt to enroll members, but as long as the notables dominate the party's operation and its policies as well as assure its finances, there is in fact no mass party.

In the face of such theoretical formulations, the financing of Wisconsin parties raises several questions. First, has the membership system succeeded in providing the necessary money to operate the political system on a mass basis, thus reducing the influence of those individuals and interests which can afford to contribute large sums? This question has public policy implications as well as meaning for the student of parties if one accepts the view, common in America, that "[the] pattern of financial support . . . is a highly significant index of who pulls the strings within the parties, and reflects the pattern of the economic structure and pyramiding of power within that structure."[11] Second, are either of the Wisconsin parties mass parties in the most widely accepted definition of that concept?

If we examine only the dues receipts of the Wisconsin parties, it is immediately clear that neither party falls within Duverger's strict definition of mass party. Table 28 shows that the maximum level of financial support accounted for by dues money was 7.6 per cent of Democratic party revenues in 1966. In other years, dues receipts were less significant. The Republican state level committees derive no support whatsoever from dues.

The recent study of comparative party finance edited by Arnold Heidenheimer concludes that in none of the eight countries surveyed were dues payments sufficient to finance the political activities of a major party. Heidenheimer suggests that perhaps a more realistic way of "identifying parties which deserve the label of 'membership party' in terms of their sources of financial support would be to determine which ones are able to cover at least two-thirds of their normal, non-election year expenses from membership dues."[12] Even applying this criterion, the Wisconsin parties would not qualify as membership parties. The annual Democratic party operating budget in 1964 was approximately $70,000 while dues receipts were $40,584 (58 per cent). In some earlier years, dues payments may have been able to pay two-thirds of the costs of maintaining the headquarters, paying the salary of the single employee, financing the membership mailings, and meeting telephone bills. No accurate report of annual operating costs in earlier years is available, but the smaller scale of party operations was matched by substantially smaller dues receipts.

Even with his modified definition of "membership party," Heidenheimer finds that only one party in the eight countries studied falls within that category, and that party is the classic case of the membership party, Germany's Social Democratic party.[13] Most parties, he reports, are able to meet about 20 per cent of their normal non-election year expenditures from dues receipts;[14] Wisconsin's Democratic party, by comparison, comes much closer to meeting this criterion of a membership party.

The inability to raise even non-election year expenses from dues has, in most countries, been caused more by the resistance to increasing membership fees than by any decline in the number of members.[15] Wisconsin's experience was similar—year after year Democratic state conventions decisively rejected leadership recommendations that dues schedules be increased. (Finally in 1967 the delegates voted to increase dues from $2 to $4 for single memberships, and from $3 to $6 for family enrollments.) The 1964 membership dues represented less than one hour's earnings for an industrial worker. This was comparable to the level of dues in the British and Australian Labor parties. Other parties collected amounts ranging from the equivalent of two hours' pay to a full day's pay. An increase to the equivalent of two hours' wages would meet the non-election year budget of the Wisconsin Democrats, but even the equivalent of a full day's pay from each member would provide less than half the amount spent at the state level in the election year of 1964.

The determination that dues do not put party financing on a mass basis is, however, only a beginning for inquiry in Wisconsin. As Table 28 illustrates, substantial amounts have been collected by both parties in direct individual contributions. Usually these funds are solicited from party members in either the form of direct campaign pleas or of appeals to purchase tickets to fund-raising dinners and similar events. Such fund drives are directed to party members and to others who are not formally affiliated with the parties.

Although there are no complete data on the relationship between party activism and campaign contributions, there are some facts which are helpful in considering the problem of whether the membership party system has put political finance on a mass basis. The University of Wisconsin Survey Research Laboratory's 1964 post-election survey asked respondents whether they had made a campaign contribution to a party or candidate. The number of contributors was 95 in a sample of 702. Thus, 13.5 per cent of Wisconsin respondents made a contribution, as opposed to 10.6 per cent in the national survey taken by the Survey Research Center of the University of Michigan. Although the numbers become too small for certainty, it can be pointed out that in Wisconsin 62.3 per cent of those who identified themselves as party members contributed money, as opposed to 10.1 per cent of the non-party members. It is possible, of course, that these party members would contribute even if they were not enrolled, but it seems a more reasonable inference that enrollment in a party increases the likelihood both of being solicited for a contribution and of making one.

Even though the mass membership party may expand the number of givers by raising money from its membership, the largest percentage of contributors (63.2 per cent) were still not party members. One additional step can be taken to investigate the relationship of party membership and mass giving. If there is a high correlation between areas where membership is great and where there is substantial giving, one might infer that the existence of membership aids in expanding the contributor base by increasing the general fund-raising efforts of the party. Even if such a correlation were found, however, it would be merely suggestive and not conclusive. The only available data on the geographical distribution of contributors is a study of the 1964 Democratic gubernatorial campaign.[16] A broadening of these data is not possible because most filed reports of both parties and their candidates do not include the addresses of contributors.

The correlation between the amount contributed per person in the population and the party membership as a percentage of the population for Wisconsin counties was −0.0009; this suggests that the amount of money raised is not related to the number of party members in the population. The correlation between the percentage of givers in the population and the percentage of party membership in the population was +0.38. While this indicates that the number of givers, though not the amount raised, may in some way be related to the number of members, the relationship is too small to argue that a large party membership can be or that it is the major factor in fund raising in Wisconsin.

A final line of argument which ought to be investigated is whether in a mass party system, politics is to a larger degree than elsewhere financed from small contributions. If this were so, then it might be tentatively argued that the existence of a mass party tends slightly to increase the number of givers and to diminish the reliance on large gifts. This is the thrust of Maurice Duverger's argument that mass parties democratize campaign finance.[17] Even if there is a tendency to be more reliant on small gifts in a mass party system, is the magnitude of this tendency great enough to warrant a finding that financing is democratic —whether by some absolute standard such as that set by Duverger or in comparison with the financing of other parties in the same or in other jurisdictions?

To determine whether the Wisconsin parties have been financed from small contributions, it is necessary to examine the sources of individual contributions according to the number of donors and the size of donations. This has been done in Table 29, which provides a picture of the number and the size of the individual contributions received by statewide party and candidate committees from 1950 to 1964. The 1966 data are not yet refined enough to permit their inclusion in this form; certain tentative findings for 1966 are reported in a later paragraph.

An examination of this table quickly reveals that the two parties relied upon different patterns of financial support. The Democrats consistently received a much larger proportion of their funds from donors of less than $100 than did the Republi-

Table 29

Number, Aggregate Dollar Amount, and Percentage of Total Amount
of Individual Contributions[a] According
to Size of Contribution, 1950–1964[b]

	$0–99.99[c]	$100–499	$500 or over	Totals
DEMOCRATS				
1950				
No. of donors	624	8	3	635
Dollar amounts	6,485	1,500	3,100	11,085
Percentage of total	58.5	13.5	28.0	100.0
1954				
No. of donors	1,895	108	12	2,015
Dollar amounts	27,341	15,067	29,433	71,841
Percentage of total	38.1	21.0	41.0	100.1[d]
1956				
No. of donors	3,819	108	4	3,931
Dollar amounts	33,278	15,880	5,338	54,496
Percentage of total	61.1	29.1	9.8	100.0
1958				
No. of donors	9,359	142	21	9,522
Dollar amounts	55,322	20,718	20,695	96,735
Percentage of total	57.2	21.4	21.4	100.0
1962				
No. of donors	22,979	1,020	86	24,085
Dollar amounts	103,993	131,521	72,995	308,509
Percentage of total	33.7	42.6	23.7	100.0
1964				
No. of donors	10,596	889	45	11,530
Dollar amounts	95,131	125,780	31,115	252,026
Percentage of total	37.7	49.9	12.3	99.9[d]
REPUBLICANS				
1950				
No. of donors	2,590	405	129	3,124
Dollar amounts	89,602	75,790	85,730	251,122
Percentage of total	35.7	30.2	34.1	100.0
1954				
No. of donors	624	1,306	73	2,003
Dollar amounts	19,541	184,708	51,130	255,379
Percentage of total	7.7	72.3	20.0	100.0
1956				
No. of donors	2,281	1,327	149	3,757
Dollar amounts	65,316	205,877	131,242	402,435
Percentage of total	16.2	51.2	32.6	100.0

Table 29 (*Continued*)

	*$0-99.99*ᵃ	*$100-499*	*$500 or over*	*Totals*
1958				
No. of donors	2,737	796	52	3,585
Dollar amounts	71,210	110,761	37,228	219,199
Percentage of total	32.5	50.5	17.0	100.0
1962				
No. of donors	3,520	1,552	176	5,248
Dollar amounts	50,128	229,481	146,690	426,299
Percentage of total	11.8	53.8	34.4	100.0
1964				
No. of donors	16,132	1,699	224	18,055
Dollar amounts	113,557	263,045	199,881	576,483
Percentage of total	19.7	45.6	34.7	100.0

ᵃ Each contributor to each statewide political committee was noted on a card; all multiple contributions by an individual were aggregated. The number of givers for each committee, and the amounts of their contributions were then grouped by size.

ᵇ 1952 and 1966 omitted (see p. 40).

ᶜ Wisconsin *Statutes*, secs. 12.09 (3) (a) and (5) (b) provide that the names of contributors of under $5 need not be listed individually. These figures are in part estimates based on a formula of an average small contribution of $1.67 divided into the lump sums reported as the total amounts received in contributions of under $5. The $1.67 average was derived from a sample of 200 small contributions which were individually listed, despite the provision of the statutes that such listings are not necessary.

ᵈ The result of rounding of figures.

cans. The Republican party, in turn, received a much larger percentage of its money in gifts of $100 to $499. Gifts of $500 or more were generally of more significance to Republicans than to Democrats, but the difference was not so great as at the other two levels and not so substantial as one might guess when considering the ideological postures of the two parties. To illustrate the differences more simply, the ratio of the Democratic percentage of income to the Republican percentage in each of the three categories was computed for the six elections under study. These ratios, set forth in Table 30, suggest the relatively greater reliance upon small gifts by the Democrats and upon larger gifts by the Republicans. A ratio of 1.0 means that the Democrats received the same percentage of their funds from

Table 30

Ratio of Percentage of Democratic Income to Republican Income
According to Size of Contribution, 1950–1964[a]

Size Category	1950	1954	1956	1958	1962	1964
$ 0– 99	1.65	5.00	3.74	1.76	2.88	1.93
100–499	0.45	0.29	0.57	0.42	0.79	1.09
500 or more	0.82	2.05	0.31	1.26	0.73	0.36

[a] 1952 and 1960 omitted (see p. 40).

gifts in a size category as the Republicans. Thus a ratio of 2.0 indicates that the Democrats collected twice as large a percentage of their funds in that category as did the Republicans, while 0.5 demonstrates that Democrats received half as large a percentage of funds in a category as did the Republicans.

The ability of the Republicans to finance their efforts from larger gifts than those available to the Democrats is probably related in part to the party's ideology. Conservative on spending, taxes, government regulation of the economy, and social welfare programs, the Republicans have a natural base of financial support among higher socio-economic groups, particularly those related to financial institutions and industrial enterprises, who can afford to make substantial contributions to sustain the political efforts of a party advancing their ideology. The relative sharpness of the cleavage between the two parties in Wisconsin and the explicitness of the Republican party's conservatism have made it easier for the Republicans to command the allegiance and the money of those capable of making substantial political contributions.

The flow of larger contributions to the Republicans cannot, however, be explained solely by the greater financial capacity of the Republican constituency. The long duration of Republican incumbency and the expectation that this incumbency would continue were probably factors in the Republican ability to command substantial donations during the 1950's. Those who were moved by other than programmatic concerns and wanted, therefore, to have access to government would certainly have found it sensible to contribute to the Republican cause during the first four elections studied here. Finally, recognition of the superior Republican fund-raising machinery gives a further clue to the Republican ability to raise money in larger sums. Not only has the Republican fund-raising machinery been better organized than that of the Democrats, especially after Daniel Parker of the Parker Pen Company assumed its leadership in 1958, but it has had available a more effective corps of fund raisers. Virtually all studies of the subject demonstrate that men who control substantial resources in other realms are effective at raising money in politics. The Republican party has been consistently able to field a large group of well-connected business and professional men to raise money from others in similarly advantaged economic positions who cannot easily refuse to heed the request of their peers or of those of superior rank in the business and professional world. The quality of the Republican fund raisers is, again, at least partly a function of that party's socio-economic constituency and its ideology. Thus, a variety of factors explain the capacity of the Republicans to raise significantly more money in large contributions than has been available to their Democratic competitors, but the ideological position of the party and its consequent constituency are a significant causal factor.

The 1954 pattern of Democratic receipts draws attention because of the sharp decline in reliance upon small gifts and the heavy percentage of funds received in gifts of $500 and over. A close examination of the contributions for that year shows that William Proxmire, the Democratic candidate for governor, his sister (Adele Baker), his father (Theodore Proxmire), and his business partner accounted for a total of $20,783 of the $26,663 in gifts of $500 or more. If these sums are eliminated from the 1954 tally, the Democratic pattern closely resembles that of the other Democratic campaigns in the 1950's. The small gift category would account for 53.5 per cent; the medium size gifts for 29.5 per cent; and the large contributions for 17 per cent of the total. The overall pattern of party support did not, therefore, change significantly in 1954.

The 1954 analysis is a useful lesson that in the area of

campaign finance the conduct of individuals may significantly affect categorization of and generalization about political phenomena. Herbert E. Alexander reports a similar instance where the shift in contributions by a single individual, Ben W. Heineman of the Chicago and Northwestern Railroad, created the appearance that members of the American Association of Railroads had, when their contributions were considered together, moved significantly from the Republican financial column in 1960 to the Democratic column in 1964.[18] The ability of a single family to shape the financing pattern of a campaign was described by Hugh Douglas Price in his study of the 1952 senatorial election in Massachusetts. By contributing more than $85,000 to the campaign, John F. Kennedy and members of his family laid the foundation for a senate campaign financed almost entirely ($324,700 of $344,660) by gifts of more than $500.[19] At a time when the systematic development of testable generalizations has become the major effort of political scientists, the campaign finance area remains one in which the impact of individual political actors may substantially hinder the ability to develop such hypotheses and may weaken the usefulness of some generalizations that appear supported by previously collected data.

A second aspect of the Democratic receipt pattern which merits attention is the tendency in 1962 and 1964 for small contributions to become less important and for the Democratic financing picture to develop a resemblance to the Republican scheme. This may be a random turn of events. On the other hand, it may be attributable to the development of certain of the same factors which permitted the Republicans to raise money in larger sums. The Democrats became more adept at raising money and developed a corps of business and professional men who, while neither so large in number nor so prominent in status as their Republican counterparts, were able to bring more success to Democratic fund-raising appeals. Furthermore, in 1962 and 1964 the Democrats were in command of the governor's office and had significant contacts with the national administration, and those seeking access rather than ideology may have found it expedient to aid the Democrats as well as or instead of the Republicans. Perhaps this condition will now become more or less permanent, for the Democrats must be considered potential winners by such interests in every election.

One further factor in the change in Democratic financing would seem to be the increase in price at the annual Jefferson-Jackson Dinner from $25 per person to $100 per person in 1962. Despite bitter criticism within the party, the then Democratic State Chairman, Patrick J. Lucey, made this change with the tacit consent of the party's major office-holders because of the need substantially to increase the sources of funds to meet spiraling costs. President John F. Kennedy spoke at the first $100-a-plate dinner, helping to assure its success, and then Vice President Lyndon Johnson spoke at the second. To mollify some of the criticism that the higher price excluded many working Democrats from participating, a $100-a-year pledge plan was created to allow Democrats to obtain a membership and a Jefferson-Jackson Dinner ticket on the installment plan. Generally the increased ticket price increased the revenue of the party, although some former contributors were not able or willing to respond to the new price. This device was, in effect, a form of increase in the assessment paid by those activists who felt committed for a variety of reasons to attend the major Democratic fund-raising event of the year. The $100 price also made it easier to obtain larger sums from non-party interests desiring to earn good will through their contributions.

Although not completely cross-checked for multiple gifts by contributors whose names appear somewhat differently in two or more reports, the 1966 contributor data reveal roughly the same pattern found in the prior elections. Of $468,719 in individual contributions by 12,245 givers to Republican state-wide committees, $84,400 or 18 per cent was in gifts over $500, $244,075 or 52.1 per cent in medium size gifts, and $140,244 or 29.9 per cent in sums under $100. The decline in the importance of large gifts is probably a result both of undiscovered multiple gifts by the same individuals and by the vigorous efforts of Ody J. Fish, Republican State Chairman in that year, to develop a larger base of contributors of medium size gifts. The Democrats show the same tendency. Their total reported individual gifts were $218,951 from 9,734 contributors. Large gifts accounted for $21,700 or 9.9 per cent of the total, while medium size gifts constituted $72,485 or 33.1 per cent and small gifts $129,766 or 57 per cent. Again, the multiple giver phenomenon probably results in an exaggeration of the importance of small gifts. However, these preliminary 1966 figures look surprisingly like those for the years in the mid-1950's, before Democratic incumbency. It might be concluded, therefore, that in 1966, both parties were somewhat less reliant on large gifts than in prior years, but somewhat more dependent on them than the figures reported here suggest.

While the two parties in Wisconsin appear to draw their financial support in different sized donations, the receipt patterns of both parties differ substantially from the size-of-contribution pattern in other states. Alexander Heard concluded on the basis of projections computed from several hundred state level campaign committees that in 1952 between 33 and 50 per cent of state political funds were received in gifts of $500 or more and between 25 and 33 per cent from gifts of $100 to $499.[20] This would leave 12 to 45 per cent to be raised in small sums.

A Connecticut study showed that the state party committees generally followed this pattern, although the Democrats tended to receive substantially more than 50 per cent of their funds from the largest givers. In that state, however, a computation of other committees brought total Democratic reliance on large gifts to less than one-third.[21] In Massachusetts, the Democratic state committee received more than 75 per cent of its money in large gifts, while the Republicans obtained only about 20 per cent of their funds from such sources. When the reports of all committees supporting major office candidates of both parties were examined, however, it was revealed that 1,384 individuals gave more than $1.3 million in gifts of over $500, accounting for slightly more than 35 per cent of all receipts reported.[22]

Wisconsin parties and candidate committees apparently raise much less of their money from large contributions than do similar organizations in other states. Table 31 sets forth the mean and the median of the percentage of income derived from gifts in each of the size-of-contribution categories for six elections. (The separate percentages for each election can be found in Table 29.) The Democrats have received much less than one-third of their funds from large gifts, while the Republicans stand at the bottom of Heard's range of one-third to one-half accounted for in other states by such contributions. Democrats stand in the lower part of the one-fourth to one-third range, which is the nationwide proportion of income received from gifts of $100 to $499, while the Republicans far exceeded the top level of that range in gifts of that size. From small contributions the Democrats have received a much larger share of their

Table 31

Mean and Median of Percentages of Receipts Derived by the Democratic and Republican Parties from Gifts of Various Sizes, 1950–1964[a]

Size Category	Democrats		Republicans	
	Mean	*Median*	*Mean*	*Median*
$ 0– 99	47.7	48.8	20.6	17.9
100–499	29.6	25.2	50.6	50.9
500 or more	22.7	22.5	28.8	33.3

[a] 1952 and 1960 omitted (see p. 40).

funds than is common in the rest of the nation, while the Republicans stand at the lower end of the nationwide range of party income generally received in small sums. The 1966 figures have not been included in this analysis because of their incompleteness; however, their inclusion would skew both distributions toward the small contribution category, thus increasing the disparity between the Wisconsin pattern and that found in other states. Generally, then, Wisconsin's lower expenditure level reported in Chapter 3 was matched by a lesser degree of reliance upon large gifts when compared to other states.

In the late 1950's and early 1960's, the use of advertising books to raise money became significant at the state as well as the national level. This practice was first used in Wisconsin in

1962. There are no available studies showing the size-of-contribution pattern created by this device in other states, but inasmuch as 27.2 per cent of Democratic receipts and 16.7 per cent of Republican income in Wisconsin came from this source in 1964, the impact of these receipts should be examined. It becomes immediately clear that the overwhelming portion of advertising book receipts was in amounts over $500, thus greatly increasing the reliance of both parties on large contributions. All of the Republican advertising books for 1964 were available to this study as were four of the five Democratic books, accounting for $137,945 of the $191,441 which Demo-

Table 32

Receipts from Advertising According to Size of Contribution:
Democrats and Republicans, 1964

Size Category	Democrats		Republicans	
	Amount	%	Amount	%
$ 0– 99	$ 4,515	3.3	$ none	none
100–499	30,880	22.4	29,500	16.4
500 or more	102,550	74.3	150,250	83.6
Totals	*$137,945*	*100.0*	*$179,750*	*100.0*

crats received from advertising. When an advertiser purchased space in more than one book, his contributions were aggregated and reported as one sum. Full-page advertisements were calculated at $1,000 apiece, with smaller advertisements figured at proportionately smaller amounts.[23] Table 32 shows the size-of-contribution pattern for receipts from advertising books for both parties in 1964.

The implications of the advertising book receipts may be better understood when the $102,550 in large purchases in Democratic books are shown to have been made by only 89 enterprises and the $150,250 in large purchases in Republican books to have been made by only 128 companies. The role of large givers in both parties was greatly strengthened by the advent of the advertising book device, especially since many of the buyers of large advertisements were businesses whose executives were also substantial givers. Thus certain large individual givers, particularly within the Republican party, greatly strengthened their positions in the financial constituencies in the political system by adding contributions from corporate enterprises to their already significant personal donations, a point which will be raised again later.

The amounts received from labor by the Democrats and from party units by the state level committees of both parties are not readily susceptible to definition in terms of size of contribution. Union political funds appear to have been drawn from a variety of sources, including an assessment of one cent per member on unions voluntarily affiliated with the Wisconsin Committee on Political Education, fund-raising events whose $10 tickets were purchased by both individuals and local unions, transfers by national COPE based on the need in key state and local races, and contributions drawn directly from union dues money.[24] It is therefore difficult meaningfully to categorize labor's contributions in terms of their size; and labor's participation in Democratic financing is more akin to the affiliation fees paid by unions achieving indirect membership in the labor or socialist parties of other countries than the direct contributions of individuals which were discussed in earlier paragraphs of this section.

The labor movement continues to assert its independence of either party and, to demonstrate this non-partisanship, labor's political efforts are occasionally directed to the support of a Republican candidate. However, the figures show clearly that the Republican candidates for governor and senator as well as the Republican state party organization have received a total of only $2,000 of labor money in the seven elections under study. Even at the congressional and legislative district levels, labor gives only token sums to a few Republican candidates. Furthermore, there is room to doubt whether labor has any meaningful choice, except in the case of a few programmatically aberrant Republican candidates, in the face of the quite distinct liberal-conservative cleavage between the two parties in Wisconsin.

The non-partisanship of the labor movement is thus largely

illusory, in both financial contributions and organizational activities. While labor does not become a formal participant in party affairs through its contributions, it nonetheless achieves an important informal voice because of the interaction between labor leaders and party leaders at all levels of Wisconsin Democratic politics. Labor's financial efforts should be seen, therefore, as a kind of affiliation payment to the Democratic coalition, yielding a substantial voice in the affairs of that party.

When the foregoing analyses of the major sources of political receipts are brought together, we have some basis for determining whether Wisconsin's mass party system has resulted in the financing of politics primarily from small contributions. Table 33 divides the funds received by the state level party committees

Table 33

Total State Level Receipts (Expressed in Percentages) According to Size of Contribution or Other Designation of Source: Democrats and Republicans, 1950–1966[a]

Source	1950	1954	1956	1958	1962	1964	1966
			DEMOCRATS				
$ 0– 99	11.5	29.6	58.1	40.0	26.3	20.0	40.1
100–499	2.6	10.7	16.7	9.9	23.9	22.3	18.9
500 or more	2.6	21.0	5.7	9.9	13.3	18.6	5.6
Labor	27.3	36.2	7.4	21.6	17.2	18.2	10.3
Party units	50.8	0.9	1.1	10.4	5.4	6.9	1.7
Other	5.2	1.6	11.0	8.2	13.9	14.0	23.5
Totals	*100.0*	*100.0*	*100.0*	*100.0*	*100.0*	*100.0*	*100.1*[b]
			REPUBLICANS				
$ 0– 99	33.8	8.7	15.6	24.9	10.4	11.8	20.2
100–499	27.1	57.0	43.6	38.8	38.5	27.3	35.2
500 or more	30.7	15.8	27.9	13.0	24.6	32.6	12.2
Party units	8.4	18.5	12.7	20.6	20.6	27.4	24.6
Other	—	—	0.3	2.6	5.8	0.8	7.7
Totals	*100.0*	*100.0*	*100.1*[b]	*99.9*[b]	*99.9*[b]	*99.9*[b]	*99.9*[b]

[a] 1952 and 1960 omitted (see p. 40).
[b] The result of rounding of figures.

and the major statewide candidates into small, medium size, or large gifts. A few fund sources, especially labor and party unit transfers, could not be categorized in this way and they are reported separately.

Even the combining of all small contributions regardless of source (dues, sales, direct gifts, advertising, etc.) does not give a definitive answer to the question of whether the Wisconsin parties are financed on a mass basis. It is clear that at no time during the period did the Republicans receive a preponderance of their funds from small contributions; this would be true even if it were assumed that all local party funds were raised in sums of less than $100, and this assumption is demonstrably untrue. Nevertheless, it is almost certainly true that the Wisconsin Republican party has drawn more of its funds from small and medium size contributions than have its sister organizations across the country. Thus the membership party system has not resulted in mass financing of the Republican party according to any absolute measure, but it has caused the party to be more nearly financed on this basis when the measure is one of comparison with other state political systems.

The Democratic financing picture is even less easily interpreted. If labor contributions and local party sources are regarded as small contributions, then the Democrats have derived more than 50 per cent of their funds from small contributions in 5 of the 7 years under study—the exceptions being 1950, the year after the party's creation, and 1964, after it had enjoyed 6 years of gubernatorial incumbency. If these sources are not considered small contributions, the Democratic party derived more money from small contributions than from other sources only in 1956, when the Catlin Act effectively banned labor contributions to the Democratic cause. It is probably fair to conclude that labor's contributions represent a mass financial base, whose resources are directed by a small group of labor leaders acting in behalf of the mass of members. This should perhaps be viewed as "indirect mass financing." The Democratic cause in Wisconsin has, by this definition, achieved mass financing to the extent of receiving more than half its income from small contributions; and it has undoubtedly been closer to the mass financing model than Democratic parties in most other American states, and perhaps in all of them.

The membership party system, when the affiliation of individuals to the party organization is seriously sought, can be viewed on the basis of the Wisconsin experience as working some alterations in the pattern of political finance in the United States. First, it may provide a mass basis for the most significant portion of the finances of the liberal party in the system, at least until that party has achieved the status of incumbency, at which point it may gain new sources from interests seeking access who contribute in large sums. Second, the conservative party draws more heavily on large contributions than on small gifts despite its attempt to move to a membership system. Third, both parties are more extensively financed from small and medium size contributions than the general run of their counterparts in other states where the membership party system does not exist.

The Programmatic Party and Political Finance

Having concluded that neither party has been primarily financed by the dues of the political activists who shape the programmatic platforms, it becomes important to assess the ideological orientations of the financial constituencies of the two parties. Financial contributors could strengthen the cleavages between the two parties if conservative givers directed their gifts to the Republicans and liberal donors theirs to the Democrats. Alternatively, the programmatic orientations of the parties could be blurred if contributors gave to both parties in hopes of gaining a hearing on specific issues.

Epstein has suggested that campaign cash for each party comes mainly from those who are its natural ideological allies: "[the] major source of Republican funds has been a few hundred corporation executives, and the Democrats . . . collected substantial sums from unions."[25] Other students of the Wisconsin party system have noted the domination of the Republican organization by conservative business and professional leaders, although not explicitly pointing out that these people also provide a conservative financial constituency of substantial means.

Studies of national campaign finance have shown that sources of campaign money for the two parties tend to be sharply different. "Campaign donors, at least, seem to think the parties stand for something."[26] Thus, after the national Democratic party became a liberal political vehicle during the New Deal, contributions from manufacturing and financial interests dropped off sharply. Every presidential election since then for which data are available, perhaps excepting 1964 when the Goldwater candidacy was apparently viewed with alarm by part of the business community, has followed the pattern of over-whelming contributions by business and financial interests to the Republicans.[27] Labor, on the other hand, has been consistent in its financial support of Democrats at the national level. In addition, the liquor industry (brewers and distillers), contractors, and owners of mass media have tended to give more to the national Democratic cause than to the Republicans, although both parties get some funds from these sources.[28]

The policy cleavages between the two parties in Wisconsin are a good deal sharper than at the national level. It would seem likely, therefore, that the sources of financial support in Wisconsin would be at least as clearly divided as at the presidential level. Such a cleavage of the sources of political money along policy lines would strengthen the programmatic nature of a party system whose candidates and activists also tend to be highly issue oriented. In this atypically ideological political system, manufacturing and financial interests should be over-whelmingly committed to the Republican cause, while labor should be strongly Democratic. Such non-ideological interests as contractors and brewers might be found giving to both parties.

There is no difficulty in contrasting labor's contributions to the two parties. As previously mentioned, union money was a significant part of the Democratic state level financial constituency in every election under study, while the Republicans received no labor money in five elections and only token gifts in two others. At other levels as well, the labor movement has been steadfastly committed to the Democrats, financially and organizationally. Inasmuch as the subsequent analysis of contributions from business to the two parties will focus on 1954 and 1964, it is appropriate to cite labor's political contributions in those years in some detail. The Republican statewide effort received no contributions from labor in 1954 and $1,000 (0.1 per cent) a decade later for the Knowles in '64 Committee. The Democratic statewide effort received $50,901, 36.2 per cent of its funds, from labor in 1954, and $127,617, 18.2 per cent, in 1964.[29] The amount of labor's contributions to specific Democratic candidates was even more impressive. The committees supporting William Proxmire for governor in 1954 reported aggregate labor contributions of $43,081, or 55 per cent of total receipts. In 1964, labor donations accounted for $32,492, or 15.7 per cent of the total campaign effort for Democratic Governor John Reynolds, and $47,475, or 23.5 per cent of Senator William Proxmire's campaign fund.

To discover the financial role in politics of Wisconsin's business and financial interests, a file of officers and directors of the 42 domestic business corporations with more than 1,000 employees (excluding 3 breweries which had this number of workers) was prepared. This group consisted of 41 manufacturing firms and 1 major insurance company. Similar information was compiled about the 11 largest banks, measured by assets, and the 8 largest utilities, measured by rate base. The contributions of these business and financial leaders and members of their families, where identifiable, were then tallied for 1954 and 1964.[30] In addition, the advertising purchased by these concerns in 1964 was calculated. Table 34 indicates the degree of support received from the business community by the two parties in Wisconsin. As expected, the Democrats received almost no financial assistance from these concerns, while the Republicans were regularly and substantially aided by them.

The figures in Table 34 provide only gross figures. A total of the contributions of the officers and directors of each company was computed. However, in the business and financial community, one individual frequently serves as an officer or director of more than one company. The contributions of such persons

Table 34

Financial Support to Statewide Party, Gubernatorial, and Senatorial Committees b
Officers and Directors of Major Business Corporations, Banks and Utilities,
1954 and 1964

	Corporations				Banks				Utilities	
	Individuals		Advertising		Individuals		Advertising		Individual	
	No.	Amount	No.	Amount	No.	Amount	No.	Amount	No.	Amou
DEMOCRATS										
1954										
Gubernatorial campaign (Proxmire)	—	$ —	—	$ —	—	$ —	—	$ —	—	$ —
Democratic party	11	801	—	—	5	301	—	—	—	—
1964										
Gubernatorial campaign (Reynolds)	5	855	2	2,750	5	195	—	—	1	20
Senatorial campaign (Proxmire)	3	550	5	3,550	4	850	—	—	—	—
Democratic Party	4	635	5	4,625	2	400	1	125	—	—
REPUBLICANS										
1954										
Gubernatorial campaign (Kohler)ᵃ	—	$ —	—	$ —	—	$ —	—	$ —	—	$ —
Republican party	39	58,360	—	—	10	22,665	—	—	8	9,3
1964										
Gubernatorial campaign (Knowles)	29	9,864	17	10,250	6	1,775	—	—	6	1,79
Senatorial campaign (Renk)	23	6,588	—	—	8	3,960	—	—	5	1,80
Republican party	41	119,090	40	40,450	8	27,400	2	2,000	8	15,03

ᵃ No committees formed in Walter Kohler's behalf. All spending in furtherance of h
candidacy was by the Republican Party of Wisconsin.

showed up several times in computing the gross totals. When
multiple contributions were eliminated, the net contribution
from the officers and directors of these 61 business and financial
enterprises in 1954 was $1,164 to the Democrats and $60,604
to the Republicans. In 1964, advertising revenues plus the

contributions to the Democrats totaled $14,200, and the net Republican receipts were $179,591.

The increase in contributions to the Democrats over the ten-year period is somewhat misleading. Of the 1964 Democratic total, $7,650 came from a single source, Patrick Cudahy, Inc., a Milwaukee meat packing and processing firm. That firm had come under the management of Richard Cudahy, one of the young members of the family, in 1961. A Yale-trained lawyer, he is by personal preference a liberal and has been a Democratic activist. In 1967, he became chairman of the Democratic Party of Wisconsin. Cudahy made personal contributions of $400, and the company purchased $7,250 in advertising. No other officer or director of the corporation contributed. Thus in 1964, as an established incumbent party controlling the governorship and both United States Senate seats, the Democrats were able to draw from the business and financial community less than $7,000, aside from the contributions of one liberal activist who had risen to the presidency of a family-owned corporation.

The extent of financial support for the Republican party by the business community is not fully described by the figures recited here. A great many persons associated with smaller manufacturing and financial institutions were substantial contributors. Furthermore, some contributions from those associated with the large concerns went to local Republican committees and therefore were reported on the state party's financial statement as transfers from other committees rather than as contributions by individuals. The Brown County Republican party's financial statement in 1964, for instance, shows that of $14,400 in receipts, at least $3,000 was contributed by those associated with the Fort Howard Paper company, one of the 61 major concerns employing more than 1,000 workers. The Racine County Republican party showed income of $41,681, of which $14,770 came from officers and directors of S. C. Johnson and Sons, Inc., and Western Printing and Lithographing Co., both of them among Wisconsin's top employers. In both county reports, officers and directors of smaller industries and banks were listed as prominent contributors. The state level report of contributions from the business and financial community is just the top of a pyramid of Republican financial support based in 72 county political organizations, only a few of which file adequate financial statements and then only in their local courthouses. In 1964, a total of $213,491 was transferred to the state level by such local committees, who accounted for 27.4 per cent of total state level receipts.

It should be noted that, while labor unions make important indirect contributions to the Democratic cause, the phenomenon described here of local business support for the Republican county units probably does not have an exact parallel in Democratic political financing. Local labor units may assist legislative candidates and congressional campaigners. However, these unions do not make very numerous or very large contributions to Democratic county and ward organizations because of their traditional non-partisan posture and because of the centralized direction of labor money by state, regional and international labor union leaders, and by state COPE officers.

In 1964, the three Wisconsin breweries that employ more than 1,000 people divided their political contributions about evenly between the two parties, in contrast to the national pattern in which the Democrats generally receive a larger share of such contributions. Wisconsin Democrats received $12,000, all of it in advertising, and the Republicans received $14,202, $10,000 in advertising and $4,202 from individuals associated with the breweries and not holding offices or directorships in any of the 61 companies previously surveyed.

The pattern of brewery contributions to the two parties differed somewhat. The Democrats received more generous assistance from the Pabst-Blatz combine, headed by James C. Windham, a Democrat, who also served as Wisconsin chairman of the President's Club. The Republicans were favored by the Schlitz Brewing Company, whose management is dominated by the Uihlein family which is closely associated with certain banking and manufacturing interests within the state. All major breweries, however, contributed substantially to both parties and their contributions are typical of the conduct of non-ideological interests which are concerned with immediate legislative matters affecting their industry. In this case, the breweries have been fighting an increase in the beer tax from $1 per barrel, set in 1933, to $2 a barrel. Approximately $3 million a year in corporate taxes is involved, after certain exemptions from the proposed tax are made. The other matter of long-term political interest to the breweries is the continual effort of church groups and temperance organizations, as well as some highway safety groups, to eliminate Wisconsin's local option beer law which permits communities to license beer taverns to serve persons of 18 years of age, as contrasted to the hard liquor law which sets a flat minimum of 21 years of age. As of this writing, a bipartisan coalition in the legislature has balked every attempt to enact either measure.

The preceding discussion of business and labor contributions to the Wisconsin parties and candidates has dealt with business as an entity and labor as an entity. It is clear that such a description oversimplifies the nature of these interests. The labor movement consists of many subgroups, each with its own leadership and internal power structure. Nonetheless, there is a clear basis for considering labor's activities in campaign finance as unified. Almost all politically active unions, except the Teamsters, are affiliated with Wisconsin COPE, whose director is also the vice president of the successfully merged labor movement. Thus a single official co-ordinates most labor political activities. No assistance of any kind is available to a candidate unless he is endorsed by the appropriate COPE committee; this clearly channels the efforts of all unions.

Money contributed directly to candidates or to political committees by unions is generally cleared with the COPE director and sometimes even inspired by him. The most active regional and international union officers are those of the industrial unions and the Machinists Union, and the directors of these unions, whose offices are located in Milwaukee, are in constant touch during political campaigns. Contributions from local union treasuries have generally been prompted either by the regional or international offices. There is, therefore, great unity in labor's political efforts, including its cash contributions, and labor as an entity should consequently be seen as a significant force in the continuing liberal orientation of the Democratic party.

It is not so easy to establish that the business and financial concerns considered in this section are also an entity whose political efforts and contributions should be considered in the aggregate in assessing their impact upon the Republican party. It can be established, however, that there is a high rate of interaction among the officers and directors of the largest firms. Seventy-one persons held 175 of the corporate posts of these 61 enterprises in 1964; 49 men participated in the affairs of 2 firms, 16 in the affairs of 3, and 6 in the affairs of 4 or more.

All of the complicated corporate interactions cannot be described, but an examination of the roster of officers and directors of 5 major banks, the state's largest insurance company, and the Wisconsin Telephone Company shows a confluence of influence in those institutions, with officers or directors of 39 of the remaining 54 companies holding corporate posts in these 7 institutions in 1964. Nor did these 7 represent separate power centers within the business community; officers or directors of the other 6 sat jointly on the board of directors of the seventh, Employers Mutual Insurance Company. Officers or directors of 5 sat jointly on the board of the Wisconsin Telephone Company. There were, in addition, a great many interactions which tied the companies together but did not involve the 7 central institutions. Thus, for example, officers and directors of 6 industrial firms were counted among the hierarchy of the Louis Allis Company. While the business and financial community has no identifiable internal structure to co-ordinate political activities, it apparently had a high rate of interaction between powerholders in the various companies and these men jointly represented a force within the Republican coalition which re-enforced the conservative, pro-business orientation of the entire party.

It is somewhat difficult to describe the exact combination of expectations about political results which have been held by business and labor. The business community has generally been conservative in a general sense, believing in limited governmental interference in the economy, governmental spending in balance with available revenues, and a tax structure which de-emphasizes progressive income taxes and corporation levies. These general beliefs have, of course, been translated into specific policy demands when governmental decisions on these subjects are made. However, there appear to be only a few of the kinds of specific demands which favor a particular industry in a particular circumstance, such as the use of state authority to deal with a strike or to rescind an anti-trust action initiated under existing laws. That is, the political approach of the business community has been to support legislation which advances general conservative principles, rather than to seek governmental actions which yield short-term profit advantages to particular enterprises.

Labor has shown a similar tendency to be more interested in programs which are related to general principles than in decisions which are of an immediate, short-term nature. Labor's outlook has generally been liberal in advocating progressive tax policies, broadening of governmental regulation of the economy, and expansion of governmental responsibility in meeting social and economic problems. Again, there are instances where labor leaders seek specific governmental action to deal with particular situations in such a way as immediately to benefit a union, but these instances must be regarded as the exception in labor's political efforts.

It appears, then, that the financial constituency of each party has to a substantial degree coincided with the programmatic nature of that party. The advent of Democratic incumbency did not alter the firm commitment of business and financial interests to the Republican cause, just as the long years of Republican triumph did not weaken labor's participation in the Democratic coalition. While business was providing 17 per cent of Republican money in 1954 and 18 per cent in 1964, it accounted for well under 1 per cent of Democratic funds in both years. Labor gave nothing to the Republicans in 1954 and made a contribution totaling only 0.1 per cent of the Republican treasury in 1964.

Thus, the major conservative economic interests in the com-

munity have reserved virtually all of their support for the conservative political party and then rewarded that party for its
conservatism with financial aid constituting a very significant
portion of all its resources. The major liberal economic interest
in the state has followed a comparable course. Political parties
composed primarily of issue-oriented activists with clearly distinct programmatic viewpoints have received substantial financial support from separate economic interests with similarly
distinct issue orientations. The failure of the issue-oriented mass
memberships to provide an adequate financial base for Wisconsin's programmatic parties did not prevent the financing of these
parties on a basis consistent with their clear and distinct ideological postures.

The Programmatic Party and the Large Contributor

The study of the large contributor has become a standard
form of analysis in the campaign finance area. It is valuable
here, as in other studies, because of the significance of the large
contributor in the financial constituencies of parties and politicians.

Political activity of every kind is a form of multiple voting,
that is, a method of achieving influence in the political system
beyond the single ballot to which an individual is entitled by
law. Campaign contributions are a form of political activity, and
a form of multiple voting on a substantial scale.[31] It therefore
becomes important to identify the large contributors to gain
some insight into who possesses this kind of significant influence
within the financial constituency. (There may, of course, also be
multiple voters of significance in other constituencies of the
candidate or party.)

The large contributor has noteworthy advantages in exercis-
ing his influence within the political system. He is generally
solicited for funds by someone close to the candidate or the
officeholder in whose behalf the funds are raised, and he is thus
recognized at the center of power as having given vital assistance. A group of small contributors, on the other hand, even
though they may give in the aggregate the same amount, are

likely to be solicited by lesser persons who are farther from those who hold ultimate decision-making authority. Furthermore, the single individual who makes a large contribution speaks his views with a single voice, whereas the many small contributors, whose aggregate gift is as large, often express conflicting viewpoints.

The large contributor also has influence of a much more subtle nature. Those charged with raising money for politics are constantly on the alert to maintain old sources of funds and to develop new ones. The fund raisers are likely constantly to remind those in whose behalf they labor of the interests of the large contributors. No bludgeon is wielded, but the reminder that certain policy decisions will adversely affect those who have given generous financial support may be cause for reassessment by officeholders and their advisors. The decision may be made to proceed with a given program anyway, but the large contributor has had his interests given additional consideration because of the multiple votes he cast by writing his check.

Of course, it is an oversimplification to see the large contributor as purchasing favors from government. Contributor motivations undoubtedly cover a wide range, and frequently a single giver is moved by a complex of motives. He may be attracted by the personal charisma of the candidate; he may be an old friend; he may approve of the candidate's ideology or program; he may glory in the friendship of the famous; he may seek social recognition by an invitation to the governor's mansion; or he may have almost no interest in politics except that a friend or colleague whom he cannot turn down solicits him for contributions. Nonetheless, the large contributor who has known policy preferences or other objectives has both direct and indirect access at the seat of power.

In addition to the multiple voting implications of large contributions, the study of large contributors has been used to test the polarization of the political parties. White and Owens have argued that in Michigan, with its highly ideological parties, the difference between the parties is more pronounced than in most states and that the economic interests in that state tend to divide sharply between the two parties as a result.[32] This type of analysis resembles the examination of the relationship of labor to the Democratic party and business and financial enterprises to the Republican party in the preceding section. In fact, the large contributor analysis is in part a retest of these findings which shows, perhaps even more fully, the divergent financial constituencies of the two parties and the relationship between the programmatic parties and their financial bases.

This analysis follows the usual guideline in defining a large contribution as $500 or more. Large contributions by individuals have usually been the focus of the large contributor studies, but, because of the significance of advertising revenue to both parties, it is necessary here to also examine the large contributions which took the form of corporate advertising. Analysis is limited to the 1964 election because of access to sources who could assist in the identification process and because of the enormity of the task of searching for the economic affiliations of 250 individuals and more than 200 corporations for more than a single year. Where a contributor held a corporate officership as well as one or more directorships, he was assigned to the classification which included the company in which he was an officer.

Tables 35 and 36 present the economic associations of those large individual contributors and advertising purchasers who gave to the state party committees, as well as to the gubernatorial and senatorial committees in 1964. These tables demonstrate the financial importance of a relatively small percentage of all contributors. A mere 208 (1.1 per cent) of the 18,125 Republican contributors gave $199,881 or 18.6 per cent of total receipts, and 128 corporations gave an additional $150,250 or 14 per cent of total receipts. The Democrats received $31,115 or 4.4 per cent of their funds from 43 (less than 0.4 per cent) of their 11,530 contributors; and 89 corporations gave an additional $102,550 or 14.2 per cent of total income. This correlates closely with the Michigan experience where, in 1956, a little more than 1 per cent of Democratic contributors gave 17.6 per cent of total Democratic funds and about the same percentage of individual Republican givers accounted for 15 per cent of total Republican contributions.[33]

Table 35

Economic Classification of Individual Contributors and Advertising Purchasers of $500 or More to State Party, Gubernatorial, and Senatorial Committees: Democrats, 1964

Classification	Advertising		Individuals		Totals		%
	No.	Amount	No.	Amount	No.	Amount	
Banking, finance	2	$ 2,125	1	$ 500	3	$ 2,625	2.0
Insurance	3	2,500	0		3	2,500	1.9
Utilities	0		0		0		0.0
Manufacturers	14	10,425	3	1,525	17	11,950	8.9
Brewers, malters	6	19,750	0		6	19,750	14.8
Contractors, construction materials	15	17,825	2	1,500	17	19,325	14.5
Transportation	6	5,600	1	600	7	6,200	4.6
Fuel (gas, oil, coal)	0		1	500	1	500	0.4
Food processors and food storage	9	15,450	5	3,625	14	19,075	14.3
Farmers	2	1,500	0		2	1,500	1.1
Farm suppliers	1	500	0		1	500	0.4
Retail stores	4	4,250	0		4	4,250	3.2
Hotels	3	2,500	0		3	2,500	1.9
Real estate	8	8,750	2	1,000	10	9,750	7.3
Mass media	1	1,500	2	1,500	3	3,000	2.2
Other business	6	3,625	3	1,500	9	5,125	3.8
Officeholders, party officials	0		3	4,340	3	4,340	3.2
Labor leaders	0		1	500	1	500	0.4
Lawyers	0		4	2,375	4	2,375	1.8
Architects, engineers	0		3	2,700	3	2,700	2.0
Other professionals	0		1	500	1	500	0.4
Party units[a]	3	2,000	0		3	2,000	1.5
Unidentified	6	4,250	11	8,450	17	12,700	9.5
Totals	*89*	*$102,550*	*43*	*$31,115*	*132*	*$133,665*	*100.1*[b]

[a] These contributions were reported as advertising revenue rather than transfers from local party units. Apparently the method of raising these funds differed from the methods used to raise money transferred directly to the state level committees.
[b] The result of rounding of figures.

A second important pattern shown by these tables is the relative importance to the two parties of individual gifts and advertising purchases. The Republicans derived 57 per cent of large contribution income from individuals and 43 per cent from advertising. The Democratic pattern was markedly re-

Table 36

Economic Classification of Individual Contributors and Advertising Purchasers of $500 or More to State Party, Gubernatorial, and Senatorial Committees: Republicans, 1964

Classification	Advertising		Individuals		Totals		
	No.	Amount	No.	Amount	No.	Amount	%
Banking, finance	9	$ 5,875	16	$ 22,880	25	$ 28,755	8.2
Insurance	3	3,500	2	1,990	5	5,490	1.6
Utilities	0		2	1,233	2	1,233	0.4
Manufacturers	91	117,750	91	99,395	182	217,145	62.0
Brewers, malters	6	11,000	4	3,300	10	14,300	4.1
Contractors, construction materials	5	3,000	3	1,850	8	4,850	1.4
Transportation	3	1,500	1	500	4	2,000	0.6
Fuel (gas, oil, coal)	1	500	2	3,200	3	3,700	1.1
Food processors and food storage	3	2,750	6	4,200	9	6,950	2.0
Farmers	0		2	1,150	2	1,150	0.3
Farm suppliers	1	500	3	1,650	4	2,150	0.6
Retail stores	0		2	2,225	2	2,225	0.6
Hotels	0		2	7,550	2	7,550	2.2
Real estate	0		2	1,100	2	1,100	0.3
Mass media	0		0		0		0.0
Other business	3	2,250	0		3	2,250	0.6
Officeholders, party officials	0		0		0		0.0
Labor leaders	0		0		0		0.0
Lawyers	0		2	1,100	2	1,100	0.3
Architects, engineers	0		0		0		0.0
Other professionals	0		0		0		0.0
Party units	0		0		0		0.0
Unidentified	3	1,625	68	46,858	71	48,483	13.8
Totals	128	$150,250	208 [a]	$200,181	336	$350,431	100.1

[a] There were 224 large contributions to the various committees, but only 208 contributors, because of multiple large contributions by a few givers.
[b] The result of rounding of figures.

versed, with 77 per cent of such receipts coming from advertising and only 23 per cent from individuals. This again illustrates the importance of advertising sales to the Democrats: it permitted them to solicit funds from corporate enterprises whose individual managers undoubtedly preferred the Republicans but were persuaded to give the Democrats some consideration in the company's corporate actions.

Most significantly, these tables point out the same kind of sharp polarization of financial sources that was found in White and Owens' study of large contributors in Michigan in 1956,[34] and indicated in Wisconsin by the review of corporate and labor giving in the previous section. A combination of financial institutions and manufacturing concerns accounted for more than 70 per cent of total Republican revenue from large contributors. The recognition that an additional 13.8 per cent of revenue came from sources which could not be identified gives this income from financial and manufacturing interests additional significance.

The Democrats, by comparison, drew the largest share of their funds from the brewing and construction industries and from food processing and storage companies. The breweries and construction companies have been found in other studies to favor the Democrats.[35] They must be put down as "internal sources"—that is, non-ideological interests with specific goals which cause them to contribute to both parties, but especially to the incumbents. In dollar terms, the breweries gave comparable sums to both parties, although their contributions were a less significant percentage of the larger Republican income from large contributors.

The construction industry gave about four times as much to the Democrats as to the Republicans. This probably reflected a contemporary political situation in Wisconsin. Democratic Governor John Reynolds proposed an ambitious highway acceleration program, involving $500 million in road construction over a six-year period. This proposal was vigorously supported by the construction industry. However, the Republican majority in the legislature determined to kill the measure in order to prevent Reynolds from winning political advantage by passing such a program in the election year. The legislature submitted the highway acceleration program to the people on an unfavorably worded referendum ballot and it was decisively defeated in April, 1964. The road construction industry apparently resolved to aid its friends and punish its enemies by withholding its usual contributions from the Republicans and directing additional money to the Reynolds campaign. Uncommitted to either party on ideological grounds, the highway construction companies could make or withhold contributions for short-term strategic purposes.

The substantial contributions from the food processing and storage industry reflects neither particular ideological commitment nor strategic maneuvering. Almost the entire $19,075 received by the Democrats came from the Cudahy interests mentioned previously, and from Francis Rondeau and his various corporate enterprises. Both are businessmen who are Democrats by personal preference and have been party activists. The Oscar Mayer Company, also a large meat packer, and its corporate officers and directors accounted for nearly all of the $6,950 received by the Republicans from food processors and storage firms.

While Michigan manufacturing is dominated by the auto industry, Wisconsin has no single industry which is so prominent. Wisconsin's major manufacturers produce automobile and truck frames and parts, paper-making machinery, hydraulic pumps, diesel motors, electronic equipment, farm machinery, and heavy construction machinery. These items were grouped together under the subheading of "heavy industry" because many major firms make several of these products or parts for them. It was then possible to reduce the general classification of manufacturing to a more refined series of subclassifications. Table 37 presents a breakdown of the economic affiliations of large Republican contributors within the manufacturing classification.

Contributions from so-called heavy industry clearly dominated the Republican receipts from manufacturing enterprises, with the paper and household goods industries playing prominent secondary roles. These heavy industries have generally been quite hostile to labor unions, yet most of their plants are organized by such aggressive unions as the Auto Workers, Steelworkers, Allied Industrial Workers, and Machinists. Both unions and management are probably inspired more vigorously

Table 37

Classification of Large Contributions from Manufacturing Corporations According to Type of Goods Produced: Republicans, 1964

Classification	Advertising		Individuals		Totals		
	No.	Amount	No.	Amount	No.	Amount	%
Printing and engraving	2	$ 3,500	7	$15,000	9	$ 18,500	5.3
Heavy industry	54	71,625	56	46,495	110	118,120	33.7
Household goods, furnish- ings, utensils	8	10,250	8	13,300	16	23,550	6.7
Leather, leather goods	4	3,750	4	7,950	8	11,700	3.3
Paper, paper goods	11	15,625	9	10,550	20	26,175	7.5
Clothing	2	1,000	0	—	2	1,000	0.3
Plumbing fixtures	1	2,000	5	4,900	6	6,900	2.0
Other manufactures	9	10,000	2	1,200	11	11,200	3.2
Total manufacturers	*91*	*$117,750*	*91*	*$99,395*	*182*	*$217,145*	*62.0*

to aid, financially and organizationally, their respective parties as a result of the sharpness of their economic confrontations.

An additional refinement of the large contributor data for the Republican party shows a significant over-lapping between sources of individual contributions and advertising purchases. Thus 40 of the 128 large advertising purchasers, accounting for $64,125 of the Republican party's $150,250 in advertising revenues, were firms with one or more officers and directors among the large individual contributors to the various Republican state level committees. These 40 firms were represented on the individual contributors' roster by 109 of the 352 large givers whose personal contributions totaled $116,700 of the $199,881 received from individual large gifts. Thus a relatively small number of corporations and their officers and directors actually accounted for more than half of the total revenue from large contributions, narrowing still farther the real base from which Republican finances were drawn.

A review of the large contributors in Wisconsin in 1964 reveals about the same pattern as found in similar studies elsewhere. A very small percentage of givers in both parties provided a disproportionately large share of the campaign funds. There were more large contributors, providing both more dollars and a larger percentage of total income, in the Republican ranks than in the Democratic. The advertising book device aided the Democrats in expanding their base of large contributors because it allowed them to seek some funds from normally Republican sources. Manufacturing and financial enterprises were the dominant source of large contributions to the Republican party, while brewers and contractors were the most significant, though not the dominant, source of large Democratic contributions.

These conclusions are not significantly altered by the preliminary data on large contributors in 1966. Of Republican large contributions identified in preliminary examinations of the filed reports, fully $79,300, or 94.1 per cent, came from individuals who had been large contributors in 1964. Furthermore, the largest amounts were received from those associated with manufacturing enterprises, who gave $56,300 or 66.7 per cent of the total, and from banks and food processors whose contributions aggregated another $7,950 or 9.5 per cent. The affiliations of those who gave $13,550 (16 per cent) of the $84,400 in large contributions could not be identified.

Similarly, the large contributions to the Democrats were, with two exceptions, from the same major sources as in 1964, but the proportion from the various sources was somewhat altered by the Democrats' loss of incumbency. Of total large contributions of $21,700, contractors gave $2,500 or 11.5 per cent, food processors (the Cudahy and Rondeau interests) $2,000 or 9.2 per cent, and transportation concerns $1,500 or 6.9 per cent. The largest source of funds was the Lucey family, whose gifts of $6,500 accounted for a full 30 per cent of the total large contribution income. Other important sources of funds were professionals, hotel operators, realtors, and farmers; each group gave $1,000 or 4.6 per cent of total large contributions. The two significant changes in the large contribution pattern are the important contributions by the candidate's family, a phenomenon which occurred also in 1954, and the virtual withdrawal of contributions by the breweries, although they may have given in forms (such as early advertising purchases) which are not apparent from the large contributor analysis. It was not possible to identify $3,200 or 14.8 per cent of the large gifts, but among those identified the continued importance of non-ideological interests, and the lack of support from the manufacturing and financial interests traditionally allied with the Republicans indicates that the nature of the large contribution base of the Democrats was not fundamentally changed.

These data strengthen the conclusion that the financial sources of the two major parties have reflected and strengthened their programmatic outlooks by making them financially dependent upon sources with the same basic ideological approaches as the party activists. Democratic reliance on labor and Republican dependence on manufacturing and financial interests increased the polarization of the two parties along liberal-conservative lines, and preserved the ideological content of the two parties even though they were not mass financed by their activists. In Wisconsin, those who cast multiple votes through party organization work and those who cast multiple votes through financial contributions have agreed on basic issues and philosophy. Those financial sources, such as carriers, breweries and contractors, which are oriented to specific short-term needs rather than general long-term programs, gave to both parties and disturbed the ideological content of neither. Wisconsin's issue-oriented politics has presented voters a choice between programmatically divergent parties, molded in large part by activist ideologues and re-enforced by quite distinct financial bases divided along ideological lines.

Party Responsibility and Campaign Finance

Frank Sorauf's analysis of the membership party system in Wisconsin led him to the conclusion that the principal force in its development was the desire of issue-oriented activists to impose responsibility on the open primary system.[36] In order to assure the conservatism of Republican candidates and the liberalism of Democrats, it was necessary for the activists in the respective parties to develop issue-oriented party machinery which would adopt ideological platforms and put both manpower and financial resources behind candidates who adhered to the general political philosophy and the specific platform planks of the party.

A second element in the theme of party responsibility in Wisconsin is found in John Fenton's recent consideration of the issue-oriented politics of the Midwest. He pointed out that the parties stand for clearly divergent philosophies and programs, and that the politicians attempt to "deliver" on these platforms when they are elected to office.[37] He emphasized the clear policy differences between the activists who support liberal and conservative candidates, and the fairly distinct electoral base upon which each party has relied.

One aspect of the idea of party responsibility which has been commonly argued is party control over finances. To the extent that parties raise and dispense campaign funds, party organizations are better able to control nominations and to be a significant influence on the officeholder elected under the party's emblem. Potential candidates may be discouraged from seeking a nomination if they know that available money generally flows to the party treasury and is disbursed to those candidates receiving the party's endorsement. Furthermore, the party platform is likely to be taken more seriously both by candidates and officeholders if the party organization provides a significant portion of campaign funds, as well as organizational efforts.

In Wisconsin, the role of parties in campaign finance has come a little closer to imposing responsibility on Republican candidates and officeholders than on Democrats. The centralized fund-raising system employed by the Republicans has meant that the party organization collected and controlled the money available from major conservative financial sources. This has permitted the Republicans to endorse candidates at their state conventions and local caucuses and to back up the endorsements with campaign cash. Those who challenged or considered challenging the endorsed candidates found that their opponents already had a substantial campaign fund to draw on and that the usual party financial sources had already contributed and could not easily be approached for a primary contest.

In most years the Republican party itself raised and ex-

pended all money in behalf of its candidates for governor and
United States senator. When candidate committees were created, they were token entities, usually formed merely for the
value of a press announcement or two. In 1962, this format
changed somewhat when both the senatorial and gubernatorial
candidates had separate committees which handled some,
though substantially less than all, of their campaign expenditures. In 1964, the Republican party required each candidate to
submit a budget and then to set up a committee to receive and
disburse funds according to that budget. This structural change
apparently occurred in the aftermath of the 1962 election when
the gubernatorial candidate ordered expenditures beyond the
limits informally established and charged these expenditures to
the party treasury. This was, in effect, a raid upon the party
coffers which crippled the party's ability to meet its commitments to other candidates or to organizational efforts. Under the
1964 system, the party guaranteed the budget and provided
transfers of a dollar amount which was the equivalent of the
difference between the amount budgeted and whatever sums
came into the candidate committee from other sources. In 1966,
Republicans began a return to the pre-1964 budgeting method,
although between a fourth and a third of gubernatorial expenditures were handled by a separate campaign committee.

The Republican financing system has instilled some measure
of responsibility in party affairs by providing party financing of
the efforts of the endorsed candidates at both the primary and
general elections. This does not, of course, mean that the party
has been able to control the nomination process. Usually its
attempts to defeat incumbent officeholders have failed. Thus in
the post-war period Governor Walter Goodland, Senator Alexander Wiley, Secretary of State Robert Zimmerman, and State
Treasurer Dena Smith survived challenges by party-endorsed
and party-financed challengers. In situations where neither candidate was incumbent, the party-endorsed candidate tended to
fare somewhat better.

The point may be, however, that the Republican organization
has been willing to put its time and money into primary fights,
thus imposing upon those who are not ideologically acceptable

the experience of a well-financed challenge for the nomination and the lingering post-primary bitterness that such a contest often causes within the party's ranks, even if the non-endorsed candidate wins. Many of the party activists, after all, are more interested in issues than in the career of one nominee, while the candidate is likely to be most interested in his own success. The willingness and the ability of the party organization to use its funds for primary fights may in fact impose some measure of discipline even on those candidates and officeholders who are not conservative ideologues.

It is difficult to assess the full extent of Republican party financial participation in the campaign of any one candidate in a primary or general election because most spending is done directly from party coffers and is reported as a party expenditure without any indication of the candidate in whose behalf the money was expended. Furthermore, in most years the Republicans have waged joint campaign efforts with mass media featuring their entire state ticket. This prevents allocation of expenditures among the various candidates. One measure of the party's financial activity may be the 1956 primary in which Representative Glenn Davis, a conservative, won the party endorsement against incumbent Senator Alexander Wiley. The major committee operating in Davis' behalf drew more than 80 per cent of its funds from the Republican party and from regular Republican contributors.

The role of the Republican party in financing its gubernatorial and senatorial candidates in 1962 and 1964 is indicated by Table 38. It shows the degree to which the separate committees supporting these candidates drew financial backing directly from party organizations and from persons who were donors to the party as well as to the candidates (implying that they gave to the candidates because they were Republicans rather than because of the candidate's individual appeal). It is important to note that in 1962 the major portion of the spending for both the gubernatorial and senatorial campaigns was handled directly by the Republican state organization, and the figures in Table 38 therefore understate the party's actual role.

The Republican finance picture has been dominated by the

Table 38

Role of Party Organizations and Party-Affiliated Donors in Financing
Gubernatorial and Senatorial Campaigns:
Republicans, 1962 and 1964

	Governor, 1962		Senator, 1962		Governor, 1964		Senator, 1964	
	Amount	*%*	*Amount*	*%*	*Amount*	*%*	*Amount*	*%*
Total candidate committee receipts	$51,569	100.0	$82,440	100.0	$226,379	100.0	$216,591	100.0
Total receipts from party sources	25,307	49.0	63,933	77.6	155,976	69.0	195,063	90.0
From state, local party units	17,815	34.5	55,783	67.7	133,846	59.1	168,528	77.8
From national party units	None	—	5,500	6.7	None	—	5,000	2.3
From party-affiliated individuals	7,492	14.5	2,650	3.2	22,130	9.8	21,535	9.9

party organization. Transfer payments from party units and direct contributions from party-affiliated individuals constituted well over half the campaign funds used in behalf of party-endorsed primary candidates and general election nominees. The bookkeeping arrangements may have varied from campaign to campaign, with the party organization actually expending the money in some years and candidate committees disbursing it in others. Regardless of the spending machinery, however, the party organization and party-affiliated individuals provided the money which was spent. The centralized financing pattern in the Republican party has been compatible with a party responsibility model and has in fact been used on some occasions to attempt to impose party responsibility in the candidate selection process. While a candidate may be concerned with many constituencies—including, for example, pressure groups, the press, and specific vote blocs—in Wisconsin, two of his most important constituencies have been merged in the party organization. A substantial share of his volunteer campaign support and most of his money come to him through the ideologically conservative

Republican party. In such circumstances it is not surprising that many Republican candidates have tended to be conservatives or at least to be attentive to conservative opinions.

The Democratic financing picture is characterized by much less distinct lines. Fund raising has not been centralized and therefore, as pointed out in Chapter 4, each candidate has been compelled to build a cadre of fund raisers and develop his own campaign treasury. Much of this can be traced to the nature of the Democratic financial constituency. As the liberal party, the Democrats have had no natural base of wealthy individuals upon whom they have been able to draw as a party. Those economic interests that need access on specific short-term problems usually preferred to give directly to the candidates since it is these men, if they became officeholders, and not the party leadership, to whom access is desired. Furthermore, the labor movement publicly adopted a non-partisan stance, and therefore usually limited its contributions to candidates selected through the endorsement process rather than giving to party organizations. As previously noted, the Democratic organization has not been able to field a significant number of prominent professional and businessmen as fund raisers, thus further weakening its ability to develop a centralized fund-raising machinery.

This sketch of Democratic financial decentralization must not, however, be overdrawn. The party headquarters has raised some money from fund-raising events, dues, advertising sales and occasionally from labor. It has expended this money in two general directions: first, to develop a strong local party organization; second, directly to aid the party's nominees. Thus Democratic candidates have drawn some financial aid, both direct and indirect, from the issue-oriented party organization. In addition, the labor movement has been an important part of the candidate financial constituency. Finally, as with the Republicans, party-affiliated individual contributors accounted for some of the funds available to the candidates. Table 39 shows the degree of financial support that Democratic candidates received from party units, party-affiliated individuals, and the labor movement.

Table 39 somewhat understates the role of both party units

Table 39

Role of Party Organizations, Party-Affiliated Donors, and the Labor Movement
in Financing Gubernatorial and Senatorial Campaigns:
Democrats, 1962 and 1964

	Governor, 1962		Senator, 1962		Governor, 1964		Senator, 1964	
	Amount	*%*	*Amount*	*%*	*Amount*	*%*	*Amount*	*%*
Total candidate committee receipts	$123,120	100.0	$171,982	100.0	$205,718	100.0	$201,950	100.0
Total receipts from party and labor sources	81,207	66.0	80,484	46.8	76,498	37.2	89,414	44.2
From state, local party units	18,807	15.3	20,406	11.9	16,298	7.9	1,509	0.7
From national party units	10,000	8.1	10,000	5.8	None	—	17,300	8.6
From party-affiliated individuals	10,698	8.7	7,881[a]	4.6	27,708	13.5	23,266	11.5
From labor	41,702	33.9	42,197	24.5	32,492	15.8	47,339	23.4

[a] This amount is probably too small. However, a significant portion of the 1962 receipts in the Nelson campaign were listed as lump sum receipts from various political events and it was not possible to calculate how much of this money came from party-affiliated individuals.

and labor in Democratic campaigns. As previously pointed out, some party contributions to candidate campaigns were disbursed directly by the party organization as directed by the candidate, rather than being transferred to his campaign committee. This bookkeeping arrangement served to reduce the level of expenditures which a candidate was compelled to report as part of his own campaign effort. It was possible to pinpoint $12,125 of such party expenditures in behalf of the 1964 Democratic senatorial candidate, and $7,500 in behalf of the 1964 gubernatorial nominee. There may be additional amounts which were not designated as candidate expenditures on the Democratic party's filed reports. Occasionally labor contributions to candidates have been directed to the party and reported as party expenditures in order to achieve the same understatement of candidate expenditures. It has not been possible to determine the magnitude of this practice.

A second facet of the Democratic party's candidate spending pattern should be noted. The Democratic party organization does not endorse candidates in the primary. However, labor frequently participates in primaries by endorsing and contributing to candidates; and furthermore, the party leadership frequently prefers one primary contestant over his opponent or opponents and attempts to influence the primary outcome by directing volunteer efforts and individual contributions to that candidate. There has not been an occasion since 1950 when a primary contest for major office was drawn along liberal-conservative lines within the Democratic party. Therefore, there has been no occasion when the liberal activists who control the Democratic party machinery were faced with the prospect of having as their nominee a person with clearly unacceptable political principles and programs. In these circumstances, the Democratic party has not developed any financial participation in primary contests and has not had to do so in order to preserve its ideological nature. Nonetheless, the failure to participate in primaries probably weakens the influence that the party exerts upon its candidates and officeholders as compared to the Republican organization's relationship to its candidates and officeholders.

While party sources have been the dominant part of candidate financial constituencies in the Republican party, this is not true for the Democrats. Of the four campaigns reviewed in Table 39, only in the 1962 gubernatorial campaign did party-labor sources constitute more than 50 per cent of the Democratic candidate's financial constituency. However, in most Democratic campaigns in the 1950's the combined party-labor sources did contribute more than half the funds. This suggests that Democratic candidates who were not holders of one of the major offices have been financially more reliant upon the ideological elements of the Democratic coalition, while incumbents have been able to broaden their financial sources as a result of the substantial resources connected with officeholding. In 1964, after two years as governor, John Reynolds was much less reliant upon party-labor sources in his re-election bid than he was in 1962 in his initial campaign for that office. Even for incumbent Democrats, however, the party-labor financial sources, which are liberal and issue-oriented, have continued to be the largest, though not the dominant, element in the financial constituency, usually accounting for at least 40 per cent of total receipts.

The financing pattern in both parties has tended to be compatible with a party-responsibility model. Not only have candidates relied upon ideological activists for volunteer organizational efforts in the campaign, they have depended on a similarly ideological base for significant financial support. Candidates may have many different constituencies, but in two of their most important ones they have been subject to clearly issue-oriented influences. The Wisconsin party system has been highly polarized, with each party organization run by issue-oriented activists and the financial bases of the two parties fairly well divided along programmatic lines. The candidates, in turn, have been subject to both organizational and financial pressures which have restrained them from moving too far away from the philosophy of their party in order to seek electoral or financial support normally associated with the other party. Once in office, the politicians have continued to look for organizational and financial help from the same programmatic sources, although incumbency has permitted Democrats to develop some new constituencies which lessen the normally heavy reliance upon the usual ideological bases of support. Generally, however, the issue orientation of the membership party and the primary sources of funds have operated in Wisconsin to re-enforce the sharpness of ideological divisions both in campaigns and in the administration of the government.

Conclusion

There is no need to repeat here the findings reported in preceding chapters. Rather, it seems useful to bring the most important of those findings together in the context of the simple input-output political resource model discussed in Chapter 1. The major thrust of such an analysis is that campaign finance is closely related to the larger political environment. Primarily, the patterns of campaign finance are a response to the political environment; but it is also true that the relationship is reciprocal inasmuch as the uses of money may within very significant limits shape the political system.

Political Resources and Campaign Funding

The funding of politics may be seen as beginning with those individuals who convert some of their personal resources, especially money, to political purposes; or, it may be viewed as beginning with the politician who seeks to convert other resources into money and to pyramid his political resources. To focus on the politician seems more realistic, since few of those who contribute would do so in the absence of his resource-gathering activities.

The nature and number of political resources was considered at length in Chapter 1. It is helpful to point out again that all resources are to some extent convertible: they can be exchanged for other resources which the politician deems useful to attain his goals. Convertibility is ordinarily a desirable attribute from the politician's perspective since it permits him to employ a resource in a wide variety of ways in response to his own judgements about the political situation and about the kind of resource use that will maximize his effectiveness in attaining his goals. Politicians also find transferability a desirable resource attribute since it permits them to deploy their resources in the locales they deem strategically significant. Politicians seek to expand or pyramid their resources in order to maximize their political strength. All resource use—conversion, transfer, pyramiding—is, of course, an act of human will, of decision-making by politicians. The amounts of resources available and the ways in which resources are used depend upon the judgements that politicians make. While the results of their decisions may be purely fortuitous, one mark of a politician's skill is the extent to which his decisions about resource use aid him in reaching his goals. It is useful to repeat, too, that there are a great many resources in politics. Not all resources are available to every politician and the amounts of those resources which are available are usually unequally distributed. In addition, not every politician has the skill or the will to use the resources which are available to him. Our study of the Wisconsin political system has suggested that some resources are especially helpful in the process of raising money, and it has provided some insight into the decisions which politicians have made in regard to the use of political resources.

Perhaps the most important political resource discovered in this study is the programmatic orientation of the political parties and candidates. As Chapter 6 clearly demonstrates, the largest share of campaign money for both parties comes from those who concur in their respective programs. The Republican party is able consistently to gain financial support from the manufacturing and financial interests in the system because its philosophy is compatible with theirs. The same is true of the Democrats and labor. The contributions of large numbers of individual party activists are apparently also in response to the programmatic stances of the parties. Financing on this basis is a re-enforcement of as well as a response to these stances. Furthermore, it ought to be pointed out that programmatic orientation is a greater resource for the Republicans than for the Democrats since those elements of the community which concur with the Republican position are also those which, for a wide range of reasons, allocate more money to politics.

Specific programs, as well as general ideologies, may have convertibility. As has been shown, the large contributions to the Democrats in 1964 by highway contractors probably resulted from Governor John Reynolds' advocacy of a massive highway acceleration program and from the Republican maneuvering to block its enactment. The contractors were moved by a specific program, and could easily change their contributing pattern at a later time in response to development by Republicans of a program consistent with their needs. Thus programs may be convertible in certain circumstances where ideology is irrelevant.

Personal charisma is also a resource which a candidate might convert into campaign cash, although there is no method available to this study for measuring its impact. Perhaps Gaylord Nelson, among the Democrats, and Glenn Davis, among the Republicans, have demonstrated the greatest ability to galvanize personal followings into action, including the making of financial contributions.

Finance organization is clearly a resource which can be converted into money. The systematic Republican canvass for funds, aided by a corps of fund raisers with the appropriate contacts, is as much a part of the Republicans' fund-raising success as is the existence of a constituency upon which this organization can call for money. The lack of organization on the Democratic side only compounds that party's other weaknesses in raising money. Party organization, aside from its finance arm, may have some effect on fund-raising ability. The development of a mass dues-paying party organization by Wisconsin Democrats has, in its own way, been a convertible resource, even if one counts only the money raised from membership dues.

Incumbency is a significant political resource, and one of its attributes is the ability to raise money. Frank Sorauf reported that control of federal patronage was a source of Democratic money in the early 1950's[1] and it again became important to the Democrats during the Kennedy administration. There is little state level patronage in Wisconsin; hence it does not constitute a major source of funds. It should be noted, however, that patronage remains an important political resource in some other jurisdictions. A recent study of Democratic financing in Indiana reports that a levy of 2 per cent on the salaries of thousands of state employees not covered by the merit system raised $275,000 in 1964, and that patronage employees were also an outlet for tickets to fund-raising dinners, rallies, raffles, and similar events which raised large additional sums.[2] Other advantages of incumbency may also be easily convertible, including the development of contacts with important interest groups during the conduct of governmental business, the occasional opportunities to perform favors, the building of a record which will be favorably viewed by those able to make contributions, and the ability to capitalize the prestige of high office by inviting potential contributors to social affairs at the governor's mansion.

Close competition may also be a resource for political figures or parties. Those who normally support them may intensify their efforts, and others who have not previously given may be motivated to contribute. Some who prefer or need to be with the winning side may find it expedient to give to both sides. Certainly part of the Democratic success in raising money in recent years in Wisconsin has been that party's newly acquired position as a strong competitor for power.

These resources appear most significant for raising money in the Wisconsin political system. It must not be overlooked that these same resources and others may have uses other than fund raising, e.g., the mass party system may significantly add to the volunteer work forces available in a campaign. It is the work of the politician to convert his resources as fully as possible into campaign cash or other desirable resources which will aid him in winning votes or gaining other campaign objectives. Furthermore, he seeks to pyramid his resources as well as to convert them. The cost to state level political committees in 1964 of the conversion and pyramiding of resources in connection with fund raising was at least 7 per cent of total cash outlays—perhaps as much as $100,000. Yet, these same committees reported raising almost $1.8 million in that year, and even conceding the heavy commitments of time by relatively large corps of fund raisers, the returns to the politicians were much larger than their investments. In short, both Wisconsin parties engaged in very intensive and quite successful efforts to convert and pyramid resources into very large campaign treasuries.

Nonetheless, it is apparent that there remained enormous slack in the political system. The 13.5 per cent of Wisconsin respondents who reported giving money to a party or candidate was substantially less than the 28.3 per cent who agreed that "even if people are not able to help their political party in other ways, they ought to contribute money. . . ." Those who do give money would probably give more in the right circumstances and with the proper solicitation. Furthermore, the total number of contributors, including dues payers, to the state level committees in 1964 was only 11,530 or about 0.5 per cent of the adult population. Yet 66 per cent of reported spending was by these committees. It would appear that because of the high visibility of the candidates involved, a much larger contributor base and a greater amount of money should be available to politicians at this level. We have, therefore, a situation in which there is both impressive conversion and pyramiding of resources in filling campaign coffers and, at the same time, great slack in the tapping of the cash resources which are apparently available.

Not only is it clear that there is enormous slack in the political system, but it is also obvious from the discussion in Chapter 4 that resources are unequally distributed between parties and between candidates. The conservative party, for instance, is advantaged because its constituents include the largest share of those who are well-off economically and thus able to make somewhat larger contributions. Furthermore, among its constituents are more of those who have the status and talents to raise funds. And finally, its constituents are those most likely to understand the importance of participating in politics by making financial contributions. Similarly, incumbency is a resource which is unequally distributed, although it may sometimes be offset by the challenger's incumbency in a different office. It is not clear whether incumbency was, for example, a greater resource for incumbent Senator Alexander Wiley or his challenger, Governor Gaylord Nelson, in the 1962 election.

Chapter 4 also demonstrated the unevenness of spending between the local and state level committees within each of the parties, and between the candidates and party committees within each party's overall effort. In large measure this unevenness can be attributed to the differences in resources possessed by the numerous centers within the political system. A case in point is the rising financial importance of the Democratic party's state headquarters as it acquired federal patronage as a resource after 1960 and as it was able to benefit from victories of some of its state level candidates, particularly its gubernatorial nominees.

The unevenness in spending is not, however, related solely to the possession of resources. Politicians must have a will to convert and pyramid the available resources into a campaign fund. A clear example of resources being available but not converted into campaign funds is that of many majority party incumbents in one-party legislative districts who are so sure of victory that they need not convert such resources as incumbency, past records, and almost certain re-election into campaign funds, unless they face a real primary challenge. Such an incumbent has one decisive resource—the party loyalty of a large majority of his constituents, which makes unnecessary any expenditure of time or skill to convert or pyramid his other resources in order to develop a substantial campaign treasury. In sharp contrast is the opponent in such a district who, while perhaps desiring to wage a vigorous campaign, is ordinarily so lacking in resources that he cannot engage in sufficient conversion and pyramiding to support a determined electoral contest. Sometimes the prospects of victory are so dim that, like his majority party counterpart, the minority party candidate has no will to engage in the process of conversion and pyramiding, even of those limited resources he has.

Although this discussion has been cast in terms of resource conversion and pyramiding by politicians, there must also be considered on the fund-raising side of the model those who contribute money in response to the appeals of the politicians. Chapter 6 demonstrated that those associated with the manufacturing and financial interests in the community are significant contributors to the Republican cause and that labor is important in financing the Democratic effort. Furthermore, party members play an important role in financing politics: while they constitute only 7.7 per cent of the adult population, party members account for 36.8 per cent of the contributors and they may be a much larger percentage of the solicitors.

All of those who contribute engage in multiple voting; that is, by allocating some of their resources to politics they have weight beyond their votes in deciding elections and perhaps policy. Multiple voting can, of course, occur through other kinds of political activities as well as contributions—by campaign work, for instance. Studies show that political activity is cumulative, "persons who engage in one political action often engage in others as well."[3] Furthermore, political action of all kinds seems correlated to education and income; those with more education and higher incomes participate more frequently and fully than those without.[4] Thus, multiple voting or resource allocation by individuals tends to be concentrated among certain classes in the community. This is of course reflected in the distinctly middle class composition of the mass parties in Wisconsin.

The tendency for political activity—and therefore for multiple voting—to be cumulative within the population is clear in Wisconsin. Of the 13.5 per cent of the population who reported making financial contributions to parties or candidates, 57.4 per cent engaged in campaign work or were party members and 19.1 per cent were political participants in both these ways. And the disproportionate representation of educated and high income groups among campaign contributors is made clear by the data in Table 40.

In summary, the input side of the political resource model has some quite clear characteristics in Wisconsin. First, there is the considerable ideological polarization of contributors, which is more marked than in most state party systems in the United States. Second, there is the importance of the mass membership party in providing a significant percentage of the total contributions and in somewhat reducing the reliance of the parties, par-

Table 40

Distribution of Contributors and the General Population by Income and Educational Attainment, 1964

Income	Contr. %	Tot. Pop. %	*Education*	Contr. %	Tot. Pop. %
Under $4000	13	23	Grade Sch.	16	29
$4000–5999	10	17	High Sch.[a]	48	54
$6000–7999	20	24	College[b]	36	17
$8000–9999	16	14			
$10,000 or more	36	16			
Not ascertained	5	7			
	100	101[c]		100	100
Total number	*94*	*702*		*94*	*702*

[a] Includes those with vocational training.
[b] Includes those with graduate work.
[c] The result of rounding of figures.

ticularly the Democratic party, on large contributions. Third, there is the somewhat more extensive financial giving among the total population than in the nation as a whole—again, probably related to the mass party system. Fourth, the givers are drawn heavily from the politically active, the better educated, and the well-off: the Wisconsin mass party system is basically a middle class politics; it does not appear, even on the Democratic side, to have activated a large base of lower class givers along the lines envisioned by Duverger. Fifth, political resources have been successfully converted and pyramided by Wisconsin politicians; nonetheless, these men have not taken up all of even the most obvious slack in the system. Ideology looms more important as a resource than in most state political systems, and patronage is less important than in a good many. Finally, the total financial resources devoted to politics in Wisconsin have increased sharply in recent years. Chapter 3 points out the sharp increases in spending in both absolute dollar terms and in comparison with spending increases in the nation as a whole. Wisconsin politicians have, as previously noted, been successful in pyramiding their resources in such a way as to sustain a quadrupling in political spending. Their resource-pyramiding activities were to a significant degree a response to a highly competitive political situation which was probably made even more competitive by their continual escalation of political activity. Two other factors, both of which were also related to the competitive political situation, may also have played a role in the politicians' resource pyramiding activities: the expansion of the membership base of the mass party system, and the development of stronger fund-raising organizations by parties and candidates.

Political Spending

As pointed out in Chapter 1, the input-output model of political resources vastly oversimplifies the process of gathering and using political resources. Resources are not simply amassed by politicians and then expended for the vote-getting activities or other objectives of the campaign. There are a good many inside expenditures for the conversion and pyramiding of resources. The cash cost of fund-raising activities by state level party and candidate committees has already been noted. Not all inside expenditures are so obvious; some expenditures may serve both indirect and direct vote-seeking purposes. Expenditures to develop party organization are an example: they develop a larger contributor base and recruit more manpower to engage in the pyramiding of resources while at the same time increasing the number of workers who take part in the canvass for votes. While the main concern of this portion of the discussion is with expenditures for vote-getting activities, it must be noted that there is a considerable amount of spending, both of money and of other resources, for purposes of resource conversion and pyramiding.

Political spending can be seen from two important angles: how much is spent and what it is spent for. Chapter 3 points out the spiraling dollar costs of politics. In Wisconsin, the increase in costs has been much sharper than the increase in the nation as a whole, whether measured on a per vote or per capita basis or in relation to a measure of wealth. Despite the sharpness of the increase, the total cost of politics is not great either on an absolute scale or in comparison with spending in other political systems. The concern about the amounts spent in politics is more appropriately related to the difficulties faced by those—candidates, their supporters, and party activists—who must raise the money than to some measure of the amount spent.

A further perspective on the costs of politics is gained by examining the political environment within which the spending takes place and the relationship of that environment to the level of spending. An intensely competitive electoral situation is one such environmental factor. It makes it imperative for the politician to finance a vigorous campaign in search of the small but critical margin of votes necessary for an election victory. A second significant factor in the environment is the existence of political resources. A politician's determination that money ought to be spent in a given political situation is actually translated into a high spending level only to the extent that resources are available to finance such an effort. Thus, the fact that there is little patronage in Wisconsin constitutes a limitation on the spending level because it denies to Wisconsin politicians a convertible resource which is available in some other political systems. A third factor is the skill of the politicians. Their capacity to pyramid resources is obviously a determinant of the levels of spending. Political skills are not uniform within a given political environment, yet it is plausible that in some environments the general level of political skill is higher than in others.

This may be related to the processes of recruitment and of socialization of political activists, which processes vary from place to place.

The nature of the offices contested and of the constituency both influence the level of spending. Campaigns for major offices are more expensive than those for lesser offices in the same constituency, as the disparity between spending levels in campaigns for governor and for lieutenant governor clearly attest. Where a large number of important public offices are contested at the polls, system-wide costs rise sharply. The Wisconsin data suggest quite clearly that costs accelerate faster when both a United States Senate seat and the governorship are at stake than in those elections when only the latter office is on the ballot. Furthermore, the larger the constituency, the greater the need for campaign expenditures. As the number of voters to be reached increases, so ordinarily does the cost: clearly it is more expensive to engage in a direct mail campaign, to use the most obvious example, in a district of 40,000 than to do so in a district of 10,000. The rise in spending is not merely proportionate to the number of inhabitants or voters in the district, however. In more populous districts personal reputation and canvassing are less important. Instead, candidates are forced to use high per unit cost media such as television and metropolitan dailies. Furthermore, there is the need to develop and maintain an extensive organization. Thus the per vote cost rises with the size of the district's electorate or population.

This discussion has measured the size of the constituency by the number of voters; a somewhat different measure might be its geographic size. The Wisconsin data cannot be manipulated to determine whether campaigns are more expensive in larger geographical regions than in smaller ones, when the size of the electorate or the population is held constant. Geographic size should not ordinarily increase costs for such items as mass mailing and media advertising. It might increase the cost of candidate campaigning, but this cost is only a small share of campaign budgets in any case. Organization expenses might be greater in a geographically large constituency, but the available data do not lend themselves to a testing of that proposition. The geographical size of the district ought, however, to be viewed as an environmental circumstance which might be relevant to campaign costs.

Another major factor in the level of campaign spending is the strength of party organization and the relative significance of other, competing channels for reaching voters. Where party organization is effective in reaching voters, other kinds of expenditures may not be so necessary. In Wisconsin, however, the mass parties tend not to perform campaign functions very well. Issue-oriented activists often prefer intra-party debating to precinct work; furthermore, they are not committed to politics on anything like a full-time basis, as are the precinct workers in parties organized on a patronage incentive. Finally, party members tend to be drawn from the middle class and are therefore to a large extent located in the wrong areas to be most effective in developing additional electoral strength for their parties. In the face of this party structure, politicians feel compelled to rely on other kinds of campaigning, especially expensive media advertising. Costs are compounded by the existence and suitability in a constituency of the most expensive alternate channels for reaching voters; thus the advent and spread of television vastly increased costs, especially for statewide and some congressional campaigns.

Furthermore, mass media, and especially television, have become effective competitors of party organization in influencing voters because of the increasingly media-oriented life style of an educated population. Thus, parties and candidates must purchase, at enormous cost, some part of the message transmitted by media in order to reach voters in the most effective manner and to offset competing political forces which are in contact with the electorate. Both the inability to rely on party organization and the existence of effective and competing alternate channels of political communication compel politicians to attempt to raise and spend more money in their quest for votes.

Not only has the trend toward mass media campaigning increased the amounts spent, it has shifted the direction of spending as well. That is to say, the emphasis in campaign budgets has now shifted to television, with other mass media also becoming a major cost item. The growing importance of mass media use in Wisconsin politics has been detailed in Chapter 5. The Wisconsin pattern is part of a national trend in which the number of television spots purchased by political campaigns at all levels increased from 9,000 in 1960 to 29,300 in 1964, and the number of radio spots rose from 29,000 to 63,000 in the same period.[5] Media advertising and publicity are the main purposes for which funds are now expended. Election day expenses continue to be important, while organization expenses have become less significant as the strength of party organization has declined. These shifts in campaign budgeting reflect an accurate assessment by politicians of the most effective ways of seeking votes in the present political context.

At the same time, their expenditures serve significant systemic functions—especially in the areas of recruiting and training political candidates and activists, of providing basic political information and a diversity of viewpoints to the public in a democratic system, and of expanding political participation and thus developing a greater sense of the legitimacy of the policies adopted by government. Almost no money is spent for purposes which are clearly banned by the democratic ethic, such as buying votes or bribing election officials. At times, of course, money spent for publicity and advertising may be used to promote messages so lacking in truth or relevancy as to threaten the integrity of the political system, but increasingly there is activity by other outlets of information as well as watchfulness by the electorate which curb such uses of money.

In sum, political spending, like campaign fund raising, is tied inextricably to the political environment. The intensity of competition, the existence of adequate political resources, the strength of party organization, the significance of the offices contested, the nature and size of constituency, the existence of a variety of channels for reaching voters—all influence the level of spending. The magnitude and direction of spending in a given environment are determined by the politicians' energy, skill, and sense of necessity. As pointed out in Chapter 5, there are severe limits on what can be achieved by campaign spending by these men; these limits range from the countervailing forces of the opposition's campaign and the other channels of information to the fixed nature of party identification and the great social and economic forces which influence the conduct of voters.

In Wisconsin and apparently in most parts of the United States few political expenditures are of a kind which can be censured as immoral per se and even fewer are of those kinds explicitly prohibited by law. Some expenditures can be shown to contribute to the operation of the American democratic political system. The criticisms of spending may, therefore, be largely misplaced. The amount of spending, when viewed in dollar terms, is not actually very high. If there is a valid criticism of the present campaign finance situation in America, it is apparently that some candidates or parties in certain jurisdictions or circumstances are unable to raise sufficient money to engage in the kinds of campaigning which in the present political environment are necessary to make a reasonably complete effort to win the support of the electorate and to perform the functions which are helpful to the maintenance of a democratic system.

Perspectives on Money in Politics

The opening paragraphs of this book noted the increase in interest in campaign finance in recent years. It will be recalled that there have been four major strands in this heightened interest in the subject: the focus on misuses of campaign gifts to influence public policy; the attention of scholars to the amounts raised and spent, the sources of money, and the purposes of expenditures; the widespread public concern about the amounts spent; the interest in various proposals to "reform" campaign financing practices. Each of these approaches has lacked the broad perspective which views money as one of many political resources in a total political system. Campaign financing has generally been viewed as a separate force or variable in the political system rather than in its proper light, as a resource whose use is largely determined by the larger political environment.

Despite the public concern about the total costs of politics, for instance, a sophisticated examination shows that by most measures Americans pay a small cost for the maintenance of an adversary political process in a complicated federal system with its many elective offices at a variety of levels of government. Seldom is the discussion of political spending placed in a perspective which reveals the relationship between such spending and the financing of activities which are essential to a democratic polity.

Even the scholarly work on campaign finance tends to concentrate on the amounts spent, the sources from which money is raised, and the uses to which money is put. These data are all helpful, but they do not show the relationship of campaign finance to the political environment—to the kinds of party systems, the available channels of communication, and other political and social phenomena. Nor is money ordinarily viewed as a form of functional representation by groups in the community and as just one of the several ways in which groups may seek their policy objectives through the allocation of resources to the political process. It seems quite clear from both the Wisconsin data and the national campaign finance studies that the most common practice is for groups to allocate resources to the support of politicians or parties whose public stances are compatible with the policy goals or other objectives of the givers. Yet much less attention is given to money as a form of functional representation than to the very infrequent instances in which campaign gifts are made for the purpose of procuring actions by public officials which would not have been forthcoming in the absence of the contributions.

Very little of the literature advocating reform in the present financing system attempts to expose the implications of such changes for other parts of the political process. Yet if money is a response to the larger political environment and is ordinarily used in such a way as to re-enforce the existing political process, reform proposals which do not take a broad perspective may actually invite changes in the political system which are not in any obvious way connected with the subject of campaign funding. This is not, of course, an argument against recommendations for reform. Rather, it is an argument that an understanding of the links between campaign financing and other political phenomena permits reform advocates to better understand the full systemic implications of their proposals and to modify their ideas where the likely consequences are contrary to the advocates' professed political values.

The major objective of this book has been to set political finance in the larger setting of the political system within which these funds are used by politicians. This effort is quite incomplete—limited by inadequate data and hypotheses about money in politics, by the incompleteness of research in other aspects of the political process, by time and energy. Yet this approach seems preferable to more limited approaches to political finance because it seeks to report the relationships between money in politics and other facets of politics. Many of these hypothesized relationships need confirmation by testing with data from other jurisdictions; others will be restated as the understanding of all aspects of the political process improves. In the short run, the approach to campaign finance expounded here should suggest a broader perspective on the place of money in politics to those who seek an understanding of American politics and to those who seek to change it. At the very minimum, it should signal attentive observers of the American system that neither an understanding of political finance nor the reform of finance practices can be achieved by the traditional approach of studying political fund raising and political spending separately from other aspects of the political system.

Epilogue: Public Policy and Political Finance

Approaches to Public Policy

The purpose of this discussion is not to enumerate in catalogue fashion all of the regulations in America which deal with money in politics, but rather to summarize the general approaches which have been used in various American jurisdictions and to evaluate those approaches in light of the role which money has been seen in the foregoing chapters to play in the American political system. Frank Sorauf recently summarized campaign finance regulation under four headings: restrictions on the sources of money, restrictions on the size of contributions, restrictions on expenditures, control by publicity.[1] A fifth category is public subsidy.

Restrictions on sources of money ordinarily ban contributions by certain interests and individuals. Regulations vary in the United States, but the most common prohibitions are those against corporate contributions which are found in thirty-three states and in the federal statutes, and the ban on union gifts which exists in four states and at the national level.[2] Some states specify particular business interests which may not contribute. Oregon, for instance, prohibits political contributions by banks, utility corporations, or a majority of their stockholders.[3] In

246

Florida, direct and indirect political contributions may not be made by those involved in the state-licensed horse- and dog-racing enterprises, those who hold licenses for the sale of alcoholic beverages, and the operators of public utilities.[4]

All of these restrictions appear to have a double purpose. First, they prevent certain interests in the community from obtaining influence in the governing process by making campaign contributions to those who seek public office. Campaign contributions are looked on as akin to bribery, except that no specific understandings between donor and recipient need be proved to make the contribution improper. Second, these prohibitions are aimed at public officials who are prevented from using their great power to extract campaign cash from unwilling enterprises, groups, and individuals who are directly affected by government.

This form of regulation raises a number of questions, aside from the obvious one of whether the kind of men willing to engage in the practices at which these prohibitions are aimed will be deterred by them. A different problem is whether the distinctions made by law are real. That is, does a ban on corporate contributions make sense if corporation officials are free to make individual contributions? Chapter 6 showed that the influence of financial and business interests in Wisconsin politics is enormous despite the statutory ban on direct corporate gifts.[5] Furthermore, there seems to be some inequality in a democratic political system which allows multiple voting in the form of campaign gifts by some interests but not by others. For instance, permitting functional representation through campaign contributions for labor unions but not for business corporations is not a policy whose rationality is apparent. Of course, those economic interests which are franchised by the government on a monopoly or quasi-monopoly basis are more needful of the kind of governmental privilege which induces them to corrupt officials and hence more vulnerable to extortion by corrupt officials than are interests chartered and regulated under laws of general application. But campaign finance regulations which discriminate against economic interests of the latter type seem to be less democratic than regulations which permit either all economic interests or none of them to seek representation through campaign giving and other forms of multiple voting.

In the second category of restrictions are those which limit the size of contributions. Seven states have such limitations, with ceilings ranging from $1,000 to $5,000.[6] Although designed to prevent particular persons from gaining too much influence in government, these restrictions are virtually useless. Ordinarily they are interpreted to set the maximum amount of a contribution by a person to any one candidate, party, or committee. This does not prevent an individual from giving sums up to the maximum amount to several committees operating on behalf of the same person, or several members of the same family from giving the maximum amount to the same candidate. As noted in Chapter 2, both of these techniques were used by members of the Kennedy family to pump an enormous amount into the successful senatorial campaign of John F. Kennedy in 1952. An attempt to reach these practices would require that individuals in the same family be prohibited from making contributions beyond the limit to a candidate or party, a rule almost certainly indefensible on both constitutional and policy grounds inasmuch as it establishes restrictions on the political activities of citizens on the basis of consanguinity.

In the third class of regulations are those which limit spending. One approach is to limit the amounts which may be spent by candidates, committees, and parties. A second is to restrict the purposes of spending, either by specifying the purposes for which money may be spent, or by enumerating those for which it may not be expended. Statutory limits on the amounts which can be spent are found in federal law, which prohibits national political committees from spending more than $3 million a year, and in thirty states, although in twenty-one the limitations apply to candidates but not to committees operating in their behalf and hence are meaningless. Limits on spending are most commonly stated in dollar terms; e.g., candidates for governor of Tennessee are limited to expenditures of $25,000 each in the primary and the general election. They are sometimes stated in terms of certain sums per vote; thus Missouri sets its limit at $8 for each one hundred votes cast in the candidate's constituency for all candidates for president in the last presidential election.[7] It is common to provide certain exclusions from these expenditure ceilings. Wisconsin, for instance, limits expenditures by candidates for governor to $10,000, but excludes the cost of mailing one communication to all voters in the state and the cost of a one-quarter page advertisement in all papers in the state or the equivalent in smaller, separate advertisements.[8]

The peculiar theory embedded in these limitations is that the expenditure of money in large sums is a public wrong per se. The establishment of absolute limits does not by itself guarantee spending parity between the candidates, for even when the limit is set at a low figure it is possible that one candidate can raise enough money to spend to the limit while others are unable to raise even a fraction of that sum. And if parity were assured, it is difficult to see what difference it makes if candidates spend small or large sums as long as they spend equally.

A different criticism of spending limitations is that they are too rigid, even where based on a certain sum per vote cast. Inflation and new campaign techniques may cause the cost of performing the same campaign functions to rise at a faster rate than the increase in the size of the electorate. Yet politicians find it difficult to alter the limits which are enacted because they fear public misunderstanding and criticism of such changes. (This situation is analogous to the difficulty in increasing the salaries of elected officials at a time when living costs and standards of living have risen steadily.)

The other variety of expenditure limits may be somewhat more defensible, at least in some of its forms. Specifying the purposes for which money may be spent neglects the steady change in campaign technology and the consequent need to spend money for new purposes. Furthermore, the attempts to be explicit about legitimate purposes of spending often lead to odd results. "Oklahoma permits, among other expenses, those for transportation of sick, poor, and infirm voters to polls; apparently expenses to transport healthy and vigorous voters are illegal!"[9] On the other hand, bans on certain kinds of spending

may bespeak community beliefs about the ethics of a democratic political system. Bans on expenditures to bribe voters are
clearly of this kind.

The fourth division of campaign finance regulations is control
by publicity. Thirty-six states require the filing of reports which
detail campaign receipts and forty-three require such reports of
expenditures.[10] There is, however, considerable variance among
the states as to whether reports are required for both primaries
and general elections, from both candidates and committees,
and both before and after the balloting. Only ten states combine
all of these by requiring the filing of statements of receipts and
expenditures for both primaries and general elections and both
before and after such elections.[11] The most comprehensive laws
also require reporting of the names and addresses of contributors and the amounts contributed as well as the amounts and
purposes for which sums were disbursed.

There are apparently two major objectives of these disclosure
laws. First, they are theoretically helpful in the enforcement of
the various kinds of limitations considered in the previous paragraphs. It seems, however, a silly expectation that candidates or
political committees which violate these restrictions would then
report these violations in their official filings. As a practical
matter, the only enforcement benefit that disclosure laws have is
the occasional reporting of a minor infraction which occurs
because the law's provisions are obscure. The second purpose of
disclosure laws is to inform the public of the amounts, purposes,
and sources of campaign funds so that voters can judge candidates with this information available.

The most widely noted disclosure law in the United States is
Florida's so-called "who gave it—who got it" law, passed in
1951.[12] The law requires that each candidate designate a Campaign Treasurer and that all contributions and expenditures in
behalf of a candidate be channelled through that Treasurer.
Gubernatorial candidates are required to report contributions
and expenditures weekly; other candidates report monthly. No
new contributions can be received during the last five days of
the campaign, and although a final expenditure statement is filed
fifteen days after the election, experience with the law indicates

that more than 95 per cent of expenditures are reported before election day.[13]

Appraisals of the Florida law have been almost unanimously favorable. In the election immediately prior to the law's enactment, two candidates for the United States Senate acknowledged spending somewhat less than $100,000 apiece. It was widely believed, however, that at least $500,000 had been spent in each campaign.[14] In subsequent gubernatorial elections, the reports of candidates revealed much higher spending. The total spending reported in Democratic gubernatorial primaries was $563,730 in 1952, immediately after the law's passage, and rose to $2,269,231 in 1966. "It is the informed judgement of those who should know . . . that Florida voters have been given an excellent profile of the financial support of all candidates before the lever is pulled in the voting booth."[15] In part this has been achieved by the vigor with which newsmen and opposition candidates comb through the reports seeking inconsistencies, suspicious contributors, and inaccuracies.[16] A side benefit of this rigorous reporting system has been a greater understanding among voters of the true cost of running for office and a greater willingness to accept the real costs of democracy.[17]

This approach to disclosure laws stresses that they keep the "voter informed of all money involved in political contests so that, *before* he votes, he can know the amount received by each candidate, the identity of contributors and the amount contributed by each donor, and the amount of expenditures and the type of expenditures made by each candidate."[18] Massachusetts sought these same objectives in its Campaign Fund Reporting Act passed just before the 1962 election. Many of its provisions closely resembled the Florida law, the major difference being semi-monthly rather than weekly reporting. Yet in Massachusetts the experiment, which has apparently succeeded in Florida, failed. The Massachusetts Crime Commission found, "[t]here is almost universal circumvention of the provisions of our Campaign Fund Reporting Act in the reporting of contributions and expenditures."[19] Murray B. Levin has reported that both Edward McCormack and Edward Kennedy and their treasurers reported receipts and expenditures far below reasonable estimates that could be made from careful observation of their primary contest for the United States Senate in 1962 and of Kennedy's successful general election campaign.[20] The press corps in Massachusetts apparently did not attempt to determine the accuracy of the reports and in the late stages of the campaign the reports received only minimal attention in the press.[21] It seems clear, therefore, that the enactment of full disclosure laws does not necessarily provide the public with full information which it can use to judge candidates at the polls. Even in the Florida case one may be skeptical about the public's actual attentiveness to campaign finance data in light of its demonstrated immunity to most news about political issues and figures.

There are constitutional problems, public policy concerns, and doubts about the feasibility of full disclosure laws. The constitutional issue centers around the campaign-treasurer provision. Can citizens be precluded from making direct expenditures in behalf of political candidates without violating their constitutionally protected freedom of speech and press? Since the campaign-treasurer provision requires that all expenditures on a candidate's behalf be made by and through the treasurer, this question requires an affirmative answer if the Florida precedent is to be followed. The issue has not reached the United States Supreme Court. The Florida Supreme Court upheld the campaign-treasurer provision in 1953 as a constitutional exercise of the state's police powers.[22] On the other hand, a similar campaign-treasurer provision of an early version of the Wisconsin corrupt practices act was struck down by that state's highest court[23] as an unconstitutional invasion of Article I, Section 3 of the Wisconsin Constitution which guarantees that "every person may freely speak, write and publish his sentiments on all subjects. . . ." At least one law review comment argues that the Supreme Court would be unlikely to find the regulation of campaign finance so important and the use of money in politics so dangerous as to justify statutory provisions which would permit candidates, acting through the campaign-treasurer mechanism, to prevent individuals from acting in their own discretion to spend money to express their opinions about political candidates.[24]

Beyond the constitutional issue, there are two questions of public policy raised by the full disclosure law. First, even if the campaign-treasurer provision is a constitutional exercise of state police powers, is it wise for a pluralistic political system to control political expressions by those who are not part of authorized campaign organizations by making the expenditure of funds by such persons and groups contingent upon candidate approval? Controls of this kind seem a high price to pay to regulate money in politics. A second policy question is whether the full disclosure scheme, standing alone, adequately confronts the main money-in-politics issue. It does not, for instance, assist the potential candidate who is deterred from running by high costs. More importantly, full disclosure does not increase the ability of political parties, particularly the minority party in one-party districts, to engage in the organizational and campaign activities which have the kinds of significant consequences for a democratic polity discussed in Chapter 5.

A fifth approach to campaign financing has been government subsidies, both direct and indirect. Wisconsin experimented for a brief time after the turn of the century with a direct subsidy, but abandoned the plan because of its cost. In 1909, Colorado adopted a program of direct subsidies based on the number of votes cast for each party's candidate for governor, but the program never went into effect because it was declared unconstitutional by the state Supreme Court and then repealed by the legislature.[25] Oregon prepares a pamphlet providing information about candidates and issues in both primary and general elections and pays the cost of distribution to every registered voter. Wisconsin provides a small amount of free radio and television time on the state-owned networks. Tax deductions for political contributions are permitted in Minnesota, California, Missouri, and Hawaii.[26]

The most important direct subsidy experiment is being tried in the Commonwealth of Puerto Rico.[27] Each party is entitled to draw up to $75,000 annually for non-election year expenses; any portion of this allowance not spent can be accumulated for use in the election year. Prior to 1964, each party was permitted an additional election year subsidy of $150,000, but this was found to be inadequate and a new law provides much more generous grants. At this writing, each party continues to receive its $75,000 for operating expenses each year; in the election year it also draws $75,000 for campaign expenses and $12,500 for transporting voters to the polls. In addition, the parties divide an $800,000 campaign fund and a $200,000 voter transportation fund on the basis of their proportionate shares of the straight-ticket votes cast in the election. They may collect only that portion of their appropriate share of each of these funds which is in excess of the already granted statutory minima of $75,000 for campaign purposes and $12,500 for voter transportation.

The rationale of the Puerto Rican subsidy plan was officially stated in the Popular Democratic Party's 1956 platform.

[The Party] favors the adoption of measures necessary to assure the proper function of political parties, which are indispensable instruments of democracy. In the fulfillment of their functions, parties incur inevitable and justifiable expenses. *In order to protect them from the risks of subordination to economic power,* the Popular Democratic Party will sponsor legislation authorizing financial aid from the State. . . ."[28]

Although the subsidy plan was justified in terms of protecting parties from economic interests, its original espousal was motivated primarily by concern about the established Puerto Rican practice of assessing public employees 2 per cent of their salaries to support the party.[29]

The most recent campaign subsidy proposal is the Long Plan, mentioned in Chapter 1, for financing presidential and congressional campaigns. At this writing, it is pending before the United States Congress. The Honest Elections Act of 1967, favorably reported by the Senate Finance Committee on November 1, 1967,[30] is actually a comprehensive regulatory scheme which includes an income tax credit for one-half of contributions of up to $50, provisions requiring the complete reporting of receipts and expenditures by presidential and congressional candidates and their committees as well as by national political committees, and an extension of federal reporting requirements to primary as well as general elections. The subsidy provision is, however, the one which has captured the most attention. It provides for candidates for president and congress to choose between public and private financing. If public financing is chosen, subsidies are provided for presidential candidates of major parties—those receiving more than 25 per cent of the vote—of 20 cents per vote for each presidential vote cast in the previous election. Senatorial subsidies are 50 cents times the number of votes up to 200,000, plus 35 cents times the number of votes between 200,000 and 400,000, plus 20 cents times the number of votes over 400,000. No formula was adopted for financing campaigns for the House of Representatives on the ground that the House itself ought to develop such a formula when the bill reaches it for consideration.

Minor parties are defined in the Act as those receiving between 5 and 25 per cent of the vote. A minor party presidential candidate would be entitled to 40 cents for each vote which the party's presidential candidate received in the prior presidential election, or which he received in the election being subsidized, whichever total vote is higher. The per-vote subsidy for a minor party senatorial candidate would be based on the number of votes for the party's candidates in the two preceding senatorial elections, or the preceding presidential election, whichever vote total was highest. The allotment would be $1 per vote for the first 100,000 votes, 70 cents per vote for the next 100,000 votes and 40 cents per vote for each vote over 200,000. While major party candidates opting for public subsidies would not be able to receive or spend money from private sources during campaign periods, minor party candidates would be permitted to do so until their total spending had reached the maximum amount of spending permitted to major party candidates who had "gone public."

As indicated in Chapter 1, a previous subsidy proposal championed by Senator Long was approved on four occasions by the Senate, but it was returned to the Finance Committee on a final roll call vote. The Honest Elections Act of 1967 was drafted in response to Senate instructions to revise the original bill. Although apparently far from passage, its provisions are an important example of the subsidy approach to campaign finance.

A Preference for Subsidies

The author's policy preference is for direct subsidies to parties and candidates at both the national and the state levels. Subsidy programs are often advocated as a remedy for the influence which interests in the community are alleged to have as a result of their campaign contributions. The Puerto Rican subsidy plan was explicitly justified as protecting parties "from the risks of subordination to economic power." There may be some merit to this argument, in a time of sharply rising political costs, if subsidies free politicians from the need to solicit funds from interests with whom they are not in agreement and whose contributions are therefore viewed on both sides as obligating the officeholder to acts which he would not otherwise perform. On the whole, however, this justification for subsidies seems misdirected.

One major point of this study is that money is only one of many political resources. To eliminate the direct flow of money from interests to political campaigns does not prevent them from multiple voting by the allocation of other resources. For example, a subsidy plan does not diminish the influence of those who control the news media. They continue to possess a significant political resource—the ability to reach the public with their opinions about candidates, officeholders, and parties. Those who lead or influence large blocs of voters organized on economic, religious, or ethnic lines will continue to have influence in politics. Even those who have traditionally sought influence by making financial contributions would not be frozen out of politics by political subsidies: instead of using their money for campaign gifts, they would use it for other purposes which would nonetheless have political effects. The political goals of unions could, for instance, be advanced by shifting money previously contributed to candidates to accelerated voter registration efforts, to get-out-the-vote drives, and to political education. By carefully selecting the vote groups which would be the targets of such activities, interest groups could aid some candidates and parties and disadvantage others. Because of its convertibility, money lends itself to a variety of uses by interests concerned with decisions made in the political arena, and the establishment of subsidy programs would not "sanitize" politics by eliminating the political influence of such groups.

A broader question is whether the elimination of functional representation for economic and other interests would be desirable, even if a subsidy program could achieve that purpose. A notable aspect of contemporary politics is that voter interests are not organized along the geographical lines which are used as a basis for the election of public officials. The most important political interests are organized around men's occupations; others are organized on such non-geographic lines as religion, national origin, and ideology. One way in which these groups can take an active part in promoting their viewpoints is by the allocation of resources, including money, to politics. It is not at all clear that the elimination of such activities improves the quality of representative government; it may indeed substantially diminish it.

In American politics, money and other political resources are for the most part used to gain representation, rather than improperly to influence decisions of public officials. Interests seem quite clearly to support the parties and candidates whose attitudes on given issues are quite close to their own. Labor support for the Democratic Party and business support for the Republican party are highly rational because the policy stances of those interest groups tend to be well represented by those parties. This is not due primarily to the financial support gained from such interests. Voting studies demonstrate that the vote bases of the parties are distinctly different; and the pattern of financing, especially in states such as Wisconsin and Michigan, tends to be consistent with the differences in their electoral support. Furthermore, studies of party leaders and of voting in legislative bodies show more division on issues between the parties than is commonly attributed to American politics. In short, campaign contributions do not on the whole buy policies or preferments in the governing process; rather they serve to re-enforce existing policy differences because the major contributors of money and other political resources tend to support the parties whose electoral bases and policy conduct are already close to their own.

Thus the case for public subsidies is not based on a belief that private financing is pernicious and should be eliminated, but rests rather on the assumption that legitimate activities are supported by political expenditures and that private financing does not yield sufficient funds adequately to provide for the conduct of such activities at even a minimum level. Clearly a preference for public subsidies is not, in this context, a protest against the costs of politics. It was argued in Chapter 3 that costs are not high from a system-wide perspective, and indeed the implication of Chapter 5 is that more money ought to be spent for political activities. Public financing may, however, be pertinent to the high level of costs as seen from the perspective of candidates because it would ease the burden of raising funds and thereby let down one of the significant barriers to candidacy by some well-qualified persons.

To make more explicit the basis on which this argument for public subsidies rests, the major findings of Chapter 5 should be restated, namely that very few campaign expenditures are for purposes which violate democratic ethics and that most political spending sponsors activities which have significant supportive consequences for a democratic political system. Foremost among these activities is recruiting. The development of a cadre of party activists and the recruitment of candidates, especially minority party candidates in one-party districts, is essential to a democratic political system as well as important to the self-promoting objectives of political parties. A democratic system works badly where the opposition is not everywhere strong enough to assure voters an alternate set of leaders to vote into office in times of discontent. Furthermore, opposition candidates and party activists are of help in safeguarding the integrity of elections and in keeping those who hold office responsive to the public by engaging in the functions of vigil and criticism which the main body of citizens is too preoccupied or disinterested to perform.

In addition to recruiting, both parties ought to have the

resources to sustain a flow of basic information to voters. There is no assurance that voters in large numbers will be attentive, but the information ought to be available for those voters and in those times when it is desired. Such basic information as the names of candidates and officeholders is not possessed by a significant share of the electorate, and many of those who do have a command of the basic information about politics are uninformed about issues and the stands of the parties and candidates on those issues. Parties can provide this kind of political information and increase the number of viewpoints available to the attentive public. To do this effectively, however, requires expenditures for such party organization efforts as canvassing, campaign materials, and, most expensively, the purchase of mass media advertising. It is clear that most campaigns, rather than performing these activities well, do so unevenly. Campaign subsidies would not assure the performance of these functions but adequate funds are a necessary condition for their performance.

Parties are also one of the major instruments for expanding political participation by the electorate. Participation not only makes the government somewhat more representative by facilitating the registering of public preferences for candidates, parties, or policies, it also strengthens the legitimacy of a democratic political system by engendering popular consent for the policies adopted by government. The cost of getting out the vote is, however, an increasingly unmanageable one for parties because of the disappearance of precinct organization and the dispersion and mobility of the urban population.

The performance of all these system-affecting functions at even minimum levels of effectiveness has become increasingly difficult and costly because of changes in the larger political environment. Old style political organizations, which were relatively efficient at canvassing and getting out the vote, are disappearing both because their organizational incentives are no longer desirable and because public attitudes have changed toward them. The electorate is now more attentive to mass media and it is therefore through those channels that parties must reach voters, if they are to reach them at all. The need to use media and to use it intensively occurs simultaneously with sharp increases in the price of radio and television time and newspaper space.

Furthermore there is apparently a nationalization of politics underway in the United States; in many formerly one-party states—though by no means in all of the legislative and congressional districts, counties, and cities within those states—the parties have in recent years become closely competitive. Not only is such competition a political reality, but it is apparently a condition preferred by a large share of the public: fully 67 per cent of respondents to the University of Wisconsin Survey Research Laboratory poll agreed that "democracy works best where competition between the parties is strong"; only 12 per cent disagreed. Yet competitive politics is substantially more expensive than one-party politics, and the rise of two-party politics in formerly one-party areas accelerates the costs of campaigns which were previously contested only as a formality, if at all. The growth of the electorate further increases political costs by requiring more elaborate and expensive campaign efforts in areas where personal contact with voters was once feasible, while increasing the price levels of the media advertising which must be substituted for personal campaigning. It should be noted also that the number of offices contested in the United States is large and that as a consequence costs are higher.

There are probably enough Americans willing to make contributions to finance the political system; in addition to the 11 per cent of Americans who report having contributed to politics, there are another 25 per cent of respondents to national polls who indicate a willingness to contribute if asked. The difficulty is that there is no effective machinery for soliciting these contributions. Parties are not organized to engage in door-to-door canvasses for funds; indeed their door-to-door and telephone canvasses for votes reach only a quarter of adult Americans. Direct mail fund appeals have met with only limited success. The proposals for tax deductions and tax credits do not address the problem; they provide incentives to contribute rather than a method of collecting the money, which is apparently the more difficult problem. Even mass membership parties, such as those which exist in Wisconsin and other states in the upper midwest, have not provided an adequate machinery for raising sufficient funds from private sources to finance the activities of political parties and the election campaigns of political candidates.

In the face of increased needs for money and the inability to raise funds in small amounts on a mass basis, parties and candidates have become increasingly reliant on large contributions. This reliance may have some of the effects feared by those who believe campaign funding is a source of undue influence in government. It is more likely to have two other effects which have significant systemic consequences. In the first instance, it discourages many potential candidates who, knowing of the need to raise enormous sums, do not enter political campaigns because they cannot or will not solicit the large contributions which are necessary in the absence of effective mass financing. For instance, a 1967 Gallup Poll of a representative sample of 61,967 individuals listed in *Who's Who in America* showed that almost a quarter of them were interested in running for office if adequate campaign funding was available. Second,

[i]ncreases in the size of individual contributions create uneasiness in the minds of the public. Actually, the exercise of undue influence occurs infrequently. Nonetheless, the circumstance in which a candidate is obligated to rely on sizable contributions easily creates the impression that influence is at work. This impression—however unfounded it might be—is itself intolerable, for it erodes public confidence in the democratic order.[31]

In summary, the case for public subsidies rests on the belief that political parties and candidates perform certain significant system-maintaining functions in a democratic polity. These activities require financing, but private financing has provided inadequate funds for their performance. Nor are parties likely to be able to develop adequate fund-raising machinery or methods to make private giving a feasible way to meet their financial needs. At the same time, the political environment is changing in such a way as to put still greater financial demands on the already beleaguered parties. Because parties "are indispensable instruments of democracy,"[32] it seems appropriate to provide them with public financing in the performance of their activities.

Problems and Implications

A major problem which has plagued discussions of campaign subsidies is whether they ought to be supplements to or substitutes for private financing of politics. Puerto Rico, for example, permits private financing in addition to public subsidies, but the Long Plan would require candidates to make a choice between the two. The considerations reviewed in the preceding section lead us to prefer the Puerto Rican approach. It would be exceedingly difficult effectively to make public financing exclusive where a candidate opted for public rather than private financing. Those who would ordinarily allocate funds to political parties or candidates could evade the system by replacing direct contributions with spending for political activities which would indirectly promote their parties and candidates. In addition, those who engaged in primary contests would be advantaged by such a system. If primaries were publicly financed, candidates who faced contested primaries would receive public money in the primary and then additional public funds in the general election. This would give them greater total resources for campaigning than if they received only a general election subsidy. Even if private money was used to finance the primary, there would still be an advantage in having primary opposition. Private money could be spent in the primary and the public subsidy would still be available in the general election; the total spending of a candidate involved in a primary would thus be some private funds plus the public subsidy, while the total spending of a candidate with no primary contest would be only the amount of the public subsidy. As a result, parties and candidates would be encouraged to sponsor nominal primary opponents so that additional money, either a public subsidy or private funds, could be spent during the primary on a campaign build-up which would be in addition to that purchased with the public subsidy during the general election campaign.

The policy implications of the "public or private" approach pose even more serious objections than the arguments of its infeasibility. There is probably too little money being spent now on American politics to perform in all of the country's political districts those activities whose consequences are useful for the political system. Since it is unlikely that any public subsidy would provide funds in a quantity sufficient to support political activities at much beyond the present levels, private financing in addition to public subsidies would increase the total amounts spent and make possible, though not guarantee, the more thorough performance of these functions. A still more important consideration is that of functional representation. It has already been argued that functional representation is probably desirable in a modern democracy and that financial contributions are one form of such representation. The granting of public subsidies should not require the elimination of such representation through private contributions.

Related to the question of whether subsidies should be instead of or in addition to private financing is the issue of disclosure. A preference for mixed public and private financing implies mandatory full disclosure of the sources and amounts of all private contributions and of the purposes, amounts, and recipients of all expenditures of both public and private funds. Private giving is justified in part as a form of representation; by this same reasoning, the general public is entitled to know who is represented and to what extent in all of the constituencies, including the financial constituencies, of those who would govern. Objects of expenditure, regardless of the source of funds, are also a matter of public interest. Continued review of financed activities is necessary to permit evaluation of whether the activities sponsored by public and private funds are those which are deemed proper by a democratic electorate and of whether public subsidies support the kinds of political activities which justify them, i.e., those viewed as helpful in maintaining a democratic society.

The monitoring of the expenditure of public funds does not pose serious technical problems. Expenditures by parties and candidates could be routed on vouchers through an appropriate public official who would regularly report the amounts, purposes, and recipients of such payments. It is more difficult to achieve full disclosure of receipts and expenditures of private funds. The Florida law described in the first section of this Epilogue provides a model on which a regulatory scheme might be patterned. Some reworking of the campaign-treasurer concept would be needed to eliminate both the constitutional and policy objections to it. A sound approach might require those who spend independently of the official campaign apparatus to file statements with the appropriate governmental agency or to channel their expenditures through the treasurer while maintaining control of the purposes of that spending.

A major weakness of most disclosure laws is the enforcement procedure. It is often placed in the hands of elected officials, but they are disinclined to prosecute violators because they fear the repercussions for their own partisans. It is impossible to prescribe watchfulness by the press and the public; but where it exists, as in Florida, it has been a major incentive for enforcement of the reporting laws. As a second-best measure, enforcement ought to be in the hands of a non- or bipartisan commission with adequate staff to receive reports, examine them, require additional information where they are inadequate, subpoena records where necessary, and prosecute violators of the full disclosure provisions. In addition, individual citizens should be given easy access to the courts either to force the commission to act if it fails to do so, or directly to enjoin candidates and parties to fulfill the legal requirements where they fail to do so. Private citizens ought also to be permitted to bring actions under whatever forfeiture provisions are included in the laws if the proper officials refuse requests to bring such actions. Private financing ought to be subject to the watchful eye of the opposition, the public, and the press before the casting of votes in an election. Such a goal cannot be perfectly attained, but every effort to provide for full disclosure before elections that can reasonably be legislated ought to be.

A second problem in the subsidy approach is the amount or level of such subsidies. Statutory establishment of lump-sum grants seems unwise because of the play of environmental factors which affect the level of costs. As previously indicated, Puerto Rico soon found its set sum subsidies woefully inadequate and was required substantially to increase the amounts. It is often difficult for political reasons to change the established grant levels. Politicians fear hostile public reactions to such expenditures of public funds; and those candidates and parties advantaged by a given situation are unlikely to be enthusiastic about changes which improve the resource situation of their opponents.

The Long Plan proposes an equal subsidy for each major party candidate based on the total number of votes cast for the office being sought. A formula based on the total number of votes cast in the constituency would be suitable for grants to parties as well. Equal subsidies for opposing candidates and parties, regardless of the political balance in the district, is of course consistent with the purpose of public financing, which is to guarantee that candidates and parties can perform certain political activities with at least a minimum level of effectiveness. Calculating subsidies on the number of votes cast recognizes that the size of the electorate is one important determinant of campaign costs.

The initial calculation of the per vote subsidy should be based on the per vote cost of political activities in fairly typical two-party competitive jurisdictions. This approach overlooks, of course, the variations in costs due to local circumstances, such as differing salary levels or advertising costs. To the extent that state legislatures might enact subsidy plans for state and local candidates and party organizations, state-to-state variations would be taken into account. It would be much more difficult to take regional differences into account in federal legislation providing subsidies for candidates for the House and Senate, since unequal per vote subsidies for different states and districts would be politically infeasible.

Inasmuch as prices of campaign materials and activities rise with other price increases in the system, a "cost of campaigning" index should be developed which would permit automatic computations of new per vote subsidy levels as price changes occur in the goods and services most commonly employed in politics. This would not, however, provide for major changes in costs resulting from the development of new and more expensive campaign techniques, such as the cost changes which occurred because of television's use as a political instrument, and those which are accompanying the use of public opinion polls and the application of computer technology in politics. An advisory board, of the kind proposed by Senator Long, ought to be established to recommend to the state and national legislatures changes in the subsidy formulae as new political techniques develop.

Public financing for both candidates and parties is by no means uncontroversial. Puerto Rico pays subsidies to parties, both for interelection operating expenses and for campaign activities. While the original version of the Long Plan provided for grants to the national committees of the political parties, the revised version provides for grants to candidates. The question of who ought to be subsidy recipients is related to the issue of party reform, which has been vigorously debated among political scientists for the last two decades. If subsidies are directed to parties, then parties will gain some additional influence with elected officials and the extent of party discipline in the American system will be increased. On the other hand, if public money is given to candidates, they will be less dependent on party than they are now, thus weakening the incentives for policy-oriented citizens to become party activists and further weakening party discipline in government. This last would, of course, have the consequence of diminishing the capability of parties to perform one of the functions or activities, already performed weakly in the United States, which it is often argued is a significant party responsibility, namely the marshalling of the various branches and segments of the government to enact and execute coherent policy.

Unless one is prepared to accept much more or much less party influence over political candidates and officeholders than now exists, some balanced program of subsidies both to party organizations and to candidates seems preferable. In the inter-election periods parties perform the significant functions of recruitment, organization, vigil, and criticism. These activities ought to be subsidized, and parties ought to be permitted to allot some share of their funds, as they now do, to campaign purposes. At the same time, during the election period candidates would receive direct subsidies so they can engage in the campaign-period activities which were described as significant for the political system in Chapter 5. A condition of payments to both candidates and party units ought to be that subsidy money should be spent in their districts or jurisdictions and not transferred to other areas; this requirement would assure that at least to the extent supportable by public grants, political activities would be performed in each locale.

An additional question in the allocation of subsidy money is which party committees or units ought to be subsidized. Again, this is related to the issue of party reform inasmuch as subsidies to the center—to state party committees or to the national committee—would strengthen those elements within the party; subsidies to local units would increase their relative importance as opposed to the central and upper level committees within the party and would increase the relative importance of those local party units which had few private resources as opposed to local units within the same party which had ample supplies of such resources. It is difficult to develop any plan which serves the purposes of public financing without substantially altering the configuration of influence within the parties.

The major layers of party organization, especially the national committees, the central party units in the states, and the most significant local units, such as the county organizations in Wisconsin, should be financed on the basis of the number of votes cast within their jurisdictions. This would channel the same aggregate amounts to the national, state, and local levels. It would tend to strengthen slightly the weakest units within any given level and the weaker layer of party units within any state. Nonetheless, the stronger elements within the party would continue to have an advantage because of their continued ability to raise money from private sources. It seems preferable to treat the two parties equally, as with candidate subsidies, since the purpose is to achieve a certain level of political activity by each party. A formula based on party strength, measured by a party's

vote or its registration rolls, would not permit the minority party
in a one-party area to perform even a minimum level of desired
political activities since it would receive a very small subsidy
and would ordinarily have little ability to convert and to pyramid resources into an adequate political fund.

Perhaps the most difficult policy question raised by public
financing of politics is whether nominating contests, especially
primaries, ought to be subsidized. In many of the nation's
political districts nomination is tantamount to election and thus
the primary in fact determines who will hold public office. Even
in a two-party district, it is often necessary for candidates to
finance primary campaigns. From the candidate's perspective,
money may be more important in the nominating process than
in the general election.[33] In primaries there is no party label
voting and less early voter decision; the electorate is more easily
influenced by the kinds of campaigning that money can buy.
Nonetheless, it is not clear that from a systemic perspective
nomination contests need be publicly financed. While the financing of minority parties in one-party districts would not, of
course, assure close two-party electoral competition in such
districts, it would permit the minority party to present candidates and programs so as effectively to offer a choice to the electorate. This is probably all that a democratic system requires.
Furthermore, a nomination contest is, from a public perspective, a battle to determine which men and issues will be identified as representing a party, and such determinations are appropriately made by the clash of elements within a party's coalition.
It artificially distorts the distribution of influence within a party
to subsidize all contestants for nomination and it does not serve
a clear public purpose, since general election subsidies assure
that there will be serious party activity in presenting choices to
voters in the final balloting. This is not to argue that there is no
public interest in the nominating process, for clearly there is.
This must be balanced, however, against the desirability of
parties determining their own nominees by internal processes
which reflect their basic internal power configurations, and the
prospect that public funds would be claimed by armies of
spurious candidates who can easily get on the primary ballot in

the overwhelming number of American jurisdictions by filing petitions signed by minimal numbers of registered voters. In such a scale, the balance seems to this author to go against public financing, but it might warrant some publicly sponsored information effort such as the Oregon voter pamphlet which is a significant indirect subsidy to serious candidates but does not seem to have been a sufficient incentive for spurious candidates to enter the electoral lists in large numbers.

The appropriate treatment of minor parties and minor party candidates has perplexed advocates of public subsidies. The Long Plan's approach to minor party candidates seems an especially suitable one. By defining minor parties as those which receive between 5 and 25 per cent of the vote, any party with a substantial body of public support is guaranteed some subsidy. At the same time, minor parties are not subsidized at the same rate as major parties. They receive a higher per vote allotment, but they receive it only for the votes they actually receive, whereas the major parties receive their allotments for all the votes cast for the office contested. This plan could easily be extended to local and state offices and to party organizations. Its greatest virtue is that it provides minor parties and their candidates with financing at a fairly low threshold of voter approval, and the financing provided is sufficient to support further appeals so that a lack of money alone does not prevent minor parties and their candidates from attaining major party status.

A strong case can be made for the theory of public financing and the provisions of such a plan can be worked out to minimize its implications for other aspects of the political system, but gaining acceptance for public financing is exceedingly difficult. In the first instance, politicians who are advantaged by the private financing system are reluctant to support public subsidies. Although they would retain their advantage in receipts from private sources, they realize that political dollars are subject to the principle of diminishing returns: where all parties and candidates are well financed, the extra dollars spent probably make less of an impact. Even though the disparity in absolute dollars might remain the same in a public-plus-private financing situation, the proportionate disparity and the real political importance of the disparity in financial resources would in fact be less than in a private-financing-only situation. These strategic calculations ordinarily mean that in the United States politicians of the dominant party in one-party districts will oppose subsidies since they will not be anxious to increase the resources of the second party lest it become more competitive. Furthermore, in the competitive districts, those who have usually had the greatest financial resources will also oppose public financing since they will not want to surrender any of their resource advantages in situations where slight alterations in resource distribution might change election outcomes. The overwhelming number of legislative districts, both national and state, will therefore be represented by men who, in considering public financing of politics, will have a sound initial reason for opposition.

These strategic considerations by politicians are re-enforced in the United States by public attitudes. Sixty-eight per cent of respondents to the 1964 University of Wisconsin Survey Research Laboratory poll disagreed or strongly disagreed with the proposition that "tax deductions should be allowed for people who contribute money to the political party of their choice" and only 19 per cent favored such a policy. Tax deductions are a much milder form of public support for politics than direct subsidies, and it seems likely therefore that hostility to public financing would be at least as great. The University of Michigan's national poll showed that in 1964 tax deductions for political contributions were opposed by 55 per cent of respondents and favored by 26 per cent, while direct subsidies to presidential candidates were opposed by 71 per cent and favored by only 11 per cent. The combination of strategic considerations and public attitudes makes the adoption of subsidy plans extremely difficult even at the presidential level where the magnitude of costs has been widely publicized and where the office and those seeking it ordinarily command considerable public respect. Subsidies for candidates for lesser offices and for political parties would be even more difficult to enact. The majorities given to the presidential subsidy plan on a series of test votes in the United States Senate indicate that political leaders, faced with the problems of rising political costs, are to a greater extent than their constituents willing to support some candidate subsidies; and that some of them at least have made their policy decisions in the face of strategic disadvantages which they or their parties would suffer as a result of a subsidy plan.

Summary

This study has directed its attention to money as a political resource. The review of political spending emphasized not only the gravity of the problem that political finance creates for politicians, but also how relatively modest is the burden that financing politics places on the whole system, and concluded that both the amount and the distribution of spending are caused by larger variables in the political system. Spending does not, as so much popular lore would have it, spring uniquely from the vicious character of politicians. At the same time that the level of spending seems only a slight cost from the perspective of the entire system, the recurring uses to which money is put by politicians in striving for their own goals have significance for that entire system. The recruitment, training, and marshalling of candidates and activists as well as the circulation of information about candidates and issues serve important purposes in a large democratic state: they assure choice at the polls and increase the opportunities for public understanding of the nature of the choices. In addition, a substantial portion of the money spent in politics promotes public participation in the electoral process, thus increasing both the representativeness of the results and the sense of commitment to the enacted policies. The evidence is that these activities are inadequately performed, primarily because politics is underfinanced, and that this is most acutely so in America's very numerous one-party districts at the state and local levels. In all districts, but in these especially, the very essence of democratic politics—a reasonably vigorous opposition—is eroded by the present system of political funding.

From these conclusions about the role of money in American

politics are derived this chapter's prescriptions for reform. The goal of such reform is a limited one. There is no intent to restructure the whole set of power relationships in American politics by extensive redistributions of political resources; rather the proposed subsidy programs would strengthen the many centers of political energy—the array of party units and army of candidates—which crowd the American political landscape. The opportunity for functional representation of groups and individuals in the political process by the allocation of their private resources to candidates and causes they prefer is not foreclosed by such a program, but the danger that large givers might improperly influence public policy by obligating candidates and officials to acts which they regard as contrary to the public interest is diminished. Indeed, even if more ambitious goals than these were desired, the advances in description and analysis of money in American politics made in this volume are not great enough to support dramatic legislative proposals with any reasonable confidence that their workings would in fact achieve such goals. The farthest reach that seems warranted by the present state of scholarly research into the role of money in American politics is a program to provide adequate financial nourishment to candidates and parties so that they will be assured that minimum supply of resources which is a precondition to their performance of political activities whose consequences are central to a democratic polity.

Appendix

This Appendix presents the data upon which the Index of Expenditure for each country reported in Table 7 is based. The data used differ in several ways from those which Heidenheimer used in his original Index of Expenditure calculations in the *Journal of Politics* symposium: Average Hourly Wage for *all* Industrial Workers has been substituted for that of Male Industrial Workers in our modified Index of Expenditure because of the difficulty of obtaining the figures prescribed by Heidenheimer. Indeed, it appears that Heidenheimer himself had some difficulty obtaining this information since in several cases, notably that of the United States, he actually made his own calculations with the same figures used here.

Although Heidenheimer reported an Index of Expenditure for India, we were unable to do so because the wage and hour materials available could not be adapted to make such calculations. Finally, there is a difference between his data and ours on the proper exchange rates for foreign currency, especially the exchange rate of the Australian dollar. The exchange rate he employed yielded a substantially higher Index of Expenditure than the one used here.

Table 41

Data Used to Calculate Modified Indexes of Expenditure
for Various Jurisdictions

	Total Expenditures[a]	*Total Vote*[a]	*Cost Per Vote*	*Hourly Wage Rate*
Australia[b]	$2.24	5.4	$0.41	$1.51
Germany (DM)	90	33	2.75	2.62
Italy (Lit.)	29,000	29.5	1,000	0.220
Israel (IL)	27	1.05	25.7	1.21[c]
Japan (Y)	6,000	40	150	150.4[d]
Philippines (P)	80	6.5	12	0.67[e]
Great Britain (£)	5.24	27.8	3s.3d.	4s.7d.
United States	$175	69	$2.53	$2.26
Wisconsin ('58)	$1.7[f]	1.2	$1.52	$2.11
Wisconsin ('62)	$3.07[f]	1.26	$2.43	$2.51

[a] In millions.

[b] Converted to American dollars.

[c] Wages reported as IL 10.2 per day; work week reported as 42 hours. Calculations assume a 5-day work week.

[d] Wages reported as Y 22,630 per month; work week reported as 47.8 hours. Calculations based on $4\frac{1}{2}$ work weeks per month.

[e] Wages reported as P 135 per month; work week reported as 44.6 hours. Calculations based on $4\frac{1}{2}$ work weeks per month.

[f] Based on "Total Expenditures: Corrected Estimates" in Table 4.

Sources: Cost estimates other than the United States, Arnold J. Heidenheimer, "Comparative Party Finance: Notes on Practices and Toward a Theory," *Journal of Politics*, 25 (Nov., 1963), 797–98.

United States cost estimates, Alexander Heard, *The Costs of Democracy* (Chapel Hill: University of North Carolina Press, 1960), p. 371.

Vote totals for other than the United States and Great Britain, Heidenheimer, "Comparative Party Finance," p. 798.

Vote data for Great Britain, *Keesing's Contemporary Archives* (Bristol, Eng.: Keesing Publications, 1959–60), Vol. XII, p. 17, 029A.

United States and Wisconsin vote data, *1958 Wisconsin Blue Book* and *1962 Wisconsin Blue Book*.

Wage rates for other than the United States, *United Nations Statistical Yearbook* (New York: Statistical Office of the United Nations, 1967), pp. 530–32.

Hours-of-work data for other than the United States, *ibid.*, pp. 107–8.

Hourly wage data for the United States and Wisconsin, *Statistical Abstract of the United States* (Washington: Government Printing Office, 1962), p. 240.

Notes

Preface

1 In Wisconsin, the filed reports are made on a form headed "Election Financial Report," which has space for previously reported totals of receipts and expenditures, itemized listings of new receipts and expenditures, and a statement certifying the accuracy of the figures.

2 These counties are Brown, Calumet, Chippewa, Dane, Dodge, Dunn, Eau Claire, Fond du Lac, Green, Jefferson, Manitowoc, Marinette, Oconto, Outagamie, Racine, Rock, Walworth, Waukesha, and Winnebago.

Chapter One

1 The best brief review of this incident is found in *1956 Congressional Quarterly Almanac,* pp. 469–78.

2 *Ibid., 1966,* pp. 494–96, 719–20, 1413–31, 1437.

3 Harry W. Ernst, *West Virginia: The Primary That Made a President,* Eagleton Institute Cases in Practical Politics, No. 26 (New York: McGraw-Hill Book Co., Inc., 1962), p. 31.

4 *Gallup Political Index,* Report No. 15 (August, 1966), p. 18; " '68 Candidates Hustle to Fill Larger Coffers," *The Milwaukee Sentinel,* Dec. 22, 1967, p. 3; Frank J. Sorauf, *Party Politics in America* (Boston: Little, Brown & Co., 1968), pp. 250–51, 304.

5 The President's Commission on Campaign Costs. *Financing Presidential Campaigns* (Washington: Government Printing Office, 1962).

6 President Lyndon B. Johnson, *Message on Election Reform* of May 29, 1966.

7 A good brief review of the maneuvering on the Long proposal and the key roll call votes is found in *1967 Congressional Quarterly Weekly Report,* pp. 775–79. See also, U.S. Congress, Senate, Committee on Finance, *Report on Honest Elections Act of 1967* (90 Congress, 1 session, Report No. 714, Washington, 1967).

8 Elston Roady, "Ten Years of Florida's 'Who Gave It—Who Got It' Law," *Law and Contemporary Problems,* 27 (1962), 434–44.

9 Henry Wells, *Government Financing of Political Parties in Puerto Rico* (Princeton: Citizens' Research Foundation, 1961); Henry Wells and Robert W. Anderson, *Government Financing of Political Parties in Puerto Rico: A Supplement to Study Number Four* (Princeton: Citizens' Research Foundation, 1966).

10 Louise Overacker, *Money in Elections* (New York: The Macmillan Company, 1932). Also, Louise Overacker, "Campaign Funds in a Depression Year," *American Political Science Review,* 27 (October, 1933), 769–83; "Campaign Funds in the Presidential Election of 1936," *ibid.,* 31 (June, 1937), 473–98; "Campaign Finance in the Presidential Election of 1940," *ibid.,* 35 (August, 1941), 701–27; "Presidential Campaign Funds, 1944," *ibid.,* 39 (October, 1945), 899–925. Additional material on the 1944 campaign is found in her *Presidential Campaign Funds* (Boston: Boston University Press, 1946).

11 Alexander Heard, *The Costs of Democracy* (Chapel Hill: University of North Carolina Press, 1960).

12 Herbert E. Alexander, *Money, Politics and Public Reporting* (Princeton: Citizens' Research Foundation, 1960); *Money for Politics: A Miscellany of Ideas,* ed. Herbert E. Alexander (Princeton: Citizens' Research Foundation, 1963); Herbert E. Alexander, *Responsibility in Party Finance* (Princeton: Citizens' Research Foundation, 1963).

13 Herbert E. Alexander, *Financing the 1960 Election* (Princeton: Citizens' Research Foundation, 1962), and his *Financing the 1964 Election* (Princeton: Citizens' Research Foundation, 1966).

14 John R. Owens, *Money and Politics in California: Democratic Senatorial Primary, 1964* (Princeton: Citizens' Research Foundation, 1966); William Buchanan and Agnes Bird, *Money as a Campaign Resource: Tennessee Democratic Senatorial Primaries, 1948–1964* (Princeton: Citizens' Research Foundation, 1966); Donald G. Balmer, *Financing State Senate Campaigns: Multnomah County, Oregon, 1964* (Princeton: Citizens' Research Foundation, 1966); H. Gaylon Greenhill, *Labor Money in Wisconsin Politics, 1964* (Princeton: Citizens' Research Foundation, 1966); Robert J. McNeill, *Democratic Campaign Financing in Indiana, 1964* (Princeton: Citizens' Research Foundation, and Bloomington: Indiana University Institute of Public Administration, 1966); John P. White and John R. Owens, *Parties, Group Interests and Campaign Finance: Michigan '56* (Princeton: Citizens' Research Foundation, 1960).

15 For a review of the literature and the recent evidence debunking the original hypothesis see Heard, *The Costs of Democracy,* pp. 16–19.

16 Robert Dahl, *Who Governs?* (New Haven: Yale University Press, 1961), p. 226.

17 Nelson Polsby and Aaron Wildavsky, *Presidential Elections* (2d ed.; New York: Charles Scribner's Sons, 1968), pp. 35–53.

18 James Reichley, *States in Crisis* (Chapel Hill: University of North Carolina Press, 1964), pp. 234–41.

19 Buchanan and Bird, *Money as a Campaign Resource,* p. 8. Party organization may be a factor in primaries, however, if one candidate receives party support denied to others. This is the case in Wisconsin Republican nominating politics, where there is pre-primary endorsement. Candidates who receive party endorsement can rely on the active support of most party leaders and workers as well as substantial financial assistance from the party treasury.

20 Dahl, *Who Governs?,* p. 226.

21 Buchanan and Bird, *Money as a Campaign Resource,* p. 8.

22 Murray Levin, *Kennedy Campaigning* (Boston: Beacon Press, 1966), pp. 289–95.

23 Dahl, *Who Governs?,* p. 227.

24 *Ibid.,* pp. 226, 308–10. Implicit in the idea that resources may be pyramided is the notion of "slack" in politics (see *ibid.,* p. 305). Simply put, this means that most people allocate to politics either a very small amount of their resources or none at

all. To the extent that the politician is successful in taking up this slack by moving people to allocate to politics their resources in amounts greater than the resources he devotes to convincing them, he pyramids his resources.

25 Buchanan and Bird, *Money as a Campaign Resource,* p. 10.
26 Dahl, *Who Governs?,* pp. 305–8, and Reichley, *States in Crisis,* pp. 234–41, consider political resources as tools in the hands of politicians whose skill and energy and predispositions affect the way in which they manage these resources.
27 Maurice Duverger, *Political Parties,* trans. Barbara and Robert North (New York: John Wiley and Sons, 1963), p. 366.
28 *Ibid.,* p. 63.
29 See, for example, Leon D. Epstein, *Political Parties in Western Democracies* (New York: Frederick A. Praeger, 1967), pp. 14–15; Frank Sorauf, "Political Parties and Political Analysis," *The American Party Systems,* eds. William Nesbet Chambers and Walter Dean Burnham (New York: Oxford University Press, 1967), pp. 50–55. This represents a departure from the structural-functional approach which attempts to identify the functions common to all political systems and then searches for the institutions and agencies which perform these functions in various political systems. See, for example, Gabriel Almond and James Coleman, *The Politics of the Developing Areas* (Princeton: Princeton University Press, 1960), ch. 1, esp. p. 17.
30 Sorauf, "Political Parties and Political Analysis," pp. 49–50.
31 Epstein, *Political Parties in Western Democracies,* p. 14.
32 See for instance: Clinton Rossiter, *Parties and Politics in America* (Ithaca: Cornell University Press, 1960), ch. 2. Also Sorauf, *Political Parties in the American System,* pp. 2–6, but note his qualification of his functional approach in his "Political Parties and Political Analysis," pp. 48–55, esp. n., p. 49, and (p. 50) his list of "functions" commonly found in the literature on political parties. Note as well Sigmund Neumann, "Toward a Comparative Study of Political Parties" in his *Modern Political Parties* (Chicago: The University of Chicago Press, 1956), pp. 396–400.
33 Sorauf, *Political Parties in the American System,* p. 3.

Chapter Two

1 This section draws heavily on Leon D. Epstein, *Politics in Wisconsin* (Madison: University of Wisconsin Press, 1958),

esp. ch. 3; also, Frank Sorauf, "The Voluntary Committee System in Wisconsin: An Effort to Achieve Party Responsibility" (Unpub. Ph.D. Diss., Univ. of Wis., 1953); and John Fenton, *Midwest Politics* (New York: Holt, Rinehart & Winston, 1966), esp. ch. 3. Helpful were Harold Gosnell, *Grass Roots Politics* (Washington: American Council of Public Affairs, 1942), ch. 4, and my own research in "The 1960 Election in Wisconsin" (Unpub. M.S. Thesis, Univ. of Wis., 1962), esp. ch. 2. Valuable information on the Wisconsin electorate can be found in Leon D. Epstein, *Votes and Taxes* (Madison: Institute of Governmental Affairs, University of Wisconsin, 1964), esp. chs. 2–3, and the survey data presented on pp. 37–76. Also note Austin Ranney and Leon D. Epstein, "The Two Electorates: Voters and Non-Voters in a Wisconsin Primary," *The Journal of Politics,* 28 (August, 1966), 598–616.

2 Complete Wisconsin vote data by county for presidential, senatorial, and all statewide constitutional offices can be found in James R. Donoghue, *How Wisconsin Voted: 1848–1960* (Madison: Institute of Governmental Affairs, 1962). Supplements have brought the data up to date for recent elections.

3 In 1948, Thomas E. Fairchild was elected attorney general on the Democratic ticket. His was not a party victory. Aided by a prominent Wisconsin political name, he was elected with the support of many Republicans and a large share of the Republican press when the Republican primary was won by an unknown named Martin whom the electorate apparently mistook for the previous incumbent Republican, John Martin, who had been elevated to the state supreme court by gubernatorial appointment.

4 Fenton, *Midwest Politics,* esp. ch. 8. See also his *People and Parties in Politics* (Glenview, Illinois: Scott, Foresman, 1966), chs. 2–5.

5 Sorauf, "The Voluntary Committee System in Wisconsin," p. 89.

6 *Ibid.,* pp. 99–101.

7 Epstein, *Politics in Wisconsin,* pp. 83–86.

8 Fenton, *Midwest Politics,* p. 62.

9 Fenton reports the preference for Goldwater among Republican leaders, *ibid.,* p. 61.

10 For roll call scores by these organizations for the 87th, 88th, and 89th Congresses respectively, see *1962 CQ Weekly Report,*

p. 2219; *1964 CQ Weekly Report,* p. 2542; *1966 CQ Weekly Report,* p. 2754.

11 Philip E. Converse, "The Nature of Belief Systems in Mass Publics," *Ideology and Discontent,* ed. David E. Apter (New York: The Free Press of Glencoe, 1964), pp. 206–61.

12 The regulations for other states are found in Herbert E. Alexander with the assistance of Laura Denny, *Regulation of Political Finance* (Berkeley and Princeton: Institute of Governmental Studies and Citizens' Research Foundation, 1963), p. 7. The Wisconsin rules are in Wisconsin, *Statutes* (1965), secs. 12.01 and 12.58.

13 Hugh Douglas Price, "Campaign Finance in Massachusetts in 1952," *Public Policy,* 6 (1955), 25–46.

14 Thus, as of 1965, the county clerk of one county had no records dating back beyond the 1964 general election, and he offered to give those records to the researcher who showed up to examine them.

15 Both Secretary of State Robert Zimmerman and the officials of the State Historical Society of Wisconsin were instrumental in making this project feasible. Without their forbearance and continual assistance during a 22-month period, I could not have developed the data upon which this study is based. Similar co-operation was received from the appropriate local officials in 19 of the 20 counties visited. Only in Milwaukee County was there official resistance to the examination of filed financial statements. Recourse to the city attorney and district attorney finally forced the county Election Commission and its staff to make the records available, but not until the staff had destroyed the 1958 records which, while technically not required to be kept, had still been in the Commission's files when the initial request to examine the records was made.

16 John P. White and John R. Owens, *Parties, Group Interests and Campaign Finance: Michigan '56* (Princeton: Citizens' Research Foundation, 1960), n., p. 9.

17 Commonwealth of Kentucky, *Election Laws* (Legislative Research Commission, Research Publication No. 52, 1957), pp. 113–19. The states were Indiana, Kansas, Kentucky, Maryland, Nebraska, and Oregon.

18 Wisconsin, *Statutes* (1965), secs. 12.01 and 12.09.

19 *Ibid.,* secs. 12.09(5) (a) and 12.58.

20 This problem is not unique to Wisconsin: 32 states require reports from candidates and committees for both primary and general elections, 10 of them both before and after each election. Alexander and Denny, *Regulation of Political Finance,* p. 7.

The advent of computer technology may ease somewhat the volume-of-data problem in the study of campaign finance. Computers cannot, however, review the filed reports of candidates and committees to select and gather pertinent data. Nor can they identify the group affiliations of individual givers. Their greatest use is, of course, in sorting and tabulating data which has been gathered and put on cards; but the enormity of the task of gathering the pertinent data to be sorted and tabulated is a deterrent to scholarly research and to effective public disclosure.

21 I wish to express my gratitude for the assistance of Sharon Bauspies, Kathleen Van Galder, and especially Alice Knight. Their efforts in putting the contributor names on cards, eliminating the multiple contributors, and categorizing the contributors according to source and size made Chapter 6 of this study possible.

22 Alexander and Denny, *Regulation of Political Finance,* pp. 14–15.

23 Price, "Campaign Finance in Massachusetts in 1952," pp. 25–26; White and Owens, *Parties, Group Interests and Campaign Finance,* pp. 9–10.

24 Alexander Heard, *The Costs of Democracy* (Chapel Hill: University of North Carolina Press, 1960), n., p. 372.

25 Wisconsin, *Statutes* (1965), sec. 12.09(3). This provision apparently requires reports of contributions in kind to candidates, their committees, and statutorily created party committees. It does not appear to apply to so-called voluntary committees which are the major spending units in Wisconsin politics.

26 Wisconsin, *Statutes* (1965), sec. 12.50.

Chapter Three

1 H. Gaylon Greenhill, *Labor Money in Wisconsin Politics, 1964* (Princeton: Citizens' Research Foundation, 1967).

2 *Ibid.,* pp. 37–38.

3 Herbert E. Alexander, *Financing the 1964 Election* (Princeton: Citizens' Research Foundation, 1966), pp. 9–10.

4 Alexander Heard, *The Costs of Democracy* (Chapel Hill: University of North Carolina Press, 1960), p. 372.

5 In 1964, Republican party membership was between 40,000 and 50,000, while the Democratic party counted 26,000 persons on its membership rolls. All of these people do not work in political campaigns, much to the regret of campaign managers, but a small proportion of them are gluttons for political work and many of the rest engage in at least modest efforts. The total manhours of labor contributed by all these political activists reaches truly Herculean proportions during a campaign, and the value of these services must reach a minimum level of at least $1 million, even at a rate of only $1.50 per hour.

6 Edmond Cahn, *The Predicament of Democratic Man* (New York: The Macmillan Company, 1961), p. 28.

7 *Ibid.*

8 Alexander, *Financing the 1964 Election,* p. 8, and *Financing the 1960 Election* (Princeton: Citizens' Research Foundation, 1962), p. 11. Also, Heard, *The Costs of Democracy,* p. 20.

9 Heard, *The Costs of Democracy,* p. 425.

10 Paul Douglas, "The High Cost of Elections," *New Republic,* 127 (December 22, 1952), 9.

11 William Buchanan and Agnes Bird, *Money as a Campaign Resource: Tennessee Democratic Senatorial Primaries, 1948–1964* (Princeton: Citizens' Research Foundation, 1966), p. 85.

12 James Reichley, *States in Crisis* (Chapel Hill: University of North Carolina Press, 1964), pp. 235–41.

13 Coleman Ransone, Jr., *The Office of Governor in the United States* (University, Ala.: University of Alabama Press, 1956), pp. 102–12.

14 Frank Sorauf, *Party Politics in America* (Boston: Little, Brown and Co., 1968), p. 304.

15 *Ibid.*

16 David Leuthold, *Electioneering in a Democracy: Campaigns for Congress* (New York: John Wiley and Sons, 1968), p. 75.

17 *Ibid.,* p. 104.

18 These data were developed by the author as part of an unpublished study, "Political Finance: Notes for a Systemic Approach."

19 Duane Lockard, "The State Legislator," *State Legislatures in America,* ed. Alexander Heard (Englewood Cliffs, New Jersey: Prentice-Hall, Inc., 1966), p. 112.

20 Donald G. Balmer, *Financing State Senate Campaigns: Multnomah County, Oregon, 1964* (Princeton: Citizens' Research Foundation, 1966), pp. 17, 22–23.

21 This figure is attributed to State Democratic Chairman Louis Hanson by political columnist John Wyngaard in his "Wisconsin Report," *Green Bay Press Gazette,* June 29, 1966.

22 "Number 1 Problem in Politics: Paying Those Campaign Bills," *Newsweek,* 59 (March 26, 1962), 27.

23 See Richard F. Schier, "Political Fund Raising and the Small Contributor: A Case Study," *Western Political Quarterly,* 11 (March, 1958), 104–12. In a solicitation of 20,000 registered Democrats for small contributions, $6,324 was grossed but only $3,541 netted after expenses of $2,783. Furthermore, a good deal of effort by party volunteers was directed to this effort and should be considered an expense inasmuch as it diverted efforts from other projects to reach the voters.

24 Heard, *The Costs of Democracy,* n., p. 373.

25 *Ibid.,* pp. 373–74, 383–84.

26 Herbert E. Alexander, *Financing the 1960 Election* (Princeton: Citizens' Research Foundation, 1962), p. 9, and *Financing the 1964 Election,* pp. 8–9.

27 Arnold Heidenheimer, "Comparative Party Finance: Notes on Practices and Toward a Theory," *Journal of Politics,* 25 (November, 1963), 796–97; Heard, *The Costs of Democracy,* pp. 372–75; Alexander, *Financing the 1960 Election,* p. 12, and *Financing the 1964 Election,* p. 13.

28 Adamany, "Political Finance: Notes for a Systemic Approach."

29 Heidenheimer, "Comparative Party Finance: Notes on Practices and Toward a Theory," pp. 799–801.

30 *Ibid.,* p. 800.

Chapter Four

1 David Adamany, "Political Finance: Notes for a Systemic Approach" (unpublished).

2 Alexander Heard, *The Costs of Democracy* (Chapel Hill: University of North Carolina Press, 1960), p. 383.

3 John R. Owens, "Party Campaign Funds in Connecticut, 1950–1954" (Unpub. Ph.D. Diss., Syracuse Univ., 1954), pp. 128, 133.

Four contests for senatorial seats in two years were the result of a set of unusual circumstances: early in 1950 the incumbent

Republican United States senator resigned the remaining two years of his term and Democratic governor Chester Bowles appointed William Benton to fill the seat until November, when both a special election to fill the seat temporarily held by Benton and the regular election for Connecticut's other seat were held. In 1952 the term of the seat filled by special election in 1950 expired, and the death of Brian MacMahon, the other incumbent, created another dual vacancy.

4 *Ibid.,* p. 126.
5 Heard, *The Costs of Democracy,* pp. 383–85. Arnold Heidenheimer, "Comparative Party Finance: Notes on Practices and Toward a Theory," *Journal of Politics,* 25 (November, 1963), 799–800.
6 Adamany, "Political Finance: Notes for a Systemic Approach."
7 The electoral effectiveness of mass parties is considered by Leon D. Epstein, *Political Parties in Western Democracies* (New York: Frederick Praeger, 1967), ch. 9. See also, James Q. Wilson, *The Amateur Democrat* (Chicago: The University of Chicago Press, 1962), chs. 8 and 10.
8 For a discussion of whether new techniques displace old ones, see Heard, *The Costs of Democracy,* pp. 403–5.
9 Leon D. Epstein, *Votes and Taxes* (Madison: Institute of Governmental Affairs, University of Wisconsin, 1964), pp. 43–45.
10 Heard, *The Costs of Democracy,* p. 82. Lester Milbrath, *Political Participation* (Chicago: Rand McNally & Company, 1965), ch. 1.
11 For a description of the special effectiveness of businessmen in raising funds for civic as well as political purposes, see Heard, *The Costs of Democracy,* pp. 220–22.
12 William Buchanan and Agnes Bird, *Money as a Campaign Resource: Tennessee Democratic Senatorial Primaries, 1948–1964* (Princeton: Citizens' Research Foundation, 1966), pp. 77–81.
13 Coleman Ransone, Jr., *The Office of Governor in the United States* (University, Ala.: University of Alabama Press, 1956), p. 105.
14 V. O. Key, Jr., *Politics, Parties and Pressure Groups* (New York: Thomas Y. Crowell Company, 1964), p. 490.
15 Heard, *The Costs of Democracy,* p. 384.
16 Heidenheimer, "Comparative Party Finance: Notes on Practices and Toward a Theory," pp. 799–800.

17 David Leuthold, *Electioneering in a Democracy: Campaigns for Congress* (New York: John Wiley and Sons, 1968), pp. 74–75, 80.

18 V. O. Key, Jr., *Southern Politics* (New York: Alfred A. Knopf, 1950), ch. 14.

19 Allan P. Sindler, "Bifactional Rivalry as an Alternative to Two-Party Competition in Louisiana," *American Political Science Review,* 49 (September, 1955), 641–62.

20 Key, *Southern Politics,* ch. 14.

21 Richard E. Dawson and James A. Robinson, "Inter-Party Competition, Economic Variables, and Welfare Policies in the American States," *Journal of Politics,* 25 (May, 1963), 265–87.

22 Richard I. Hofferbert, "The Relation Between Public Policy and Some Structural and Environmental Variables in the American States," *American Political Science Review,* 60 (March, 1966), 73–82.

23 John Fenton, *People and Parties in Politics* (Glenview, Illinois: Scott, Foresman, 1966), chs. 2–5. Also, Fenton, *Midwest Politics* (New York: Holt, Rinehart, and Winston, 1966), ch. 8.

24 Heard, *The Costs of Democracy,* p. 21.

25 *Ibid.* Labor spending is included in the Democratic share of spending.

26 John P. White and John R. Owens, *Parties, Group Interests and Campaign Finance: Michigan '56* (Princeton: Citizens' Research Foundation, 1960), p. 16.

27 Adamany, "Political Finance: Notes for a Systemic Approach."

28 Herbert E. Alexander, *Financing the 1964 Election* (Princeton: Citizens' Research Foundation, 1966), p. 8.

29 V. O. Key, Jr., *Public Opinion and American Democracy* (New York: Alfred Knopf, 1960) ch. 6. Also, Angus Campbell et al., *The American Voter* (New York: John Wiley and Sons, 1960), ch. 13.

30 Milbrath, *Political Participation,* ch. 1.

31 Epstein, *Votes and Taxes,* pp. 43–45.

32 Louise Overacker, *Presidential Campaign Funds* (Boston: Boston University Press, 1946), p. 15; and Heard, *The Costs of Democracy,* pp. 123–24.

33 White and Owens, *Parties, Group Interests and Campaign Finance,* pp. 30–31.

34 Adamany, "Political Finance: Notes for a Systemic Approach."

35 Heard, *The Costs of Democracy,* p. 124; see also my Chapter 6.

36 Heard, *The Costs of Democracy*, pp. 213–24.
37 *Ibid.*, p. 130.
38 H. Gaylon Greenhill, *Labor Money in Wisconsin Politics, 1964* (Princeton: Citizens' Research Foundation, 1967).
39 In Wisconsin, the law has permitted unions to contribute dues money to candidates for state and local offices, except for one interlude from 1955 to 1959 when the so-called Catlin Act made such contributions illegal. See Donald P. Kommers, "Organized Labor's Political Spending and the Catlin Act" (Unpub. M.A. Thesis, Univ. of Wis., 1957), for a discussion of the background, passage, operation and effect of the Catlin Act.
40 Apparently the situation is substantially different in Michigan where Democratic party organization leaders play the leading role in raising money for statewide candidates. The money goes through the candidate committees rather than the party organization, but the organization leaders are nonetheless instrumental in finance matters. White and Owens, *Parties, Group Interests and Campaign Finance*, p. 17. Although Wisconsin Democratic party leaders may be active in candidate fund raising, the party leadership in a corporate sense does not act as the fund-raising cadre for the gubernatorial or senatorial candidates.
41 Heard, *The Costs of Democracy*, p. 7.
42 Leon D. Epstein, *Politics in Wisconsin* (Madison: University of Wisconsin Press, 1958), ch. 3, esp. pp. 82–86.
43 Frank Sorauf, "The Voluntary Committee System in Wisconsin: An Effort to Achieve Party Responsibility" (Unpub. Ph.D. Diss., Univ. of Wis., 1953), pp. 140–41.
44 *Ibid.*, pp. 55, 140.
45 *Ibid.*, p. 140.

Chapter Five

1 Louise Overacker, *Money in Elections* (New York: The Macmillan Company, 1932), pp. 5–14.
2 *Ibid.*, p. 7.
3 Quoted, *ibid.*, p. 8.
4 *Ibid.*, p. 9.
5 Alexander Heard, *The Costs of Democracy* (Chapel Hill: University of North Carolina Press, 1960), n., pp. 395–96.
6 *Ibid.*, p. 394.
7 *Ibid.*, p. 393.

8 *Ibid.*, n., p. 394.
9 Richard Rose, *Influencing Voters* (New York: St. Martin's Press, 1967), pp. 79–80.
10 Wisconsin, *Statutes* (1965), secs. 12.09 (3) (d) and 12.09 (5) (b).
11 Heard, *The Costs of Democracy*, p. 393.
12 *Ibid.*
13 *Ibid.*, pp. 403–5.
14 Ten of the state's 14 television stations provided the requested information, although only 5 of them had been operating in 1954 and 8 of them in 1956. Other stations which had been on the air in those years had been bought by or merged with other television corporations and data for them were not available. Sixteen of the state's 41 daily newspapers responded with the desired data.
15 Nineteen weekly papers chose to and were able to provide full cost data going back to 1954, while 431 such papers operate in the state. Many of these outlets, however, do not take political advertising because they are organizational bulletins, college newspapers, etc. Eight of the state's 75 commercial radio stations provided the requested information.
16 U.S. Congress, Senate, Committee on Privileges and Elections, *Report, 1956 General Election Campaigns* (85 Congress, 1 session, Washington, 1957); Federal Communications Commission, *A Survey of Political Broadcasting* (Washington, D.C., 1965).
17 Daniel Katz and Samuel J. Eldersveld, "The Impact of Local Party Activity upon the Electorate," *Public Opinion Quarterly*, 25 (Spring, 1961), 11–12.
18 Phillips Cutright and Peter Rossi, "Grassroots Politicians and the Vote," *American Sociological Review*, 23 (April, 1958), 179.
19 Raymond E. Wolfinger, "The Influence of Precinct Work on Voting Behavior," *Public Opinion Quarterly*, 27 (Fall, 1963), 387–98.
20 Leon D. Epstein, *Politics in Wisconsin* (Madison: University of Wisconsin Press, 1958), p. 81.
21 *Ibid.*, ch. 4. Also, David Adamany, "The Size-of-Place Analysis Reconsidered," *Western Political Quarterly*, 17 (September, 1964), 477–86.

22 Epstein, *Politics in Wisconsin,* pp. 82–86.
23 Leon D. Epstein, *Political Parties in Western Democracies* (New York: Frederick A. Praeger, 1967), p. 125.
24 Cutright and Rossi, "Grassroots Politicians and the Vote," p. 179.
25 Warren Miller, "One-Party Politics and the Voter," *American Political Science Review,* 50 (September, 1956), 707–25.
26 *Ibid.,* p. 715.
27 Samuel J. Eldersveld, "Experimental Propaganda Techniques and Voting Behavior," *American Political Science Review,* 50 (March, 1956), 160.
28 Katz and Eldersveld, "The Impact of Local Party Activity upon the Electorate," p. 17.
29 *Ibid.,* p. 11.
30 John Wyngaard, "Wisconsin Report: Party Leaders Find Value in Filling Local Tickets," *Green Bay Press Gazette,* June 18, 1966, Editorial page.
31 H. Gaylon Greenhill, *Labor Money in Wisconsin Politics, 1964* (Princeton: Citizens' Research Foundation, 1966), p. 31.
32 Katz and Eldersveld, "The Impact of Local Party Activity upon the Electorate," p. 17.
33 M. Margaret Conway, "Voter Information Sources in a Nonpartisan Local Election," *Western Political Quarterly,* 21 (March, 1968), 75.
34 Epstein, *Political Parties in Western Democracies,* p. 233.
35 These data were collected by the University of Michigan Survey Research Center and are reported in Frank Sorauf, *Party Politics in America* (Boston: Little Brown and Co., 1968), p. 249.
36 Bernard Rubin, *Political Television* (Belmont, California: Wadsworth Publishing, 1967), p. 3.
37 *Ibid.,* p. 4.
38 William A. Glaser, "Television and Voting Turnout," *Public Opinion Quarterly,* 24 (Spring, 1965), 73–74.
39 Avery Leiserson, *Parties and Politics* (New York: Alfred A. Knopf, 1950), p. 75.
40 Paul Lazarsfeld, Bernard Berelson, and Hazel Gaudet, *The People's Choice* (New York: Columbia University Press, 1948), p. 50.
41 *Ibid.,* p. 51.
42 Bernard Berelson, Paul Lazarsfeld, and William McPhee, *Voting* (Chicago: University of Chicago Press, 1954), pp. 110–12.

43 Lazarsfeld et al., *The People's Choice,* p. 50.

44 *Ibid.,* p. 151.

45 Berelson et al., *Voting,* pp. 118–20.

46 *Ibid.,* p. 254.

47 V. O. Key, Jr., *Public Opinion and American Democracy* (New York: Alfred Knopf, 1960), pp. 360–61.

48 The two-step flow of communication was suggested by Lazarsfeld et al, *The People's Choice,* p. 151. The most important work modifying this hypothesis is Elihu Katz and Paul F. Lazarsfeld, *Personal Influence* (Glencoe, Ill.: The Free Press, 1955), esp. ch. 14. This volume also confirms findings that public affairs opinion leaders tend to be somewhat older than those they advise, to be somewhat more gregarious, and to have somewhat higher social status. They are also shown to be much greater users of the media as a source of information than others in the population, while nonetheless also relying more heavily on personal contacts for the same purpose. Additionally, public affairs opinion leadership is found to be disproportionately an activity of men in the community. *Ibid.,* esp. chs. 12, 14, and 15.

49 Berelson et al., *Voting,* pp. 248–50.

50 Lazarsfeld et al., *The People's Choice,* pp. 152–53.

51 Fred I. Greenstein, *The American Party System and the American People* (Englewood Cliffs, New Jersey: Prentice-Hall, 1963), p. 31.

52 *Ibid.*

53 Angus Campbell, Gerald Gurin, and Warren Miller, *The Voter Decides* (Evanston, Illinois: Row, Peterson and Co., 1954), p. 18.

54 Leon D. Epstein, *Votes and Taxes* (Madison, Wis.: Institute of Governmental Affairs, 1964). Also Jay G. Sykes, *Wisconsin Gets a Sales Tax,* Eagleton Institute Case Studies in Practical Politics, No. 38 (New York: McGraw-Hill Book Co., 1965).

55 *Ibid.,* pp. 1–18 describes the enactment of the compromise tax bill and the subsequent maneuvering within the Democratic party.

56 *Ibid.,* p. 18.

57 *Ibid.*

58 *Ibid.*

59 Epstein, *Votes and Taxes,* pp. 23–24.

60 *Ibid.,* p. 25.

61 *Ibid.,* p. 29.
62 Sykes, *Wisconsin Gets a Sales Tax,* p. 29.
63 *Ibid.,* p. 26.
64 *Ibid.,* p. 30.
65 Berelson et al., *Voting,* p. 236.
66 *Ibid.,* p. 202.
67 Epstein, *Votes and Taxes,* p. 54.
68 *Ibid.,* p. 57.
69 Rose, *Influencing Voters.*
70 Joseph Schumpeter, *Capitalism, Socialism and Democracy* (New York: Harper and Bros., 1950), p. 269. Also, R. T. McKenzie, *British Political Parties* (New York: St. Martin's Press, 1955), pp. 585–91.
71 Epstein, *Politics in Wisconsin,* p. 93. Note that his data show that only 40 per cent of legislators reported such contacts by party leaders. This figure does not, however, contradict the responses of party leaders concerning their recruitment activities because their efforts are likely to be greatest in opposition-dominated districts where "self-starting" candidates do not come forward and ticket-fillers must be recruited. The defeated legislative candidates were not included in Epstein's data, yet they were the most likely to have been encouraged or persuaded by party leaders.
72 Julius Turner, "Primary Elections as the Alternate to Party Competition in 'Safe' Districts," *Journal of Politics,* 15 (May, 1953), 201.
73 Berelson et al., *Voting,* ch. 14. Lester Milbrath, *Political Participation* (Chicago: Rand McNally, 1965), ch. 6.
74 *Ibid.,* p. 149.
75 *Ibid.,* p. 150. Also, Herbert McClosky, "Consensus and Ideology in American Politics," *American Political Science Review,* 58 (June, 1964), 361–82; James W. Prothro and C. M. Grigg, "Fundamental Principles of Democracy: Bases of Agreement and Disagreement," *Journal of Politics,* 22 (Spring, 1960), 276–94.
76 These data were obtained from the Survey Research Center at the University of Michigan and the University of Wisconsin Survey Research Laboratory, respectively. Other survey data on Wisconsin used in this chapter are also from the latter source unless otherwise attributed.

77 V. O. Key, Jr., *The Responsible Electorate* (Cambridge: Harvard University Press, 1966), passim.

78 Angus Campbell, Philip Converse, Warren Miller, and Donald Stokes, *The American Voter* (New York: John Wiley & Sons, 1960), ch. 9, esp. pp. 201–2; and Greenstein, *The American Party System and the American People*, pp. 88–89.

79 *Ibid.*, pp. 11–17.

80 Coleman Ransone, Jr., *The Office of Governor in the United States* (University, Alabama: University of Alabama Press, 1956), pp. 374–78.

81 Berelson et al., *Voting*, pp. 246–50.

82 Key, *Public Opinion and American Democracy*, p. 346.

83 Jack Dennis, "Support for the Party System by the Mass Public," *American Political Science Review*, 60 (September, 1966), 600–615.

84 Milbrath, *Political Participation*, p. 106.

85 *Ibid.*, p. 105.

86 Richard Rose and Harve Mossawir, "Voting and Elections: A Functional Analysis," *Political Studies*, 15 (1967), 189.

87 *Ibid.*, pp. 190–91.

Chapter Six

1 Leon D. Epstein, *Politics in Wisconsin* (Madison: University of Wisconsin Press, 1958), p. 77.

2 Wisconsin, *Statutes* (1965), sec. 12.56.

3 *Ibid.*, sec. 12.09.

4 H. Gaylon Greenhill, *Labor Money in Wisconsin Politics, 1964* (Princeton: Citizens' Research Foundation, 1966), pp. 23–24, 30–31.

5 *Ibid.*, pp. 36–39, contains the best summary of labor's direct political activities and their costs.

6 *Milwaukee Journal*, March 21, 1966.

7 Frank Sorauf, "The Voluntary Committee System in Wisconsin: An Effort to Achieve Party Responsibility" (Unpub. Ph.D. Diss., Univ. of Wis., 1953), p. 140, reports a contrary finding, but his impressions were based on party situations in the early 1950's, when the structure and tools of fund raising were substantially different in both parties.

8 For a more complete discussion of the Wisconsin parties, see my Chapter 2. Also, Frank Sorauf, "Extra-Legal Parties in

Wisconsin," *American Political Science Review*, 48 (September, 1954), 692–704; Epstein, *Politics in Wisconsin*, ch. 5; John Fenton, *Midwest Politics* (New York: Holt, Rinehart & Winston, 1966), chs. 3 and 8.

9 Sorauf, "The Voluntary Committee System," pp. 52–55.

10 Maurice Duverger, *Political Parties*, trans. Barbara and Robert North (New York: John Wiley and Sons, 1963), p. 64.

11 Louise Overacker, *Presidential Campaign Funds* (New York: The Macmillan Company, 1932), p. 19.

12 Arnold J. Heidenheimer, "Comparative Party Finance: Notes on Practices and Toward a Theory," *Journal of Politics*, 25 (November, 1963), p. 792.

13 *Ibid.*

14 *Ibid.*, p. 793.

15 *Ibid.*

16 Linda Reivitz, "Campaign Contributions to Governor John W. Reynolds: 1964" (Unpub. Senior Honors Thesis, Univ. of Wis., 1965).

17 Duverger, *Political Parties*, p. 63.

18 Herbert E. Alexander, *Financing the 1964 Election* (Princeton: Citizens' Research Foundation, 1966), p. 93.

19 Hugh Douglas Price, "Campaign Finance in Massachusetts in 1952," *Public Policy*, 6 (1955), 36–39.

20 Alexander Heard, *The Costs of Democracy* (Chapel Hill: University of North Carolina Press, 1960), pp. 49–50.

21 *Ibid.*, n., p. 50.

22 Price, "Campaign Finance in Massachusetts in 1952," pp. 31, 42.

23 This method of calculation may lead to some imprecision because of the practice of charging additional amounts for premium locations in certain advertising booklets. However, rate cards were not available, and the estimates are probably in error as to only a very few ads, e.g., those on the back covers of booklets.

24 Greenhill, *Labor Money in Wisconsin Politics, 1964*, pp. 40–42.

25 Epstein, *Politics in Wisconsin*, p. 79.

26 Heard, *The Costs of Democracy*, p. 124.

27 *Ibid.*, pp. 120–24. Also, Herbert E. Alexander, *Financing the 1960 Election* (Princeton: Citizens' Research Foundation, 1962), pp. 63–66, and Alexander, *Financing the 1964 Election*, pp. 90–95.

28 Heard, *The Costs of Democracy,* pp. 123–25.

29 These 1964 figures differ slightly from those reported by Greenhill, *Labor Money in Wisconsin Politics, 1964,* because different time periods and different committee reports were used for the computation. Even with these differences, the estimates of the two studies vary by only slightly more than 2 per cent.

30 Republicans have generally filed only the first initials and last names of their contributors. Identification of business leaders and their families was, therefore, in some instances quite difficult. In cases of doubt, contributions were excluded from these tallies, and there is thus likely to be some underestimation.

Contributions from those associated with breweries were excluded because of the previously noted non-programmatic orientation of brewery political objectives. See pp. 207–8 for a discussion of their Wisconsin contributions.

31 Heard, *The Costs of Democracy,* pp. 48–49.

32 John P. White and John R. Owens, *Parties, Group Interests and Campaign Finance; Michigan '56* (Princeton: Citizens' Research Foundation, 1960), pp. 10–11, 34.

33 *Ibid.,* p. 30.

34 *Ibid.,* pp. 29–34.

35 Heard, *The Costs of Democracy,* pp. 123–25, n., p. 124; White and Owens, *Parties, Group Interests and Campaign Finance,* pp. 32–33.

36 Sorauf, "The Voluntary Committee System," pp. 55, 65.

37 Fenton, *Midwest Politics,* pp. 68–72, 224–31.

Chapter Seven

1 Frank Sorauf, "The Voluntary Committee System in Wisconsin: An Attempt to Achieve Party Responsibility" (Unpub. Ph.D. Diss., Univ. of Wis., 1953), p. 141.

2 Robert J. McNeill, *Democratic Campaign Financing in Indiana, 1964* (Princeton: Citizens' Research Foundation, and Bloomington: Indiana University Institute of Public Administration, 1966), pp. 16–19.

3 Lester Milbrath, *Political Participation* (Chicago: Rand McNally, 1965), pp. 17–18.

4 *Ibid.,* pp. 120–24.

5 Herbert E. Alexander, *Financing the 1964 Election* (Princeton: Citizens' Research Foundation, 1966), p. 54.

Epilogue

1 Frank Sorauf, *Party Politics in America* (Boston: Little, Brown and Co., 1968), pp. 316–18.

2 Herbert E. Alexander, with the assistance of Laura Denny, *Regulation of Political Finance* (Berkeley and Princeton: Institute of Governmental Studies and Citizens' Research Foundation, 1963), p. 13.

3 *Ibid.*

4 *Ibid.*, p. 12.

5 Wisconsin, *Statutes* (1965), sec. 12.56.

6 Alexander and Denny, *Regulation of Political Finance*, p. 12.

7 For a review of these specific regulations and a compendium of others in the American states, see, *ibid.*, pp. 10–11, 59–61.

8 Wisconsin, *Statutes* (1965), sec. 12.20.

9 Alexander and Denny, *Regulation of Political Finance*, p. 11.

10 *Ibid.*, p. 7.

11 *Ibid.* The 10 states are: Kentucky, Minnesota, New Hampshire, New Jersey, New Mexico, New York, Texas, Utah, West Virginia, and Wisconsin.

12 Elston E. Roady, "Florida's New Campaign Expense Law and the 1952 Democratic Primaries," *American Political Science Review,* 48 (June, 1954), 465–76. Also, his "Ten Years of Florida's 'Who Gave It—Who Got It' Law," *Law and Contemporary Problems,* 27 (1962) 434–54.

13 *Ibid.*, p. 438.

14 *Ibid.*, p. 436.

15 *Ibid.*, p. 434.

16 *Ibid.*, pp. 438–39; Roady, "Florida's New Campaign Expense Law . . . ," pp. 475–76.

17 Roady, "Ten Years of Florida's 'Who Gave It—Who Got It' Law," p. 445.

18 *Ibid.*, p. 434.

19 Quoted in Murray B. Levin, *Kennedy Campaigning* (Boston: Beacon Press, 1966), p. 250.

20 *Ibid.*, ch. 5.

21 *Ibid.*, n., p. 284.

22 *Smith v. Ervin* (1953) 64 So. 2d 166.

23 *State v. Pierce* (1916) 158 NW 696, 698.

24 "Statutory Regulation of Political Campaign Funds," *Harvard Law Review,* 66 (1953), 1267–68.

25 Alexander and Denny, *Regulation of Political Finance,* p. 29.
26 *Ibid.,* p. 24.
27 Henry Wells, *Government Financing of Political Parties in Puerto Rico* (Princeton: Citizens' Research Foundation, 1961). Also, Henry Wells and Robert W. Anderson, *Government Financing of Political Parties in Puerto Rico: A Supplement* (Princeton: Citizens' Research Foundation, 1966).
28 Wells, *Government Financing of Political Parties in Puerto Rico,* p. 10 (emphasis added by Wells).
29 *Ibid.,* pp. 8–11.
30 U.S. Congress, Senate, Committee on Finance, *Report on Honest Elections Act of 1967* (90 Congress, 1 session, Report No. 714, Washington, 1967).
31 *Ibid.,* p. 4.
32 Wells, *Government Financing of Political Parties in Puerto Rico,* p. 10.
33 Alexander Heard, *The Costs of Democracy* (Chapel Hill: University of North Carolina Press, 1960), ch. 12.

Index

–